DATE DUE

MR 30 '98			

CUMBE REBORN

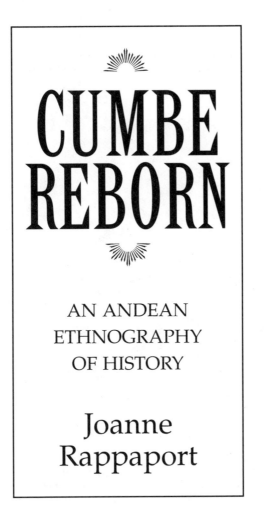

CUMBE REBORN

AN ANDEAN
ETHNOGRAPHY
OF HISTORY

Joanne
Rappaport

THE UNIVERSITY OF CHICAGO PRESS
CHICAGO AND LONDON

ropology at the University of Maryland,
of Memory (1990).

The University of Chicago Press, Chicago 60637
The University of Chicago Press, Ltd., London
© 1994 by The University of Chicago
All rights reserved. Published 1994
Printed in the United States of America
02 01 00 99 98 97 96 95 94 1 2 3 4 5
ISBN: 0-226-70525-0 (cloth)
        0-226-70526-9 (paper)

Library of Congress Cataloging-in-Publication Data

Rappaport, Joanne.
    Cumbe reborn : an Andean ethnography of history / Joanne
        Rappaport. p.   cm.
    Includes bibliographical references and index.
    1. Indians of South America—Colombia—Cumbal—History—Sources.
2. Ethnohistory—Colombia—Cumbal.   3. Indians of South America—
Colombia—Cumbal—Social life and customs.   4. Cumbal (Colombia)—
History—Sources.   I. Title.
F2269.1.C93R36   1994
986.1'62—dc20   93-4909
                                                                    CIP

⊗   The paper used in this publication meets the minimum requirements of the American National Standard for Information Sciences—Permanence of Paper for Printed Library Materials, ANSI Z39.48-1984.

To my father,
Irving Rappaport

Memory believes before knowing remembers.
Believes longer than recollects, longer than
knowing even wonders.

WILLIAM FAULKNER, Light in August

Contents

Illustrations

Figures

Plates follow p. 122

Acknowledgments

THIS BOOK IS THE product of collaborative research with the indigenous community of Cumbal, Nariño, involving the collection of extensive oral history recordings and transcripts. These were returned to the community and are currently being studied by the indigenous leadership in preparation for the territorial reorganization plan that will define the nature of local political process, pursuant to the 1991 Colombian constitution. Therefore, it is fitting that I pay my first debt of gratitude to the Indians of southern highland Nariño. I would like to thank the cabildos of Cumbal, Panán, Mayasquer, Colimba, and Muellamués, which welcomed me into their midst, scoured the countryside in search of me to take me to meetings and ceremonies, and shared with me their historical texts, their political strategies, and their dreams for the future. In particular, I am indebted to the cabildo of Cumbal and its leadership from 1986 to 1989, including José Elipcio Chirán (Cuaical, 1986), Alonso Valenzuela Taramuel (Quilismal, 1987), Manuel Jesús Tarapués (Nazate, 1988), and Luís Arcesio Cuaspud (Cuaspud, 1989). I am also grateful to the families of the six *veredas* of Cumbal, of Panán, and of Mayasquer, who invited me into their homes and their lives, sharing conversation by the fireplace, roasted *cuyes, hervidos,* and continued friendship.

I am deeply indebted to *memoristas* doña Lastenia Alpala (Quilismal) and don Benjamín Cuaical (Cuaical) who introduced me to the richness of Cumbal's oral history. Other memoristas, to whom I am also grateful, are included in the list of narrators. Exegetical discussions with Miguel Taimal (Guan); José Abrahán Mimalchí and Julio Paguay (Tasmag); Maximiliana Alpala, Bernardita Chirán, Salomón Cuaical, and Gilberto Valenzuela (Cuaical and Quilismal); Carmen Colimba, José Amador Peregüeza, Isabel Peregüeza, and Moisés Tapie (Nazate); Luís Arcesio Cuaspud (Cuaspud); Raúl Fueltala (La Libertad, Panán); and the late Ramiro Muñóz (Colimba) enriched my understanding of Nariñense history, as I hope it did theirs. I am especially grateful to my collaborator, Helí Valenzuela Mites (Nazate), who collected and reflected upon oral histories in Cumbal and Mayasquer and was a constant companion and interlocutor. I will always appreciate the hospitality of Aura Rodríguez, Helí's wife, whose house in Puebloviejo was a home away from home.

Members of the Pasto-based Committee in Solidarity with the Indian Struggle, especially Adela Bravo, Luz Angélica Mamián, Iván Villota, and the late Glauco Villota, played a central role in collecting data and discussing Cumbal history and politics; they also gave me a place to hang my hat in Pasto. Most important, Adela and Angélica provided the guidance and dedication needed so that indigenous readers can begin to use the data we collected.

My various stays in Cumbal and visits to archives were sponsored in 1986–87 by the Council for the International Exchange of Scholars (American Republics Program), the National Science Foundation (grant no. BNS-8602910), and the Social Science Research Council; by a U.S. Department of Education Fulbright-Hays Postdoctoral Fellowship in 1988; by the Wenner-Gren Foundation for Anthropological Research in 1989; and by the University of Maryland, Baltimore County (Designated Research Initiative Fund) in 1990. The University of Maryland also provided funding for work-study and graduate research assistants—Pamela Burkins, Diana Digges, Susan Huizar, and Brenda McMahon—who diligently catalogued a great deal of the data. A debt of thanks is due especially to Diana and Susan for their suggestions and commentary on various chapters.

The research upon which this book is based was conducted under the supervision of the Instituto Colombiano de Antropología and its various directors between 1986 and 1990, Roberto Pineda Giraldo, Ana María Groot de Mahecha, and Myriam Jimeno. During the research period I was affiliated with the Department of Anthropology, Universidad de los Andes (Bogotá), whose directors, Carlos Alberto Uribe and Roberto Pineda Camacho, provided me with office space and, more important, with a forum for analyzing the material I had collected.

The various archives in which I collected documentary materials are listed in the bibliography. Thanks goes to their directors and staff, particularly to Grecia Vasco of the Archivo Nacional del Ecuador (Quito) and Jorge Isaac Cazorla of the Archivo Histórico del Banco Central del Ecuador (Ibarra), who were especially helpful in searching out and reproducing historical documentation. Work in a few of the Colombian archives was conducted by Luz Angélica Mamián Guzmán. When Cristóbal Landázuri and the associates of Marka, Instituto de Historia y Antropología Andina, discovered that we were all after the same documents pertaining to the Pastos, we began collaborative research in various Ecuadorian archives, pooling our materials and initiating what I hope will be a long and fruitful relationship.

The bulk of this book was prepared during sabbatical leave from the University of Maryland, Baltimore County in 1990–91, for which I am grateful. It was written while in Rome, where I was made to feel welcome by Marco Curatola and his colleagues at the Museo Nazionale Preistorico ed Etnografico "Luigi Pigorini." The chance to coordinate graduate seminars partially based on my research at the Facultad Latinoamericana de Ciencias Sociales (Quito, Ecuador), the Universitetet i Oslo (Norway), and the Universidad de Nariño (Pasto, Colombia) afforded me the welcome opportunity to test my ideas in group discussion.

A vast number of colleagues were generous in their commentaries on portions of this book. I would especially like to thank Catherine Allen, Ruth Behar, Deborah Caro, Thomas Cummins, Robert Dover, Andrés Guerrero, Catherine LeGrand, Dana Leibsohn, Enrique Mayer, the late Ann Osborn, Roberto Pineda Camacho, Deborah Poole, Frank Salomon, Linda Seligmann, Sarah Skar, Carlos Alberto Uribe, María Victoria Uribe, and R. Tom Zuidema. The reviewers for the University of Chicago Press provided insightful commentary on my manuscript, helping it on its way to becoming a book. Ellen Feldman expertly touched up my prose, making the book more readable. Finally, I am especially grateful to Jean-Paul Dumont for taking this book so seriously, and to T. David Brent of the University of Chicago Press, who has made it a reality.

Maps and illustrations were prepared by Julie Perlmutter.

Chapter 4 appeared in a slightly different version as "History and Everyday Life in the Colombian Andes," in *Man* (n.s.) 23 (1988): 718–39, and is reprinted here by permission. An earlier verison of chapter 5, coauthored with Diana Digges, appeared as "Literacy, Orality and Ritual Practice in Highland Colombia," in *The Ethnography of Reading,* ed. Jonathan Boyarin (Berkeley and Los Angeles: University of California Press, 1993), 139–55; excerpts are used with the permission of the University of California Press. A Spanish translation of chapter 6 was published as "Toretes y bramaderos: visiones entrelazadas de la historia nariñense" in *Identidad*, ed. M. Jimeno, G. I. Ocampo, and M. Roldán (Bogotá: ICFES, 1989), 221–43.

David Gow accompanied me on a brief visit to Cumbal and later, through multiple drafts of *Cumbe Reborn*, patiently reading and rereading my words, listening to my ramblings and speculations, offering thoughtful suggestions and commentary, keeping my feet on the ground. Most important, our conversations about how anthropology might be turned to people's advantage have motivated me to continue to explore ways of making my research relevant to the Indians of southern Colombia.

Introduction

In an entry in her diary, Joyce Carol Oates reflects upon her father's recounting of a failed attempt at raising pigs in rural New York many years before, when she was still a child. As he spins his yarn in a comfortable suburban living room, Oates's father delights his audience with his vivid descriptions of how the pigs tried to run away, how he chased them and caught them, how he finally slaughtered them and cured their meat, how the meat rotted; in short, a hilarious image of what was, at the time, a disastrous effort to pull his family out of poverty. For Oates, the story is meaningful on two levels:

> It was a sort of domestic tragedy; a blow to *machismo*. Now of course all that is gone, like the old farmhouse and the old barns, old even during my childhood; any humiliation is forgotten as if it had never been; Frederic Oates tells his story as delightfully as anyone, even a professional, might tell it, and we are all laughing, and we are all sympathetic, and I sit there contemplating how, for us, yes for all of us, what is passed is retrieved only by way of language artfully selected; the past is in fact simply the consequence of a series of presents palimpsestically overlaid upon it; and that past, which had once seemed so inviolable in its reality, its concreteness, even its smells, is now erased as "history" surrenders to "story." And now that my parents' lives—the lives of the Oatses—have so clearly changed, now perhaps we are ready to surrender the past to story, even to anecdote; past griefs to present laughter. And the truth came to me how if you survive, all things in time become narrative, that artful selection of words, words

1

that do your bidding, not *This happened to me* but *I did this.* If
you survive. (Oates 1990, 134)

This book examines another set of experiences-turned-stories, those
told, sung, written, and performed by the people of Cumbal, an indigenous community in the highlands of southern Colombia. Unlike the
tale told by Joyce Carol Oates's father, however, the stories of Cumbal
are meant to do more than delight: they spur people to action. They
are not yarns of long gone and forgotten disasters, but reflections on
events that still impinge upon everyday life. In this sense they are
much more than stories, although they have certainly grown and
changed with the years since the original events they record transpired. Like Oates's story, they are palimpsests, whose multiple presents overlay the pasts they seek to represent, pasts conveyed through
the careful selection of words and images that help their tellers to remember why they are important at all.

These Colombian narratives recount the loss of aboriginal lands. The
Cumbales live on the high slopes of two volcanos, Mount Cumbal and
Mount Chiles, just to the north of the Colombia-Ecuador border, in the
department of Nariño (see figure 1). Their homes, once smoke-filled,
dimly lit wattle and daub huts thatched with straw, now two- or three-
room adobe brick houses with whitewashed walls, red tile roofs, and
electric light, are perched amidst the purple blossoms of potato fields
and the golden tassels of barley on mountain slopes at 3,000 meters
(9,900 feet) or more above sea level. Buffeted by the winds of summer
and drenched by the rains of winter, the dairy cattle that provide many
Cumbales with an entry into the regional market economy graze at
even higher altitudes, picking their way through the broken, rocky, and
marshy terrain of the Andes. Although these pastures are located below the tree line, Cumbal has been largely deforested by agricultural
expansion; the eucalyptus prominent on the horizon were planted during the past twenty years. Below, an hour or more by foot along uneven
dirt roads traveled by motorcycles, jeeps, and the *escalera,* an ornately
painted open-air bus, are flat and fertile valley bottoms once monopo-
lized by the cattle of non-Indian absentee landlords.

Increasingly, however, militant Cumbales, guided by anually elected
leaders organized in a *cabildo* or council, are repopulating the valleys
with smaller, more rustic versions of their houses. The adjacent fields
are planted in maize, a favored item in the local diet that does not
grow on the higher slopes. The transformation of *mestizo* cattle ranch
into indigenous smallholding is the product of a series of land occupations in which Indians named Tarapués, Malte, or Tupue, their claims

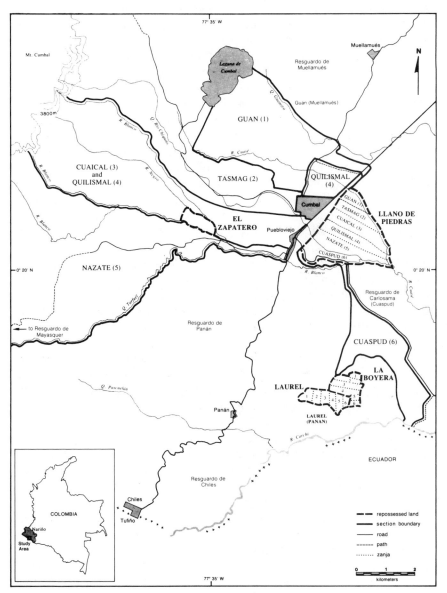

1. The six sections of Cumbal, Nariño

authenticated by historical documentation from the seventeenth and eighteenth centuries, reclaimed lands usurped from them more than three hundred years ago by the Erazos and the Trejos, Spanish landowners and colonial officials. Once called Guamialamag, Cuchicuelán, and Nazate, the ranches of the valley have been carved up over the years by inheritance and by sale, passing into the hands of people named Arellano, Pantoja, Revelo, even White. At the advent of the land struggle in the mid-1970s, the largest landowning families, representing one percent of the population, owned almost 50 percent of the land, holding deeds to properties averaging slightly over 400 hectares or 1,000 acres, while most Indian smallholders made do with 1.2 hectares or three acres (Zúñiga 1986, 15).

Given the magnitude of the land problem, the less than 2,000 hectares reclaimed since 1975 can go only so far in improving the lot of the 16,000 Indian smallholders who live in the municipality of Cumbal. The struggle to restore stolen lands to their rightful owners continues to preoccupy cabildo leaders and their followers. The process of land claims is slow, however, retarded by bureaucratic red tape: INCORA, the Colombian Institute of Agrarian Reform, recompenses the landlords or *hacendados* for their loss at slightly less than market value. But what constitutes ownership in Cumbal is different from the meaning mestizo hacienda owners attach to the word.

The municipality of Cumbal, frequently called Gran Cumbal or Greater Cumbal, is composed of four constituent communities—Cumbal, Panán, Chiles, and Mayasquer—the first three occupying the high mountain slopes that descend to the valley where Guamialamag once lay.[1] Mayasquer is located on the other side of Mount Cumbal, facing the Pacific Ocean, at a lower and warmer elevation of 1,500 to 2,000 meters. It is a steamy and heavily forested region where a sparse population of native Mayasqueres and Cumbal, Panán, Chileno, and mestizo colonists cultivate maize, sugar cane, and tropical fruits. The four communities of Gran Cumbal are *resguardos*, communally owned and politically autonomous landholding corporations enjoying title to lands granted their *caciques*, or hereditary chiefs, by the Spanish Crown in the eighteenth century (see González 1979). Individual resguardo members, called *comuneros*, possess only use rights to their plots. Thus, when the cabildo occupies and successfully reclaims an hacienda, after its former owner has received the first installment of government bonds, signed an agreement with the indigenous community, and finally vacated the land, the acreage is reincorporated into the resguardo. No longer private property, it is now collectively owned territory.

The dream of recovering aboriginal territory is not new to Cumbal.

The documentary record contains thousands of pages of transcripts of court cases heard over the past four centuries in which cabildos waged legal war on Spanish authorities and the Colombian state to restore indigenous ownership to the land. The Cumbales have consulted some of these papers themselves, and their contents have been absorbed into the oral tradition. The memory of other legal battles has been transmitted by word of mouth across the generations. These stories and the documentary sources upon which they are based build one upon another, palimpsestically, so that one could trace any given narrative of a particular land struggle back through its multiple sources: the oral accounts of various attempts at reclaiming a given plot across time, the crosscutting paper trails that each consecutive effort left behind, the vestiges and scars that persist in the land itself. Ultimately, as narrators interweave oral, written, and tangible evidence of their heritage of land claims, they attest to the futility of a legal solution to what is, in essence, a problem of the distribution of political and economic power. Far from being mere artful selections of words about the past, their stories stand as evidence of the need for militant action in the present.

In order to recoup territories that are legitimately theirs by colonial title, the Cumbales must assert a distinctly indigenous identity, for according to Colombian law, only Indians are entitled to enjoy the communal protection of the resguardo. Yet while many comuneros proudly bear the surnames of the eighteenth-century caciques Cuaical or Alpala, they no longer speak the Pasto language in which they conversed until the nineteenth century.[2] Neighboring mestizos, enraged over the land occupations, accuse the Cumbales of having "lost" their indigenous culture. It is by telling stories, whose contents are local in nature and whose structure is culturally distinctive, that the Cumbales find a medium in which they can express their relationship with their forebears, at the same time as they engage in the cultural invention that frequently accompanies such programs of resurgent ethnicity.

The tellers of these tales are local intellectuals, people who enjoy access to varied forms of oral and written historical documentation, but who also are skilled at interpreting evidence and are good at spinning yarns. Many narrators, especially the older ones, are recognized as historians by their neighbors, a convention I will maintain in the following pages. Some, like the elderly doña Lastenia Alpala and don Benjamín Cuaical, whose voices will appear repeatedly, are highly skilled storytellers drawing upon decades of experience with the cabildo, hours spent listening at the feet of their politically active parents and grandparents, and miles trodden on the paths linking the four resguardos, loaded with cheese, meat, potatoes, firewood, or other items to be bartered or sold. Others, such as don Benjamín's son, Valentín Cuaical, once active in leftist peasant organizations and later in mainstream political parties, recast their historical knowledge in song. Young people, like Miguel Angel Alpala, his political career just beginning in the ranks of Acción Comunal, a grass-roots public works committee, write historical plays. And yet others incorporate history into written legal briefs, as did Agustín Colimba, former secretary of the cabildo, or into treatises, like Panán shaman José Delfín Canacuán and national officeholder Helí Valenzuela, or even into poetry, like Efrén Tarapués, one of the comparatively few to complete high school, now employed by a local development organization. The range of genres of historical expression, like the array of narrators, is indeed broad and flexible.

Although indigenous intellectuals are the primary focus of this book, I will also explore the ways in which their contributions are absorbed by other community members, who remember history primarily through images and clichés. The nature of popular historical memory is, as I hope to show, very different from historians' tales. It is not made up of carefully woven narratives but of a series of brief and incomplete images, which are never developed in any detail. Instead, these images are lodged in the minutiae of everyday life: in mundane ceremonies, in place names, in objects, in the very organization of space itself.

The history of Gran Cumbal is told differently depending upon the narrator: the aged community leader or the young activist, the apolitical farmer, the former sharecropper. The multiplicity of voices we will encounter in the following pages extends, nevertheless, beyond contemporary community boundaries. Cumbal's narrators are dispersed not only in space but in time. The written record upon which local intellectuals depend goes back as far as the seventeenth century. The names and sometimes the signatures of distant hereditary chiefs, such as don Pedro Alpala or don Bernardo Tarapués, jump out at us from the tattered pages of the notarial record. These same documents were studied in the nineteenth century by people like Manuel de Jesús Tarapués, who left his mark on them, peppering carefully preserved copies with notes and addenda, saving for posterity only those records that were of use to him in his efforts to win back haciendas in the Supreme Court chambers in Bogotá. Nineteenth-century readings determine, moreover, the ways in which the colonial record is understood by contemporary intellectuals, because individuals like the nineteenth-century governor Manuel de Jesús Tarapués recast their contents in oral form. When a contemporary historian, such as Nestor Tarapués—

no relation to don Manuel de Jesús—peruses an old document, he already knows what he will find there, having heard so much from his grandparents. And his own retelling of what he has read will be grounded in the realities of everyday life, which are, for his listeners, the stuff history is made of. Don Nestor's account of how colonial chiefs lost their land will be embedded within a wealth of detail describing the recent past of those who were forced to survive on the remaining tiny plots of land. He embellishes his narratives with tales of civil war, famine, wage labor, lists of the crops his ancestors planted, the clothing his grandparents wore, the Catholic festivals they sponsored. The sources and the final products of Cumbal's historians are thus palimpsests in which the distant past, the recent past, and the present are layered, in which the political maneuvers of ancient chiefs and the labors of artisans of just thirty years ago complement each other, and in which written and oral modes of communication are interwoven with practical action.

These histories of heroic forebears and of potato farmers spring from the interface of the indigenous community and the state, for national legislation requires that Indians submit particular forms of historical evidence to substantiate their claims to land or political authority. For this reason, many of the stories I heard in Cumbal are couched in the language of jurisprudence or are organized as though they constituted evidence for legal briefs. The bridge that connects community and state is paved with papers and with interpretations of them. The very communal organization that the Cumbales perceive as making them culturally distinct is, moreover, a product of Spanish colonial and Colombian national Indian policy. The very fact that they call themselves Indians is a reaction to efforts by the state to legislate them out of existence. The traditions of everyday life within which history is lodged derive from customs introduced by the Spanish administration. And the recent memories that provide the foundations upon which far-reaching historical interpretations are built are drawn from experiences within a regional market economy and national political life.

Cumbal is an Andean community. In many ways, the Cumbales live like the Quechua-speaking peasant farmers just over the border in Ecuador or further to the south, in Peru and Bolivia. The models that structure the organization of topographic space and temporal memory are common to other Andean settings. The Cumbales grow the same crops, perform the same ceremonies, and most of the metaphors they use to recount historical experience appear, time and again, in other Andean narratives, as the following chapters will demonstrate. In other ways, however, the Cumbales are quite different from their southern neighbors. Their pre-Columbian Pasto ancestors resisted the advances of the Inca empire, maintaining their decentralized chiefdoms until the arrival of the European invaders in 1536. Their colonial-era forebears were assigned to a very different political jurisdiction from that of the Incas' northern capital, Quito. Attached to the Spanish city of Pasto, they were never touched by colonial appeals to the Incaic past or by the Spanish-imposed spread of Quechua. And once Colombia gained political independence in the early nineteenth century, the Cumbales enjoyed the dubious distinction of being highland Indians in a country whose majority thought only mestizos lived in the highlands. Ethnographies of places on the periphery, like Cumbal, help us to expand our definitions of culture areas: in this case, to move beyond a Cuzco-centric notion of Andean culture.[3]

This book does not, however, focus on the persistence of Andean lifeways in Cumbal. Instead, it explores their emergence over time by concentrating on how a specific community has resisted, capitulated, and accommodated to the state, looking in particular at the communal pasts that its inhabitants constructed and the political context in which they deploy this knowledge. The numerous sources of history, the various genres in which historical referents are cast, and the contradictory ways in which they are used constitute the principal focus of my exploration of the past in Cumbal. Far from a seamless whole, it is from those points at which the fabric of everyday life has been rent or stretched by colonial domination and by confrontation that this ethnographic essay springs, for this is the past that is foregrounded in contemporary Cumbal. Before I turn to consider the broader political context in which Cumbal's militancy unfolds, it would be useful to look a bit more closely at how this ethnic ideology is expressed.

Recuperación and the Politics of History in Cumbal

The Politics of History

July 1, 1987—the cabildo of Cumbal is meeting with the directors of the Colombian Institute of Agrarian Reform (INCORA) and the Division of Indigenous Affairs, both flown in from the capital city of Bogotá to hacienda La Boyera. From atop the hill crowning the reclaimed hacienda they look out upon the valley once called Guamialamag. The eighteenth-century battle over this huge expanse of land culminated in the signing of the resguardo title.[4] Today portions of Guamialamag are once again resguardo territory, recovered during fifteen years of land claims: El Laurel, shared by Cumbal, Panán, and Chiles; La Boyera, now part of Cumbal; and La Poma, repossessed by Panán, to name just a few. But directly below La Boyera the valley is still ruled by landlords.

Suddenly a host of men, women, and children armed with agricultural implements descends upon Pueipiza, the hacienda of Laureano Alberto Arellano, national senator from the Liberal party and member of the Cumbal mestizo elite. Furrows are carved into the cattle pasture as Arellano's land is reclaimed by the sweat of the brow. Fifteen minutes later, the group moves on to neighboring Las Playas, where an identical scene is repeated. In the following months Las Playas will be returned to the cabildo, although the political influence of Senator Arellano will block the transformation of Pueipiza from private property into resguardo.

The peaceful repossession of Las Playas took only fifteen minutes, unlike the months and years of struggle and bloodshed that culminated in the reincorporation of El Laurel and La Boyera. Propelled by the political connections of the cabildo and by the national government's recent adoption of a pro-Indian policy as a hedge against the expansion of guerrilla movements into indigenous areas, land claims have become a matter of sometimes interminable negotiations with government officials. Nevertheless, at the cabildo meeting the following Sunday, triumphant governor Alonso Valenzuela traced a connection between the event and the glorious exploits of national heroes:

> On October 12, 1981, we entered Boyera. If on October 12 the invader arrived, on October 12, 1981, Gran Cumbal confronted this invasion.
> On July 1, 1987, we entered in battle, as did Simón Bolívar on July 20 in the Battle of Boyacá. All Colombians could then say that we were finished with the Spaniards.
> But this July 20, 1987, we will say to Colombia that we will once again tell the landlords, in the face of landlord aggression, Gran Cumbal answers, "Landlords, get out!" (Alonso Valenzuela, Vereda Tasmag)[5]

Appealing to his authority as governor in 1981 and in 1985, Valenzuela likens himself to Simón Bolívar, the father of Colombian independence, and likens the repossession of the two haciendas to the end of Spanish domination in America, which he glosses as the Battle of Boyacá. History is recapitulated by manipulating significant dates associated with key phrases. Valenzuela gives the date of the cabildo's entry into La Boyera as October 12, 1981, associating it in the minds of his listeners with Columbus's October 12, 1492 landfall. This is clearly an ironic gesture, given that the October 12, 1981 cabildo occupation of the hacienda was, in his eyes, much more of a liberation than an "invasion," as landlords and neighboring mestizos prefer to call it. His second reference to the calendar is an association by proximity of the July 1, 1987 occupation of Pueipiza with Colombia's independence celebration, the July 20 anniversary of the Battle of Boyacá. This time irony and incongruity are laid aside with the celebration of a dual independence: Bolívar's break with Spain and Cumbal's political emancipation from the Liberal party faction led by Arellano, Pueipiza's owner.[6] History intrudes even into political oratory, articulating the ideology of *recuperación* that has fueled indigenous militancy for the last fifteen years.

Recuperación

Recuperación is the term used to describe the act of reclaiming territory by occupying usurped lands, a concept best translated into English as "repossession," the term Native Americans use to refer to the same process in the United States (Landsman 1988). By calling their activities "recuperación," the cabildo distinguishes its discourse from that of the state and the landlords, who commonly label these actions "invasions."

The ideology of recuperación revolves around the collective repossession of land, the transformation of private property into communal resguardo territory. This stands in contrast to other concepts of agrarian reform operating in Colombia, in which independent cooperatives of peasant property owners are created on former haciendas. The meaning of recuperación in Gran Cumbal is best exemplified by the repossession of El Laurel. Once occupied by a landlord, INCORA transformed El Laurel into a cooperative farm for landless peasants from neighboring communities; some of these people are close relatives of resguardo members. Notwithstanding the efforts of the agrarian reform agency, however, El Laurel remained beyond the sphere of cabildo authority, even though the resguardo title includes the farm within its colonial boundaries. This is why the cabildos of Cumbal, Panán, and Chiles, whose territories are validated by that document, united forces to reincorporate Laurel into their communal holdings. Recuperación thus signifies the collective repossession of land in the name of correcting history, an activity that emphasizes indigenous agency validated by collective sentiments that are themselves supported by common descent and written documentation.

Recuperación is also used as a gloss for the process of strengthening cabildo authority. In Gran Cumbal, this has involved the consolidation of power by pro-repossession sectors of the population, or *recupera-dores*. The revitalization of cabildo authority is equated with the restoration of historical conditions in which colonial caciques enjoyed greater power than twentieth-century cabildos. This sentiment can be explored most fruitfully in metaphor. For example, in his political oratory Alonso Valenzuela calls the mythical cacique Cumbe the "first organizer," comparing the colonial chief to the recuperadores of today. At a 1987 possession ceremony in which the use rights to a small plot of land were transferred from a comunero to the cabildo in preparation for the construction of a collecting tank to water the Llano de Piedras, the first large piece of land repossessed by the cabildo, a comparable statement was made likening the contemporary cabildo to its colonial forebear. All observers were asked to roll on the ground and be whipped by the *teniente*, the governor's lieutenant who keeps orders at meetings, as is customary in such ceremonies, while cabildo president Gilberto Valenzuela recalled the colonial formula the resguardo title recorded, transferring the plot to all the "indios, indias, chinos, y chinas" of Gran Cumbal.

But recuperación means more than reclaiming lands or reconstituting indigenous political authority. The term also has been used as a gloss for economic innovation, such as the development of new agricultural techniques promoting self-sufficiency, regardless of whether these methods actually find their roots in the past. As such, recuperación is at once a return to the past and a masking of innovation by reference to history (Hobsbawm 1972; Hobsbawm and Ranger 1983).[7] A good example is the introduction in Cumbal of datura—a hallucinogenic plant of the nightshade family—as a fumigant against potato rust (see plate 1). Although the use of datura is called a recuperación, the plant has never before been employed in this way.[8] However, the use of datura as a fumigant is a kind of return to the past, a return to a time when potato rust did not exist and when comuneros were not heavily indebted by their dependence on chemical fumigants.

Finally, recuperación encompasses multiple forms of cultural revitalization, including the reacquisition of historical documentation and its reinterpretation in the leaflets, songs, and dramatic presentations described in the following chapters. Once again, "recuperación de la historia" is not so much the retrieval of the *letter* of the historical past as the reincorporation of the *spirit* of the forebears in the context of the present. In 1982, under the leadership of governor Manuel Jesús Tarapués, great-grandson of nineteenth-century hero Manuel de Jesús Tarapués, some thirty comuneros decided to relive their history by retracing the boundaries recorded in their title, thus reinventing a tradition that is common to other Andean communities.[9] The *recorrido*, as the expedition was called, also led to the creation of new customs. One of the participants explained to me why, for example, when they reached the boundary marker called the Piedra de los Siete Alhueros [Agujeros], the Stone of the Seven Holes, they drank the water that had collected in the crevices of the rock:

> M.T.: Because when we saw how beautiful the holes were, it was worth drinking the water from there. The rest of the comrades drank water.
>
> J.R.: So this wasn't something that the elders had told you, but that you yourselves decided to do?
>
> M.T.: We ourselves decided to do it that way. That's what happened. (Moisés Tapie, Vereda Nazate)[10]

As with so many contemporary activities, the ritual was recorded on film and on audiotape, new forms of inscription.

The militant ritual of retracing resguardo boundaries was accompanied by a reading of the title. For this group of comuneros, whose command of the written word was imperfect, the act of experiencing the boundaries through movement and through sight afforded them a more immediate means of reliving history and of comprehending the enormity of their undertaking:

> M.T.: We took the deed there, we took it, and looking at the deed, following the deed, we would see the place, and we looked at the deed and saw the place where the site was.
>
> At least, the next day we went to the Cerro Doña Juana, as it's called—today they've given it another name, Doña Luisa—but in any case, the deed names the mountain. And we had the opportunity, we were even doing it with acts.
>
> J.R.: What do you mean, with acts?
>
> M.T.: With acts. That when we got to the point, we didn't just look at it from here, but we arrived there, we had the chance to arrive at the very Cerro de Doña Juana.
>
> From there you can see another boundary marker called the Cerro del Rollo, and the Cerro del Rollo looked so far away. There was good weather, you could see it in the morning—at just nine in the morning, and then it's covered, that happens there in the mountains where it's covered with clouds and you can't see anything.
>
> From there we could, we followed the boundaries: not by

the Miraflores road but down a ridge that delimits Deed 228 [the title]. (Moisés Tapie, Vereda Nazate)[11]

Recuperación is assessed in cabildo rhetoric as a successful project, a simple matter of redistributing lands and reclaiming authority by appealing to historical documentation. Nevertheless, it is a complex process fraught with contradictions. The question of how a pro-recuperación movement is to be organized—whether it should operate parallel to the cabildo or within it, whether or not it should be integrated within a centralized regional bureaucracy, whether it should focus exclusively on indigenous demands or, alternatively, should ally itself with other oppressed sectors, such as the peasant movement—has been broached differently by the various groups that have sprung up in Colombia over the past twenty years in defense of indigenous rights. Cumbal's cabildos do not operate in a vacuum; their struggle grew against a broader backdrop of Indian militancy in other parts of Colombia.

Studying Ethnic Militancy

Indigenous Militancy in Colombia

Unlike its Andean neighbors Ecuador, Peru, and Bolivia, which have large indigenous populations, only two percent of Colombians are Indians. Given this state of affairs, it is indeed remarkable that three indigenous delegates were elected to the Constituent Assembly that wrote Colombia's 1991 constitution and were instrumental in redefining Colombia as a pluriethnic nation (Colombia 1991, 2 [art. 7]).[12] As a result of their newly minted constitutional status, three Indians are now members of the Colombian Senate (Colombia 1991, 45 [art. 171]), entrusted with key roles in the drafting of new indigenous legislation; one of these positions is shared by a Guambiano senator from Silvia, Cauca with Helí Valenzuela of Cumbal, who was elected as an alternate for the senate seat.[13]

The opening that permitted the participation of a subordinated minority in the national political process was in part motivated by the historical juncture in which the Colombian government finds itself. Four decades of violence came to a head during the 1980s, forcing the state to extend its control through direct intervention in zones of conflict. State intervention, once wholly military, has taken more positive forms lately: the state has been willing to acknowledge indigenous territorial demands in those areas in which frictions are rooted in confrontations over land, in large part because there is no significant private investment in these marginal areas. Under other circumstances, economic interests would force the government to assign a higher value to these lands (Gros 1991, 322–25).

But if areas with indigenous populations have been identified by the state as zones of conflict, it is also because a mature Indian movement has grown there, responding to the threats posed by land loss, capitalist development, and population growth (ibid., 315–16; Jimeno and Triana 1985, 143). In effect, indigenous organizations have forced the government to seek them out as interlocutors, much as have guerrilla movements, such as the M-19, now a legal political party and ally of the Indian senators.

The Indian militancy of the past two decades arose in those parts of highland Colombia where indigenous communities had been locked in struggle with landowners for centuries, regions that had provided fertile soil for the growth of a range of militant strategies since the 1900s. The contiguous departments of Nariño, Cauca, and Tolima, which together contain the majority of Colombia's highland Indian population, were foci in the early part of the century of an indigenist movement headed by Páez leader Manuel Quintín Lame, whose principal aims were the expansion of resguardos, the political consolidation of cabildos, the abolition of sharecropping, and the reaffirmation of indigenous cultural values (Bonilla 1979; Castillo-Cárdenas 1971, 1987; Castrillón Arboleda 1973; Fajardo 1981; Lame 1971 [1939]; Rappaport 1990b). The Lamista movement met with severe repression.[14] The more integrationist strategy of peasant organizing followed by José Gonzalo Sánchez, a Lamista turned Communist, which was attempted in the same areas in the 1930s and 1940s, also encountered violent governmental opposition (Bonilla 1979; Findji and Rojas 1985; Sánchez 1977). From the 1930s to the 1950s, cabildo organizing skills were honed by resistance to government-supported privatization of resguardo lands.[15]

The 1970s witnessed the development of the contemporary Indian movement in Cauca and Nariño in particular. The land struggles of Guambiano and Páez sharecroppers, and the labor conflicts of caneworkers around Corinto, provided the political context for the founding of the Consejo Regional Indígena del Cauca (CRIC) (Regional Indigenous Council of Cauca), whose seven-point program built upon Manuel Quintín Lame's indigenist demands: (1) repossession of resguardo lands; (2) broadening of the resguardo land base; (3) strengthening of cabildos; (4) cessation of sharecropping; (5) popular education on Indian legislation and the promotion of its just application; (6) defense of indigenous history, languages, and customs; and (7) formation of Indian teachers.[16]

According to Christian Gros, from the start CRIC exhibited an innovative form of distinctly indigenist organizing:

> And in effect, the originality and efficacy of the movement issues in great measure from the ability to reappropriate this "indigenous" institution [the cabildo]—whose origin is colonial, as is well known. In place of innovating by making space for the creation of an alternative organization at the heart of the resguardos, the demand now is the reconstruction of cabildos (if they have disappeared), their reconquest (if they still exist but remain under the tutelage of whites or of minority interests hostile to the movement), in all cases, to provide them with new attributes and place them at the service of the organization and the land struggle. CRIC will present itself as a federation of cabildos, its general assembly as its direct expression. (Gros 1991, 216)

CRIC promoted numerous occupations of haciendas, by 1974 effectively repossessing some 10,000 hectares or 25,000 acres (ibid., 189), organizing cooperatives in reclaimed lands during the mid-1970s (ibid., 190), and promoting bilingual education and development projects in the 1980s.

At the same time as CRIC pursued what it felt to be an indigenist strategy within Cauca's Indian communities, it allied itself to the broader peasant movement. In 1972 it established an Indigenous Secretariat within the Asociación Nacional de Usuarios Campesinos (ANUC) (National Association of Peasant Users). Originally created in the late 1960s as a state-sponsored organization promoting peasant participation in agrarian reform activities, by the early 1970s ANUC had become an independent peasant movement organized around demands for land and the protection of colonists and smallholders (Zamosc 1986). CRIC's efforts at pan-Indian organizing, which included periodic meetings, advising new indigenous organizations, and the establishment of the national Indian newspaper, *Unidad Indígena*, placed them in contact with burgeoning Indian organizations in Tolima and Nariño as well as with groups from the more distant tropical lowlands and northern coast, also under the tutelage of ANUC. By 1977, however, the leadership of CRIC felt that ANUC was ignoring indigenous concerns and was attracted to the Indian struggle for purely propagandistic reasons (Morales 1979). In Nariño, where independent cabildos, such as that of Cumbal, had organized themselves to reclaim lands under the tutelage of ANUC, many indigenous leaders made similar complaints about the opportunistic tendencies of the national peasant organization, which by the late 1970s had adopted a Maoist orientation.[17]

During this period, the Colombian state was moving toward a growing recognition of the specificity of indigenous needs and demands, embodied in the creation of a number of institutions dedicated to Indian issues, including the Division of Indigenous Affairs in the Ministry of Government and a specific division of INCORA that purchased lands for the establishment of community enterprises, which remained, nevertheless, independent of cabildos (Jimeno and Triana 1985). But the repressive government of President Julio César Turbay Ayala (1978–82), alarmed at the deepening guerrilla struggle and its presumed links with the Indian movement, attempted to increase state control of resguardos through the introduction of a highly unpopular Indian statute that would supplant all previous legislation (Gros 1991, 226–28). The vacuum created by the demise of ANUC's Indigenous Secretariat was quickly filled with alliances dedicated to overturning Turbay's project. The organizations that participated in the resistance met in 1980 to form a National Indian Coordinating Committee, which by 1982 had become the Organización Nacional de Indígenas de Colombia (ONIC) (National Organization of Colombian Indians).

When Turbay's government was replaced by the populist presidency of Belisario Betancur in 1982, state policy once again turned favorable to Indians, recognizing ONIC as the representative of Colombia's indigenous communities. Under the Betancur presidency, seventy-eight new resguardos were established, turning millions of hectares over to indigenous control (ibid., 279–81). As a result of this policy, the national Indian movement became highly heterogeneous, incorporating both the organizations of highland regions, which had been forged in decades of agrarian struggle, and lowland associations, some of which had been founded under the supervision of the Catholic Church (Jackson 1991); unlike the centuries-old Andean resguardos, lowland organizations represented resguardos and reserves recently created at the instigation of the state (Gros 1991, 293–94).

CRIC's success at land claims and at pan-Indian organizing was rewarded by the growing support of international donors, ultimately leading to a large, centralized organization with a growing body of full-time staff and an office in the departmental capital of Popayán. By the late 1970s, several Páez communities in Cauca and the nearby Guambianos had grown highly critical of CRIC's burgeoning bureaucracy, accusing the by-then-famous Indian organization of creating a political force parallel to the cabildos. Although these groups originally saw themselves as an opposition faction within CRIC, by the early 1980s these forces created a parallel traditionalist organization, the Autoridades Indígenas del Sur Occidente (AISO) (Indigenous Authorities of the Southwest)—now called Autoridades Indigenas de Colombia (AICO) (Indigenous Authorities of Colombia)—to which the cabildos of Gran Cumbal and of other Nariñense communities allied themselves.[18] AISO, in contradistinction to CRIC, advocated that repossessed lands be reincorporated into resguardos rather than reconfigured as INCORA-sponsored community enterprises independent of cabildos, a strategy CRIC has long since abandoned. They also rejected CRIC's bureaucratic orientation, limiting their organizing to the level of individual cabildos; the cabildos would meet periodically, and communicate and collaborate with their counterparts under the umbrella of the broader organization. Finally, they eschewed CRIC's organizational apparatus, which survived because of donations from charitable foundations and aid agencies, preferring instead to direct outside funding toward specific projects. In effect, AISO rejected CRIC's development into a nongovernmental organization, instead asserting their intention to remain rooted in the traditionally indigenous institutions of resguardo and cabildo.

It is indeed intriguing that Cumbal and its neighbors, as highly integrated as they were into the dominant culture, should choose a traditionalist organization such as AISO as an ally instead of ONIC, which served as an umbrella for other, even more acculturated communities, such as those of Coconuco, Cauca (Jimeno and Triana 1985), and Tolima (Fajardo 1981). I suspect that the Indians of Nariño opted in favor of AISO precisely because of its emphasis on the cabildo, the institution that had ensured continuity of their territorial autonomy and ethnic identity over the centuries.

The Ethnography of Militancy in Cumbal

The quincentenary celebrations—or, more appropriately, the commemoration of five hundred years of resistance—and the prominence of ethnic rights movements have prompted many anthropologists to turn their research interests toward indigenous resistance, including the phenomenon of Indian political organizing. In many instances, this research takes the form of historical studies of the development of ethnic ideologies within a comparative framework (Barre 1983; Gros 1991; Mejía Piñeros and Sarmiento Silva 1987; Schroder 1991) or a concentration on changing state policy toward indigenous communities (Fundación para las Comunidades Colombianas 1987; Jimeno and Triana 1985; Triana 1980). When Indian demands come to the forefront of national consciousness, as they did in the 1990 Indian Uprising of Ecuador (Cornejo Menacho 1992; Field 1991; Rosero 1990) or in the participation of indigenous people in Peru's Shining Path (Degregori 1989, 1990; Mayer 1991), anthropologists have been forced to reconsider their traditional focus on bounded communities anchored to an imaginary ethnographic present; they have turned their sights instead toward the interaction between indigenous communities and the national society (Urban and Sherzer 1991).

An alternative course for antropological study is the detailed analysis of a resistance movement at the local level. Such an analysis might explore the symbolic dimension of ethnic organizing, the growth of an ideology at the grass-roots, and how militancy is embedded within the texture of everyday life. In a study of the Mohawk occupation of Ganienkeh, located on the U.S.-Canada border in upstate New York, for example, Gail Landsman (1988) concentrates upon the conflicting symbols wielded by Iroquois and non-Indians in a yearlong dispute over indigenous sovereignty. Kay Warren (1978) investigates the changing nature of indigenous identity as revolutionary Catholic Mayas confront their traditionalist compatriots in Guatemala. Martin Diskin (1991) and Jean Jackson (1989) approach the difficult question of cultural invention in their analyses of the rhetoric of Miskito and Tukanoan ethnic politics in Nicaragua and in lowland Colombia; Alcida Ramos (1988) undertakes a similar, albeit more general, evaluation of indigenous political discourse in Brazil.

Microlevel studies in the Andes have concentrated both on peasants' land struggles and on proletarian organizing, frequently from a historical perspective. Although these scholars choose to interpret events in the local arena, they remain highly sensitive to how national economic and political trends affect individual communities. Gavin Smith (1989) is particularly successful in his use of people's daily economic activities as a starting point for a history of the reposession of an hacienda by Quechua-speakers in the Mantaro Valley of Peru. June Nash (1979), working with Bolivian proletarians in the tin mines, and Mary Crain (1989), studying Quichua land struggles in northern highland Ecuador, underscore the significance of the relationship between historical consciousness and forms of resistance in the Andes.

It is this last theme—the generation of political strategy through recourse to historical knowledge—I will develop in this book. I will explore the rebirth of Indian identity and the constant reinvention of culture over time by examining how historical consciousness nourishes the struggle for land in Cumbal. I am particularly interested in how Cumbal's political history, especially the history of the land disputes of the distant colonial period that culminated in the granting of the resguardo title, furnishes a framework through which an experiential knowledge of the past transmitted through personal recollection can be harnessed in the context of political action. The distant past is embodied in the name of cacique Cumbe, the hereditary chief who ruled Cumbal at the time of the Spanish invasion. The documentary record yields no trace of him; Cumbe is best grasped as representing the multiplicity of political leaders across time whose existence is legitimated by legal papers. Cumbal's chiefly forebear is reborn each time a local historian weaves a tale about him, with every song that calls him back to the living, in every instance that he lends his name to a community organization.

This book explores how that rebirth takes place by concentrating on three key themes, which I examine ethnographically and historically in the following chapters and situate within a broader theoretical discussion in the conclusion. By viewing indigenous resistance through the lens of these three areas of inquiry, I hope to contribute not only to our understanding of the mechanics of ethnic militancy in the Americas, but also to a broader methodological discussion concerning the nature of historical consciousness under colonial domination.

1. *The construction of indigenous identity:* The fact that the Cumbales see themselves as Indians is the product of a specific historical moment when ethnic activism and government policy have imbued indigenous identity with a positive content. Precisely how Cumbales define Indianness is determined by a number of factors, including the depth of their historical consciousness, which registers what being an Indian meant at specific junctures in the past. Across time, Cumbal notions of self have been influenced by the modes used by the dominant society to define indigenous identity as they are applied in specific microcontexts in which Indian identity is asserted.

2. *The orality-literacy divide:* Although it is common for anthropologists who study both historical consciousness and ethnic militancy to confine their inquiries regarding popular memory to its oral manifestations, the realities of colonialism require a more careful investigation into how overlapping discursive systems are harnessed in and generate the process of change. The oral and literate channels of communication, as well as such nonverbal modes as the deciphering of material culture, are not discrete structures; they reciprocally influence one another. They are expressed, moreover, in a multiplicity of overlapping genres, each characterized by its own criteria for selecting historical

referents. In Cumbal, where the land-claims process requires a knowledge of legislation and the rules of presenting evidence, legality is a major determinant of the intermingling of the various genres of oral, literate, and nonverbal communication.

3. *Methods for studying historical consciousness:* The centrality of legality to Cumbal historical consciousness and indigenous militancy has various methodological implications. Native historiography cannot be understood as a series of unchanging and timeless texts but must be viewed as a process rooted in time. It is studied most effectively as the product of a historical process, which requires the analysis of both oral and documentary sources. There are, however, myriad forms of returning the interpretation of Cumbal historiography to the flow of time. Historical sources, whether oral or literate, are more than mines for facts: they must be studied ethnographically, because Cumbal's political actors interpret them within particular cultural frameworks. Such ethnographic study can be achieved only by breaking out of the illusory enclosure of orality that limits so many anthropological investigations, by considering the sometimes daunting mountain of legal papers that are so fundamental to subaltern senses of history throughout the world.

Methodological Considerations

The three themes I have outlined presuppose a radical reevaluation of the types of data that must be collected for the study of historical consciousness as well as of the form of analysis to which this data should be subjected. Not only must we consult a broad array of unfamiliar documents, but we must treat them as ethnographic data. Ethnographic information is not, however, the product of a single cultural community. Rather, it must be approached as the vestiges of communication across cultures, a sometimes hostile conversation in which each group appropriates, manipulates, misconstrues, and reapplies the discursive rules of the other.

It is not easy to get at this sort of information. Community historians may not always be willing to share their sources or might not be aware of the origin of the information they interpret. Alternately, most ethnographers do not have the archival expertise needed to locate such evidence. The methodological contribution of this book resides in its juxtaposition of a broad range of information in an attempt to understand how an indigenous community living under particular social constraints and historical conditions learns and interprets its own past.

The net I cast includes far more than oral narrative and ritual; my catch ranges from man-made features of the landscape to publicity posters, touching upon legal documents from the past three centuries and mid-twentieth-century inventories of community archives. In other words, by treating historical materials as grist for the mills of local intellectuals instead of as evidence for my own historical reconstructions, I try to situate contemporary Cumbal history-making in the foreground of my analysis, in a historical time that is of its own making.

My approach is largely the product of the relationship I established with the community of Cumbal as a corporate whole and with many of its individual members. Their eagerness to collaborate with me stems from the fact that ethnic militancy there has bred an intense desire to know the past. Following my own assessment of the ethics of the field situation as well as the suggestion of the cabildo, I agreed to share the fruits of my research with the community, although the form this collaboration would take was not specified in the public meeting at which I was introduced to the council. Tapes and transcripts of the three hundred-odd hours of oral history interviews I conducted were deposited with community authorities, with individual historians, and with non-Indian supporters of the land struggle, as were the notes I took during the course of archival research in Quito, Bogotá, Popayán, and other cities. This, along with my decision to leave copies of my Spanish-language articles and audiotape translations of English-language publications, was, I suspect, what the Cumbales hoped I would do, although they appeared to be pleasantly surprised at the volume and seriousness of the material I turned over to them.

The Cumbales probably did not expect I would routinely share my interpretations, play tapes, or read transcripts at cabildo meetings or at local gatherings I arranged at people's houses. This strategy allowed me to share the results of my investigations with those who were not activists, especially women and youth, as well as with those who were on the outs with the cabildo leadership at any given moment. In addition, it afforded me the opportunity to hear and record their voices.

I trained several people in the methodology of oral history interviewing. Some of them, such as Helí Valenzuela, are from Cumbal; others, including Angélica Mamián and Iván Villota, belong to the Pasto-based Committee in Solidarity with the Indian Struggle. Close collaboration with Cumbal activists permitted me to engage in more profound exegesis, a process that was mutually satisfying. I also felt that training researchers would be the most useful contribution I could make to the community, because they would no longer be passive re-cipients of my data, but active participants in the revitalization of local historical knowledge.

As a result of my policy of returning results to the Cumbales, I was afforded a number of important privileges. First, I encountered almost no difficulty in collecting oral histories, since the narrators knew that copies of tapes or transcripts would remain in Cumbal. Second, ca-bildo and household archives were opened to me, providing keys to how documentary evidence is interpreted and deployed in the political arena. Third, I found myself welcome at any number of meetings where I could observe the formulation of historically informed strat-egy. Finally, I was able to engage in countless exegetical discussions with community authorities, local intellectuals, and indigenous collab-orators, and to develop an analytical language that they could compre-hend. Most important, by acknowledging the value of historical infor-mation both to the Cumbales and myself, I could situate us in a common historical moment where we could share common evidence of the past, evidence we approached in similar, but also in different, ways.

Unfortunately, I received more than I could give. It quickly became apparent that much of the information I returned was not easily ab-sorbed by Cumbal as a whole, nor by a significant sector of the political leadership. Many neither had the time nor the inclination to study the mass of data I left them. The tapes I gave to cabildo archives disap-peared days after they were deposited or were hidden away for con-sumption by the few. While this heightened my understanding of how history is constructed and transmitted, it also left me with a feeling of impotence and with the suspicion that many of my intentions had been presumptuous at best.

I have received thus far a few dispersed indications that what I have to contribute has been of interest to some. Helí Valenzuela taped a June 1988 cabildo meeting in which references were made to some of the historical documents I had collected. Young people sometimes write to me requesting copies of my articles. The governor of neigh-boring Colimba, Ramiro Muñóz, consulted some of my documentary research in preparation for a regional meeting called to settle border disputes between communities. Ramiro and I had been planning to conduct archival research together when his life was taken by a death squad in April 1990.[19] A Pasto-based solidarity group has incorporated some of my data into the curriculum that they are developing for an agricultural high school that Ramiro founded in Colimba. A committee of representatives of various cabildos in Nariño is currently working through my interview transcripts as part of a larger project of restructuring local political authority under the 1991 Constitution.[20]

This process will clearly take much longer than I naively expected when I agreed to share my data with the cabildo. In addition, it undoubtedly will follow avenues that I still cannot foresee. The use that the Cumbales ultimately make of these materials is, however, a question to be explored in the future, perhaps the theme of another book.

ONE

Law and Indian Identity

MIGUEL TAIMAL, GOVERNOR OF Cumbal in 1984 when the campaign to recover the hacienda La Boyera was at its height, once told me how the law arrived in America aboard Columbus's ships:

> At first the Spanish people in Spain, in Europe, over there, made war and the people lived crowded over there. They didn't have any lands to work.
> So Christopher Columbus spoke and he thought, and with others he set sail. And they said that there were lands.
> So they navigated for six months.
> Then the other companions were going to kill Christopher Columbus, but where were they going to kill him if there wasn't any land?
> So, now that they'd come close, from afar they could see, they could see a light shining and the light shined at them. And then they saw that there was land.
> So they got out onto the shore. They brought down the three sheets of paper of Law 89 of 1890. And then they saw and they said that there was land.
> In those days in Colombia there were no white people. In Colombia it was all Indian people. (Miguel Taimal, Vereda Guan)[1]

The advent of law, for don Miguel, is bound inextricably with Spanish conquest and European colonialism, an imposition upon Indians by the dominant society.

Yet it is through recourse to legislation that the Cumbales and their

25

neighbors justify their land-claims strategy in the eyes of the national government. Law constitutes a common idiom employed by community and state to formulate demands and to fashion and implement policy. In other words, the repossession of the Llano de Piedras, El Laurel, and La Boyera was by necessity framed within a body of legislation on the basis of which the Division of Indigenous Affairs and INCORA could transfer title to the cabildo. If the occupation of haciendas provides the necessary push to prompt a recalcitrant government to take action, appeals to national legislation provide significant justification for implementing policy.

At the core of the juridical idiom shared by Indians and the state is an acceptance of a legal definition of indigenous identity, one that originated in Bogotá but has been internalized by resguardo members (Gros 1991; Rappaport 1990a). In effect, the European construction of the other, as it is interpreted in law, is basic to an indigenous definition of self.

Law 89 and Indian Identity

History and Law

Until 1991, when the new Colombian constitution (Colombia 1991) replaced all previous Indian legislation, Law 89 of 1890 constituted the centerpiece of resguardo law. Originally enacted to safeguard the resguardo as an institutional support during the transitional period in which Colombian Indians would be integrated into the dominant society, Law 89 delineated the administrative contours of communal property. While Law 89 has certainly served as a support over the years for the numerous indigenous communities intent upon preserving their territorial autonomy, this piece of legislation grew out of a very different set of political priorities than those of contemporary ethnic militants. It was born of political struggles at the heart of the nineteenth-century dominant society.

Post-independence Colombia was governed for the most part by the Liberal party, whose laissez-faire economic philosophy motivated legislators to enact laws aimed at dismantling the resguardo system in the interests of freeing up land for private ownership. During the first six decades of independent rule Colombia was governed by a federal system. But the devastation of a century of civil war and poor economic policy led some Liberals to ally themselves with members of the Conservative party and, in the 1880s, to establish a stronger, centralized, and paternalistic government. In the realm of Indian affairs this meant the enactment of protectionist laws such as Law 89, legislation that insured the temporary survival of the resguardo on the one hand, but that, on the other, also legislated its demise.[2]

Given the vital importance of Law 89 for maintaining a communal identity, it is not surprising that many Cumbales frequently confuse it with Deed 228, the colonial-era land title that codifies the boundaries of the resguardo, confirms the existence of the cabildo, and legitimizes the very indigenous identity that the Cumbales embrace.[3] Deed 228 also constitutes an important source of historical evidence for native historians. For the many who are not acquainted with cabildo procedure and Indian legislation, Law 89, like Deed 228, is believed to demarcate indigenous autonomy by virtue of its historicity, not its juridical force. In other words, history and law are synonymous for most Cumbales.

Myriam Jimeno and Adolfo Triana have shown that the Indians' fetishizing of the law is rooted in the realities of the colonial period. They argue that the central government, has been obliged—first by a federalist system and later by civil war, violence, and intense regionalism—to relinquish power to local authorities so as to conserve national unity. The indigenous communities' almost single-minded embrace of Law 89 is a form of circumventing the absence of effective national rule by law on the regional and local levels (Jimeno and Triana 1985, 272).[4]

Law 89

Law 89 of 1890 specifies "the manner in which savages in the process of being reduced to civilized life should be governed" (Colombia 1983, 57). It situates indigenous communities beyond the pale of general Colombian law, within the jurisdiction of a special legal corpus. It codifies the structure and organization of the resguardo, stipulating the annual election and obligations of the cabildo, the distribution to resguardo members of usufruct rights to communal lands, limitations on the legal jurisdiction of the cabildo in the settlement of disputes, and the minority status of comuneros, who are placed under the tutelage of the state. The primary intent of Law 89 is the integration of Indians into the dominant society; it also provides for the ultimate privatization and sale of resguardo lands within the space of fifty years.

Of particular interest here is how Law 89 is employed to determine who can claim Indian identity, and the basis upon which that identity is founded. At the time of its inception, Law 89, like subsequent pieces of indigenous legislation, was nourished by an evolutionary philosophy in which Indians were perceived as moving up the cultural ladder toward Western civilization (Correa 1989). Although the original intent of Law 89 was the *cultural* integration of indigenous peoples, however, it ultimately defines the Indian as a *legal* rather than a cultural being. The legal construction of indigenous identity affects the form in which local history is remembered, since it limits the types of historical evidence that can be offered to substantiate membership in, or the very existence of, a community. In essence, then, a European legal format and trait list are provided to determine who can be classified as an Indian and which historical sources can be used as evidence of identity.

How has law defined Indianness in the recent past? Case studies from other Nariñense communities to the north of Cumbal provide us with answers to this question.

Case Studies

The Battle over Ancuya

Lying on the western slopes of the cordillera overlooking the Pacific lowlands, Ancuya has always been a crossroads and a marketplace for the multiple ethnic groups that inhabited Nariño in the pre-Columbian period. The early colonial *visitadores* Tomás López (1558) and García de Valverde (1570–71) classified Ancuya as a Pasto chiefdom, but it nevertheless was understood to be a multiethnic meeting ground and was subject to tributary requirements very different from other Pasto communities.[5] Its very multiethnic nature would provide grist for the mills of nineteenth-century mestizos intent upon usurping resguardo lands. Colonial Ancuya was founded, moreover, at what would become an economically significant crossroads in the post-Independence era.

Turn-of-the-century Nariño was virtually isolated from the rest of the Spanish-American world, separated from Quito to the south and from Popayán and Bogotá to the north by vast intermontane desert valleys, the Chota and the Patía, respectively. All commerce was channeled, instead, toward the Pacific coast via the Camino de Barbacoas, on which numerous Cumbales, Guachucales, and Colimbas worked as carriers (see chapter 3). The road was a major focus of governmental concern; repeated attempts to upgrade it for use by mule teams were unsuccessful until 1893 (Gutiérrez 1897). With the completion of this vital link between the sierra and the outside world, the need to develop the backward highland region was felt in all its urgency; this included the commercialization of its small farms. The city of Túquerres, a major stopping point on the road, is located near Ancuya, whose warm and productive lands were now coveted by mestizos and outsiders alike.

The problems of Ancuya's Indians were twofold. As was the case in neighboring localities, valuable indigenous lands were being usurped by local mestizo townspeople and had to be defended by indigenous authorities. But the only line of defense available to the Indians, their cabildo, was not recognized by municipal authorities. What had begun as a dispute over land was swiftly transformed into a battle over ethnic identification. The controversy, as it can be read in the words of its protagonists, unfolded as follows.

Ancuya mayor Modesto Portilla, a mestizo who disputed the cabildo's legitimacy, had the following to say:

> Considering the third article of Law 89 of 1890, in which one observes that a cabildo can be formed where an indigenous *parcialidad* [community] has been established, moreover it expressly states that the former will be founded provided [the latter] was established; moreover, as in this place there has not existed nor exists to this day such a parcialidad as you refer to in your note, consequently they cannot practice any installation [of cabildo authorities] as they are not recognized by any authority in this District and for the same reason, this functionary cannot attend to the demand made of me because the possession to which it pretends is illegal.[6]

Under direct attack from the mayor's office and anxious to reclaim its lands, the cabildo appealed to the provincial government in Popayán. They asked that a government representative attend the investiture ceremony for the cabildo of 1895 to demonstrate the fact of official recognition of the resguardo.

Mayor Portilla, under pressure from the provincial government to recognize the cabildo, went to great pains to justify his claims. Considerable economic interests were at stake, as we learn from a brief written by the cabildo: the municipal mayor was himself guilty of stealing resguardo lands. In May 1895, Portilla sent a communiqué to the provincial government, stating that there were no Indians in Ancuya. He demanded that those who called themselves Indians prove themselves so:

> Considering that an indigenous parcialidad never before existed in this District, there being no evidence in this office, those who presented themselves with the character of Indians of Ancuya will prove the fact of so being in order to be treated according to the law.[7]

The task of ethnic definition was to be undertaken by the mayor's office itself:

With respect to the individuals presented today at this office with the character of Indians of Ancuya, the secretary will draw up proceedings in which each one is considered individually in order to designate the place in which [he] has existed and from what date [he] has knowledge that a parcialidad ceased to exist in this District.[8]

The mayor then drew up a list of those who claimed to be Indians and required that they testify to their identity. Threatened with criminal proceedings, the frightened witnesses swore that they were not native to Ancuya and could not recall the existence of a cabildo there.

The kinds of accusations leveled by Mayor Portilla, as well as the forced testimony that supported them, stand in contrast to the historical consciousness of the cabildo itself. The council drew an obvious connection between the politicians' ethnic taxonomies and the realities of land loss in the community:

10,000 Indians live in these two provinces, including Ipiales, Túquerres and Ancuya, [and] we are persecuted and harassed and devastated by those who envy our resguardo lands, who with the pretext of purchases and sales have taken the greater part of our resguardo lands that the King of Spain left in our favor.[9]

The cabildo recognized that the mayor's claims were based on a series of weak arguments. From Portilla's standpoint, the cabildo members were not Indians because they did not live on their land, because they testified to belonging to other communities, and because they swore that they did not remember the existence of a cabildo. But the reason many comuneros did not reside on their lands was that the mayor had usurped them. Their claim to the land, the Indians declared, was of considerably longer duration, going back to the grants given them by the Spanish Crown.

In November 1895, the cabildo wrote to the governor of Cauca, denouncing the mayor, who had sent the police after the Indians as though they were criminals. The letter also indicated that mestizo townspeople had enlisted the services of the Liberal party in support of their claims.

The indigenous authorities sent documentation to Popayán proving that they were, indeed, Indians from Ancuya. They included a statement indicating that the cabildo met regularly each year, despite the fact that the mayor consistently refused to recognize its existence. The cabildo also disputed the mayor's allegations regarding the origins of several Indians, who had come from outside Ancuya, emphasizing that these were individuals who had married comuneros. Ten usufruct documents were presented as evidence of the continuing existence of the resguardo. The cabildo also provided what they conceived to be the ultimate certification of their Indianness: as stipulated by legislation, they would furnish colonial documentation attesting to their resguardo status. That is, they perceived their land rights and their claim to political power as stemming from their descent from the original founders of the resguardo: "But we are all descendants of our ancient tributaries from whom we have our titles that secure our lands."[10]

There ends the documentation for Ancuya. It is no longer a resguardo and few, if any, of its inhabitants still consider themselves to be Indians. The tug-of-war between the local and provincial governments and the lack of resolution of the 1895 case undoubtedly sounded the death knell for indigenous identity in this Pasto community.

Several dimensions of the legal definition of the Indian are apparent in the Ancuya material. Using the same juridical source, the two parties to the dispute constructed radically different definitions of ethnicity. The Indians built their identity upon their descent from colonial tributaries to whom they were linked through their colonial title. The political viability of the community was maintained through the issuance of usufruct documents. Such forms of evidence of indigenous identity are founded upon Law 89 of 1890.

The mayor also drew upon Law 89, although he based his argument upon different aspects than did the cabildo. Modesto Portilla appealed to a portion of Law 89 requiring that cabildos be established in existing indigenous communities to justify his claim that the Indians of Ancuya had no right to a cabildo. In Portilla's view, if he could prove that Ancuya had long ceased to operate as an indigenous community, then it would be within his rights to refuse recognition of the cabildo. Only on this basis could he defend the deeds of non-Indian property holders who had illicitly purchased resguardo lands. His evidence of a presumed lack of continuity of the resguardo system in Ancuya was drawn from the testimonies of Indians living in neighboring towns. That is, Portilla conflated residence with membership in the ethnic-legal category of "Indian."

Significantly, the mayor collected his evidence through individual interviews, not through a communal affirmation by the collectivity. This stands in contrast to the cabildo's defense, based on communal documents (colonial title and nineteenth-century usufruct documents) and a collective history (recognition of descent from colonial tributaries). Finally, the mayor used a manipulative technique that is still practiced in Nariño: since he found no documentation proving the Indians' identity in his archive, he assumed that it did not exist.[11]

The Extinction of the Quillacinga Resguardos

Surrounding Pasto are a series of towns—Anganoy, Catambuco, Consacá, Chachagüí, La Cruz, La Laguna, Pandiaco, and Tangua, among others—that were resguardos until the first half of the twentieth century. From before the time of the Spanish invasion, the Quillacingas, the ethnic group to which these townspeople belonged, inhabited the valleys surrounding what is today the city of Pasto. The Pastos, with whom the Cumbales identify, lived in the high mountains of the Ipiales-Túquerres plateau to the south. By the twentieth century the Quillacingas, like the Pastos, had lost their aboriginal language and many of their lands; in the course of three centuries of European domination, they had become culturally similar to their Pasto neighbors.[12]

By the 1930s, as the fifty transitional years specified by Law 89 for the extinction of resguardos were drawing to a close, government authorities turned their attention toward the department of Nariño. The economy was now booming, thanks to a highway built in 1932 connecting Pasto to the rest of the country to the north. The land needed to supply goods for export and pasture for cattle was quickly identified and made available: the Quillacinga resguardos. By 1950, almost all communal Indian lands surrounding Pasto had been freed up for commercial exploitation as a result of the liquidation of their communal status.[13]

The history of the termination of the resguardos of Pasto is of interest here insofar as it illustrates how legal definitions of indigenous identity, aspects of which I already have examined for Ancuya, operated in tandem with changing concepts of identity among Indians themselves. In other words, the legal basis for Indian identity supplied by Law 89 was no longer entirely external to the indigenous community; it had been embraced as a form of self-definition by Indians themselves. Guillermo Bonfíl Batalla's notion of deindianization is useful for understanding the process of indigenous internalization of the dominant society's legal interpretation of ethnicity. Bonfíl Batalla coined this term to characterize processes of ideological change in Mexico, in which communities divest themselves of their indigenous identity in response to outside pressures (Bonfíl Batalla 1987). Deindianization, in his view, is a purely ideological phenomenon; it does not necessarily imply a consequent rejection of elements of indigenous culture. In fact, many of the deindianized communities he observed in Mexico continued to maintain a culture similar to that of neighboring villages, which still considered themselves to be Indian.

The historical record poignantly illustrates the role of deindianization in the demise of the Quillacinga resguardos. The same economic factors that caused local mestizos to covet indigenous lands propelled Indians to approve almost overwhelmingly the extinction of their resguardos. Comuneros were persuaded by the government that their holdings would be more secure under deeds than under usufruct documents; bureaucrats argued that the cabildo was a source of disputes within the community, due to its unethical ways of distributing land. In some cases, such arguments were channeled through deindianized comuneros or local mestizos whose own Indian identity had only recently been lost. The extinction of Consacá, for example, was brought about by a narrow sector of the resguardo, some of whom were not actually resguardo members but had manipulated the census rolls so that they appeared on paper as comuneros.[14]

The deindianized Quillacingas believed their Indian identity to be a transitory and strictly legal phenomenon. This is evident in the words they choose to describe themselves. For instance, in a 1944 letter to the Minister of National Economy, the cabildo of Consacá called itself "los que hasta hoy llamados indios"—"those who until today were called Indians"—as though indigenous identity could be effaced by government decree.[15]

The evolutionary perspective that guided the values of most government authorities fostered the use of cultural arguments to persuade comuneros that they were no longer Indian. In a study of the resguardo of Chachagüí, for example, Bogotá observers concluded that "its members enjoy a level of culture similar to that of the rest of the country's peasant population."[16] The official study of Males alleged that Spanish monolingualism revealed an absence of indigenous culture, echoing early twentieth-century arguments in favor of a policy of acculturation through language teaching; similar contentions fuel modern criticism of Cumbal's continued resguardo status.[17] High educational levels and cultural attributes similar to those of other peasants led the municipal mayor of Consacá to argue that for all intents and purposes, the comuneros were not Indian at all: "The number of inhabitants in this Community is one hundred sixty-eight persons, these being people who are all completely civilized, given that they are all white and are all more or less educated."[18] Clearly, the authorities perceived these

comuneros as well placed on an evolutionary ladder that, in their be-
lief, divided Colombians into the "savage" and the "civilized." Race,
culture, and legal identity were understood to be equivalent categories.

It is evident from the historical record that deindianized Indians
drew upon the same evolutionary theories that nourished the hopes
of Colombian officials. The cabildo of Males, anxious to free itself from
the clutches of Law 89, echoed government sentiments with the following plea:

> Law 89 of 1890 was issued for uncivilized Indians, semi-
> savages, who had only just been reduced to civilized life,
> when they were considered incapable of administering their
> property themselves, and when the first Indians of a tribe were
> of a reduced number, and all has changed with modern sys-
> tems of education and their facilities, an Indian is a true man,
> sufficiently educated, capable of administering his properties
> himself.[19]

Similarly, those of Consacá perceived their legal and ethnic status as
an atrophied and nonvital link to their past: "And for this reason, it is
unjust that we continue to live the ignorant life of the aborigine, although that is only understood today as a tradition of the origins of
the peoples of South America."[20]

Nevertheless, only some comuneros approved of the liquidation of
their resguardos. This is evident in a letter from a group of embattled
smallholders from Consacá:

> But, unfortunately, with the current change in the government,
> the authorities from this locality such as the Mayor and Munic-
> ipal Deputy who sponsor the indigenous Cabildo upon whose
> administration we depend, are waging a vulgar campaign of
> persecution against us, attacking us in our economic activity,
> paralyzing our labors and depriving us of the right to produce
> foodstuffs, thus: they attempt to steal our lands under the pre-
> text that we are no longer Indians, according to the vulgar am-
> bition of the thieves who are grabbing the plots that they take
> from other Indian farmers, in an abusive and arbitrary manner,
> [stealing] all the fruits of our labor.[21]

This letter also indicates that the most politically powerful were frequently also the most deindianized. In such instances, ethnic boundaries can be comprehended most clearly in terms of the distribution
of power and not of cultural repertories.[22]

Today the peasants around Pasto have relinquished their indigenous
identity completely, although their life-styles are essentially identical

to those of the self-identified Indian agriculturalists of the Ipiales region. In fact, in all of the discussions I have had with middle-aged peasants from Catambuco, Consacá, and Tangua, none identifies him- or herself as Indian nor remembers anything beyond the fact that in the dim and distant past a resguardo existed in the municipality.[23]

Indian Identity in Contemporary Cumbal

Juan Bautista Cuaicual

One of the most popular tales told around the fire on cold evenings is that of Juan Bautista Cuaical, who was drafted into the Colombian army sometime around the turn of the century. Juan Bautista was not cut out to be a soldier; he was ultimately relegated to kitchen duty. After six wasted months in the bar racks, he was sent home to Cumbal. Juan Bautista's father traveled to the city of Pasto to meet his son, who was now unrecognizable. He no longer spoke with a characteristic Nariñense accent and had changed his name from "Cuaical" to "Cuaicual":

> He'd gone to the barracks, and even his language, his very language, he'd lost it. He didn't introduce himself properly, but he said Juan Bautista Cuaicual. He didn't say Cuaical. (Benjamín Cuaical, Vereda Cuaical)[24]

Imitating the accent of the northerners, whom they call "Paisas" after the epithet given to colonists from Antioquia, storytellers remember a host of incidents in which Juan Bautista denied his identity.

For example, there is the bittersweet recollection of how Cuaical did not recognize his own father when he arrived to take him home from the barracks:

> When his father arrived at the barracks, then he asked for Juan Bautista Cuaical, and then the guard told him, "Here's a man looking for you, who says he's from Cumbal, and that you should go."
> Then they would say—well, sure, could it be true or not?—that when he left in this manner, he looked there through the door and the little old man was standing there. And they say he saw him there. They say he said to him, "Who do you see, my son? I'm your father, Juan Ramón Cuaical."
> "Ah! Cuaical, right?"
> They say he said, "I came to see, to see if we could go now."

"Let's see, then," he said. Then he played dumb. "What-ever you say, commander," he said. "Whatever you say. Let's see, then, if you'll give me my discharge, then we'll go," he said.

And then, "You, little old man, might you be my father? Then I should kneel [and ask for a blessing]." (Benjamín Cuaical, Vereda Cuaical)[25]

Juan Bautista's father had brought toasted fava beans for the long walk home, but his son threw them away, calling them *pepas bobas* or silly seeds. And once he arrived home, he recognized nothing:

Well, he entered the kitchen and, as we keep guinea pigs, which scurried around there in the parlor, they say he said, "And that little animal that runs around there, down in the corner, saying 'Lui, lui,' what kind of little animal is it?"

"Those are guinea pigs, my dear son," they say his mother said.

And then, "Don't you remember? Those are guinea pigs."

And they say that his mother said to him, "They are to be caught and skinned."

"Hum!" they say he said, "Let's see, then, hum! Let's see, catch one. Let's see, then, skin it." (Benjamín Cuaical, Vereda Cuaical)[26]

Later Juan Bautista tried to attack an animal he saw in the rafters; he could be calmed down only when told it was not an invader but cheese. And when he asked who the monkey was in the kitchen, and was informed that it was his sister Melania, he responded with a word-play on her name, "Mil años que no la he visto," that he hadn't seen her for a thousand years.

What Juan Bautista had forgotten were all those customs and life-ways that the Cumbales perceive as making them culturally distinctive. In a play on how comuneros understand the everyday workings of an indigenous identity, Juan Bautista is cast as the ultimate buffoon who has forgotten his roots. In reality, however, non-Indian peasants from surrounding communities—including Juan Bautista's imaginary com-panions in the barracks—speak with the same accent, ask blessings of their parents, eat guinea pigs, and produce cheese for the market.[27] What constitutes identity within the community is precisely that which identifies comuneros as non-Indians outside. Neighboring mes-tizos proffer these same cultural attributes, including Spanish mono-lingualism and articulation within the market economy, as examples of the Cumbales' loss of indigenous lifeways in the hopes of persuading government authorities to extinguish the resguardo and free its lands for privatization.

The Legal Basis of Identity

Political activists in Cumbal frequently offer alternative definitions of indigenous identity for the consumption of outsiders, since they understand that what binds people together on an everyday basis is not necessarily the same as what unites them in the eyes of the dominant society. When asked by a visiting bureaucrat to explain what made him an Indian, 1986 governor José Elipcio Chirán pointed to the existence of Deed 228, the memory of colonial-era hereditary chiefs, and the continued occupation of the land by families with the same surnames, generation after generation: in other words, the legal and communal definition of Indian required by legislation. This political identity informs all efforts at historical recollection in Cumbal, whether the narratives of memoristas, legal briefs composed by cabildo members, local histories written by ethnic activists, or the plays presented by militant youth. Central to all these historical representations are the same images: the title, the chiefs, the surnames.

Nevertheless, an everyday identity of the sort described in the Juan Bautista Cuaicual story is articulated with this political identity in most of the historical representations that I encountered in the course of my research. Narrators, writers, and actors all contextualize their evidence of the distant political past within the more familiar imagery of the recent past and even the present. As a result, they frequently cite lifeways common to their mestizo neighbors as evidence of their cultural distinctiveness. That is, although Cumbal political identity is founded upon the requirements of the law, it is grounded in a perceived cultural specificity marking the comuneros as Indians.

Thus, when viewed from the outside, it appears as though the Cumbales objectify their culture by transforming Indianness into a kind of a trait list, a bounded and distinguishable thing, composed of abstract and timeless characteristics (see Clifford 1988; Handler 1988; Jackson 1989). Perhaps the objectification of Cumbal culture is an inheritance from the philosophies of the dominant society and from the requirements of law. But indigenous identity is also grounded within a specific storytelling tradition centered around the cabildo and its activities. This narrative tradition has developed, as we shall see in the following chapter, within the context of a model of spatial organization characteristic of southern Nariño.

TWO

The Path of the Three Staffs of Office

WHEN I FIRST ARRIVED in Cumbal I visited the cabildo to request permission to conduct fieldwork. Cumbal's cabildo meets every Sunday afternoon in a cement-block house perched on a hill above the cemetery. On Sundays, the horses grazing around the building are a signal that the cabildo meeting has begun. The first time I approached the *casa de cabildo* or cabildo office I was greeted by small groups of men, whose wives sat patiently on the steps of the patio. Their hospitality was contagious and, I was to discover, constant: handshakes, greetings, and perhaps even a shot of *aguardiente* welcomed me on subsequent visits.

Upon entering the office I was told to remove my hat, under pain of a fine or a whipping by the teniente or lieutenant of the cabildo, one of whose responsibilities is to maintain order during the meeting. When I approached the table at which the eight cabildo members were seated, their staffs of office laid on the surface before them, I was told to greet the authorities one by one, beginning with the governor and ending with a general salutation to the comuneros or resguardo members present in the hall. I was invited to take a seat and observe the proceedings. As I was an unusual guest, I was offered a place on the benches immediately within the the low fence enclosing the cabildo table. Had I been a comunera, I would have hunted for a space on one of the many benches filling the room, or I might have been forced to take my place with the crowd standing at the back.

The cabildo of Cumbal is composed of eight elected officials: six *regidores* or aldermen, an elected governor, and his appointed lieutenant; the governor appoints a secretary to take charge of all paperwork.

The president, vice-president, and treasurer are chosen from among the six regidores by all eight members at the first meeting of the year.[1]

On the day of my visit, as at all cabildo meetings, once the comuneros had submitted their multiple requests for hearings to the secretary, a young man seated at a small desk next to the cabildo's table, and the *cabildantes* or cabildo authorities had finished conferring over the order of business, the public meeting began. The various parties to land transfers or disputes, the representatives of *juntas de acción comunal* or grass-roots public works committees, even a visiting government official, approached the table to have their case, their complaint, their request, or their suggestion heard. Some matters were discussed and resolved, punctuated by shouting matches and oratory, while special meeting times were designated for further consideration of other problems. After a number of visits to the cabildo, it became apparent to me that real decision making does not take place here, although opinions certainly are aired at these assemblies. In my case, the decision was immediate and unanimous: I was to be permitted to conduct fieldwork so long as I shared my data with the cabildo. How I was to do this was never discussed but was developed over the course of the year.

Occasionally cabildantes are requested to address the public on any one of a variety of issues. The six regidores representing the six *veredas*, the broad territorial divisions of the resguardo, will stand at their seats and one by one eloquently express their views on the matter at hand. On my first visit to the cabildo, I noticed that the cabildantes spoke in a designated order, beginning with the representative from the vereda Guan, moving on to the delegate from Tasmag, continuing through the authorities from Cuaical, Quilismal, and Nazate, and ending with the regidor from Cuaspud. This order of presentation, I was to discover, replicates the organization of topographic space in the resguardo, a series of five parallel bands of territory that radiate out from snow-capped Mount Cumbal, beginning with Guan in the north and ending with Cuaspud in the southeast. Cuaical and Quilismal share a common territory, with vereda membership defined by house plot (see fig. 1). Subsequent visits to the secretary's table provided further evidence of the ubiquitousness of the section order. The handwritten documents the young man prepared all closed with spaces for the authorities' signatures, which were arranged according to the same scheme.

Anyone who spends any amount of time in Cumbal is bound to notice that the section hierarchy pervades daily life. Until comuneros were sure that I was acquainted with the community, I was told, day after day, that there are six veredas in Cumbal, after which their names were listed in order—Guan, Tasmag, Cuaical, Quilismal, Nazate, Cuaspud. In all official activities, whether they be cabildo meetings, *mingas* or collective work parties, the distribution of festival sponsorship, or land claims, the sections are clearly ordered, with Guan first and Cuaspud last.

Even everyday conversation commenting upon events in the six veredas follows this model, idealizing a social reality that hardly conforms to such harsh generalizations: Guan is frequently referred to as the "best section," with the wealthiest and most hardworking comuneros who are also *buenos recuperadores* or active participants in the land struggle; the Cuaspudes are believed to be incompetent *contrarios*, enemies of the land struggle, because many of them are poor and have worked as servants for the landlords. Indeed, the Cuaspudes feel that they are consistently slighted by others.

Jokes also obey the section hierarchy, as I discovered when Alonso Imbago, 1986 cabildo president, asked me about the many foreigners he noted crossing into Ecuador at the nearby border checkpoint of Rumichaca. He called them "globetrotters," a special breed of long-haired young people, laden with backpacks. Alonso said he planned to become one. But he did not propose to follow the usual itinerary from Colombia to Ecuador, to Peru, and finally to Bolivia; instead, he would begin his voyage in Guan, moving on to Tasmag, through Cuaical and Quilismal, crossing Nazate, and finally to Cuaspud.

The section system that organizes topographic and social space in Cumbal and in several neighboring communities also provides a template for structuring temporal process, both for short-term everyday experience and for long-range historical time.[2] Over the half hour or so dedicated to the discussion of a single point in the cabildo meeting, for instance, time is divided into six units, permitting regidores to speak in order. Longer stretches of time, ranging from a week to several years, and even to the four and a half centuries since the Spanish invasion, are all made meaningful through application of the same model. This template for the past also provides the Cumbales with a pattern for structuring land claims. In other words, the section hierarchy is more than a model of reality that makes sense of the world and motivates routine process within it; it also provides a model for initiating far-reaching changes in the economic and political environment, particularly the reincorporation of usurped lands into the resguardo.

Andean Perspectives on Time and Space

Similar models for organizing topographic space and historical time can be found throughout the Andes. R. Tom Zuidema's pioneering work on the *ceque* system of Cuzco reveals how the Incas conceptually organized their capital into a series of political and ritual units bounded by imaginary lines marked by shrines, leading from the capital of Cuzco to the horizon. This spatial model, which when mapped divides the Inca capital into subunits that look like slices of a pie, was used to encode dynastic history as well as to structure calendrical knowledge acquired through astronomical observation along the sight lines constituted by the ceques (Zuidema 1964, 1982a, 1982b, 1990; Sherbondy 1979; Wachtel 1982). Ethnographic research in contemporary southern Andean peasant communities underlines the persistence of these geographic schemes. To varying degrees in different communities extending from northern Chile to Peru and Bolivia, we find territorial models organized according to a hierarchical section order that governs political life, ritual, and productive activity (Albó 1972; Barthel 1986 [1959]; Urton 1984, 1988, 1990).

It is impossible to trace the persistence of the section system among the Pastos back beyond the colonial period, as scholars have been able to do for Quechua speakers. Colonial-era Pasto *cacicazgos* or hereditary chiefdoms were independent political units distributed across the terrain according to a pattern somewhat similar to the parallel bands of territory that comprise today's veredas (Landázuri 1990; Rappaport 1988; Salomon 1986). In the colonial period, the territory now called Gran Cumbal—made up of the resguardos of Cumbal, Panán, Chiles, and Mayasquer—was composed of a number of independent but interlinked cacicazgos. In those days, Cumbal was much smaller than it is today, counting among its *parcialidades* or sections only the modern-day veredas of Guan, Tasmag, Cuaical, and Quilismal as well as parts of Panán and Chiles; at that time, Cuaical and Quilismal occupied distinct bands of territory.[3] What is today Nazate was then an independent cacicazgo that also contained portions of modern-day Panán and played host to migrants from Chiles. Cuaspud was similarly an autonomous entity. In the sixteenth century, Mayasquer belonged to the chiefdom of Tulcán, in what is today Ecuador, but two hundred years later was claimed as part of Cumbal.

We can see the roots of the section system in colonial descriptions of the parcialidades of Cumbal, which were tenuously linked within the decentralized cacicazgo. Parcialidades were always listed in these documents in a strict order, suggesting that when native authorities were called upon to prepare lists of their subjects, they accomplished this task in keeping with a widely known social and territorial model. Similarly, a 1722 census from nearby Ipiales cites the component parcialidades in an order surprisingly similar to the one that appears in a 1940 document.[4]

The colonial period was a time of massive land loss and of political and territorial consolidation for the Pastos. By 1810, Cumbal had been transformed into a larger cacicazgo of eight parcialidades, including not only the four original sections of colonial Cumbal, but also Nazate, Cuaspud, Panán, and Chiles. At the end of the colonial period the component sections of the broad cacicazgo followed much the same order as they do today, with the difference being that at that time the tail end of the hierarchy was brought up by Panán and Chiles.[5]

Throughout the nineteenth century Cumbal was composed of eight parcialidades, including Panán and Chiles, both of which became fully independent only at the beginning of the twentieth century. This is undoubtedly the reason why section hierarchies do not exist there today. That the section order functioned as a conscious governing model for political and territorial organization is clear from Republican-era cabildo documents, which regidores signed according to their places in the hierarchy. The nineteenth-century Cumbales perceived their section system as ancient, as is apparent in the following explanation provided to the municipal government:

> Those of us who are registered as members of the section "Tas-mag" respectfully declare: that it is clear that the communal lands of this district form a single body, and that this land is distributed to all those who have no means of maintaining themselves; but we must caution you, Mr. Mayor, that this portion of territory is divided into small sections, called "parcialidades," and each of them is demarcated by its own boundaries, and is represented by a Regidor, and so that it can pursue its domestic governance and so that it can observe its ancient customs, we need to know the boundaries of each parcialidad.[6]

While Cumbal has always been divided into sections, their order and number has varied over the centuries. Nevertheless, by the nineteenth century, Cumbales accepted that their model of territorial organization was ages old and unchanging.

Time and Space in Everyday Experience

Experiential Time and the Six Sections

The section scheme organizes practical time for comuneros and their cabildo. As I noted earlier, regidores' interventions at cabildo meetings faithfully obey the hierarchy. Similarly, cabildo elections are organized by section, so that in reality a series of six consecutive elections take place for the six veredas, beginning with Guan. When all regidores have been elected, the entire community votes for governor:

> Come noon, the whole community, with its veredas and others, came together.
> Then, there they were in the convent: there was the municipal mayor with his secretary. There they drew up the document of the appointment of the cabildo.
> Then they followed with [those candidates named by] the regidores, then those named by the community, for so-and-so, for so-and-so.
> Then they started with Guan, for so-and-so. They passed in front of the priest, the mayor, telling them, "Another [vote] for so-and-so." And with that, he who ended up with the greatest number of votes was decided for sure.
> And it went on this way until the arrival of the hour of [voting for] governor. When they arrived at governor, they would say so-and-so, and the whole community would agree. (Benjamín Cuaical, Vereda Cuaical)[7]

Communal projects are organized in the same fashion as cabildo elections. Time is divided into periods lasting a week, with Guan working on Monday, Tasmag on Tuesday, and so on.

The section structure is mirrored in practical activity. Agricultural labor, for example, is organized according to a rotational scheme. Potatoes are planted in rows, called *guachos*. At a minga two men will take a guacho, one opening the ridge and leaving seed there while the other covers the seed with soil. Each pair is assigned its own guachos and will not encroach on those of its neighbors. If there are five pairs of workers, each pair will work one guacho in five. Moreover, they will not continue on to their next guacho until all the workers have completed their rows:

> So, everyone goes along, making guachos at the minga, of course.
> Then some leave the others behind.
> When they finish there, their row, the workers leave.
> They say, "I'm going to rest." They say, "I've finished up. Bring me the boss so he can tell me to turn around and return [in the next row]," they say, "to help out the slow ones." (José Abrahán Mimalchí and Mercedes Cuaical, Vereda Tasmag)[8]

Similarly, at community-wide mingas, distinct bands of land are assigned to work groups, replicating the organization of the resguardo.

I observed this on the slopes of Mount Cumbal, at a minga convoked to open canals to irrigate the valley below. When a group completed the task assigned to it, the participants refused to join in to help their comrades from other sections, stating that they would only work that stretch of territory supplying water for their own vereda. Thus, a very clear configuration of distinct and autonomous sections, repeated over and over, is reproduced in the course of the labor process.[9]

Territorial Hierarchies and the Structure of Authority

The shape of long-term experiential time is also determined by the section system. Each year the governor is elected from a different vereda, moving in order. Thus, in 1984 he was from Guan, in 1985 from Tasmag, in 1986 from Cuaical, in 1987 from Quilismal, in 1988 from Nazate, and in 1989 from Cuaspud. Each year that the governorship falls in a particular vereda, that entity has three representatives on the cabildo: the governor, a regidor, and a teniente or lieutenant appointed by the governor. Since each cabildo member carries a staff of office, the rotational system is interpreted metaphorically in terms of the movement of the three staffs of office around the circuit of the six veredas.

The same rotational system cannot be traced for chiefly successions in the pre-Columbian or early colonial periods for lack of historical evidence. Nevertheless, within the Spanish-derived administrative scheme governing colonial Indian communities, the designation of annually appointed governors rotated from parcialidad to parcialidad in a sequence that roughly followed the section order existing at the time. We do not know whether such a rotational scheme was a pre-Columbian tradition or a Spanish introduction. In order to ascertain the origins of the system, data regarding political authorities other than those encompassed by the Spanish gubernatorial system would be needed.[10]

But it is immaterial whether or not the system of political rotation that characterizes modern Cumbal is pre-Columbian in origin. What is of greater significance is how this mode of selecting political authorities colors the contemporary memory. Instead of locating events by their calendrical dates, it is possible for individuals to situate experiences by reference to the vereda that occupied the governorship at the time. Such a dating scheme would be useful only for the period in which the speakers were eyewitnesses to cabildo succession, a span of roughly forty years cut into six-year periods. In fact, I heard many of the more politically active comuneros construct historical chronologies in just this fashion.

Flexibility in Territorial Models

The ten months I spent in Cumbal in 1986–87, the three months in 1988, and the years since, during which I made annual visits and maintained constant telephone communication with cabildo authorities, have been characterized by intense factionalism and power struggles. Members of the various currents of the Colombian Liberal party have practiced a game of one-upmanship that in 1987–88 almost divided the resguardo. An ever-diminishing cross section of families still opposes the policy of land claims pursued by the cabildo since 1975. Numerous comuneros from less wealthy and less politically powerful families have never had much voice in cabildo decisions, beyond the more passive strategies of refusal to participate in cabildo functions. Women have never occupied positions of authority in the cabildo, and gossips frequently criticize those women who are vocal at meetings.[11] In other words, Cumbal is by no means a harmonious or homogeneous community.

Beneath the presumed equality of the rotational system, which insures access to the governorship for all veredas and provides each section with a measure of political autonomy through the offices of the regidor, lies a more profound sense of inequality. The formal hierarchy that places Guan at the apex and Cuaspud at the bottom of the path of the three staffs of office, and that implicitly values the contributions of Guan over those of Cuaspud, is but one of a series of inequalities characterizing resguardo life.

The rotational system is not as egalitarian as it appears: instead, it masks inequality. While each vereda claims the governorship for the space of a year, this does not mean that political power is enjoyed equally by all governors. As I will describe in the next chapter, certain families exert considerably more influence within cabildo circles than others. Until the governorship became a coveted office with the advent of the 1975 land struggle, these families controlled the cabildo's everyday functioning through their domination of the secretary's office. Since 1975, a few groups of ethnic rights militants, only some of whom come from these same powerful families, dominate the cabildo and political process in general.

It is thus surprising that in such an environment of factionalism, gossip, and general discord over almost any issue, every adult I met accepted the rotational hierarchy as a basic fact of existence and as a general organizing scheme for making sense of experience. This might be due to the fact that until the wave of land occupations that began in the 1970s, most comuneros did not participate in cabildo activity and, as veredas were largely endogamous until recently, tended to perceive their world in terms of section boundaries. What transpired in cabildo meetings became relevant only after 1975.

On a deeper level, the generalized acceptance of hierarchy can be traced to the porous nature of the system. Considerable leeway for manipulation exists within the broad limits of the rotational structure. Although section membership is determined largely by residence, it is possible to shift affiliations or to belong to two veredas simultaneously if one owns lands in various locations. This flexibility of affiliation has increased in recent years with a rise in veredal exogamy, but a long-standing tradition of inter-vereda land sales has always served as a means of establishing multiple residences. Consequently, in a number of instances, individuals have secured the governorship twice in a six-year rotational period by claiming membership through land ownership in more than one vereda. Moreover, since 1975, the porous nature of vereda boundaries has facilitated the acquisition of political power by families that traditionally shunned the cabildo. By claiming simultaneous residence in a number of sections and creating alliances with relatives in other veredas, these families have secured the administrative continuity necessary for the consolidation of their authority over the cabildo.

On the other hand, the vereda hierarchy has proved an effective weapon against unusually blatant claims to power. For example, in 1989, when a charismatic former governor from Tasmag attempted to wrest power from Cuaspud, to which the three staffs of office had passed, the community opposed him almost unanimously, appealing to the sanctity of the rotational system, despite the fact that he had always enjoyed a high level of popular support.

Geography and History

A Template for Memory

The organization of the six veredas furnishes a model for a more general interpretation of history: the past is remembered, recounted, relived, and corrected in section order. Numerous memories, ranging from the sponsorship of feasts to colonial-era resistance to Spanish rule, are interpreted as having occurred according to the order of the six veredas.

History itself is depicted as though it were cyclical, literally moving from one section to the next. In the past, before the cabildo office was constructed, the archives storing years of political and administrative documentation had to be carried from vereda to vereda, moving from year to year as the governorship moved. But if the movement of the governorship and the archives is described as a cycle, this does not mean that time is literally perceived as cyclical, just that the six sections are a template for organizing a more open-ended temporal experience. The archives are in a constant state of flux, with new documents added and old ones deleted—or stolen—each year. Thus, in the days before the cabildo office was built, the archive that completed the rotation from Guan to Cuaspud was not the same one that began the circuit.

A good example of the influence of the section hierarchy on historical memory can be found in accounts of the administration of feast days at the beginning of the twentieth century, when regidores were also responsible for selecting *fiesteros* or fiesta sponsors, individuals who spent considerable sums of money on lavish feasts and processions for their veredas. Contemporary storytellers maintain that fiestero selection followed vereda order. In the cabildo archive there are a number of notebooks, called *libros de devoción*, that record festival sponsors from each of the sections from 1919 to 1951. For many of the fiestas, including the Immaculate Conception, the Presentation, and the Virgen de las Mercedes, there were six sponsors a year, one from each section, named in order. Frequently, the entries treat the appointments as though they moved each year to a new vereda, stating that the sponsorship "falls in" (*recae en*) a given section.[12]

The appointment of fiesteros for certain special celebrations, such as the Nativity and Corpus Christi, was also supposed to have obeyed the six-section scheme, thus reinforcing the division of time into six-year periods. But information contained in the libros de devoción does not entirely bear out this stylized version of the past. Lists of sponsors for the feasts of the Nativity and Corpus Christi for 1921–35, the most continuous data existing on fiestero appointments, shows that although such obligations rotated from vereda to vereda, they did not necessarily move in strict section order.[13] Contemporary historical consciousness thus recreates an ideal that did not always bear out in reality.

The history of festival sponsorship is, nevertheless, central to an awareness of the past. When I asked Benjamín Cuaical, one of Cumbal's foremost historians, to comment on a draft of my analysis of the section hierarchy, he suggested that I add detail on the interaction of the section order with the appointment of festival sponsors. Contemporary reconstructions of fiestero appointments are significant in that they provide information on cabildo functioning across a range of domains of community life, extending well beyond the strictly political sphere. During the past century the impact of the cabildo on the everyday life of the community has diminished, and for many it was almost a chore to find candidates for cabildo office. Today, however, broadranging authority is being recuperated through the land-claims movement. The memory of the rotation of historical festivals is thus an element in the cabildo's revitalization of its earlier authority, an attempt to reclaim symbolic ground as well as territory.

Geography and the Recapitulation of History

While the section hierarchy governs the nature of the memory of particular events, it also organizes the general historical memory, juxtaposing key images of the communal past in a hierarchical configuration that is itself historically derived. The path of the three staffs of office recapitulates the order in which the three pre-Columbian cacicazgos of Cumbal were integrated into a single entity in the late colonial period. The four original sections of the colonial cacicazgo of Cumbal are now the first four sections of the modern resguardo. Nazate, which joined Cumbal in the seventeenth century, is now the fifth section. Integrated into Cumbal at some point in the eighteenth century, Cuaspud became the sixth section. Both Nazate and Cuaspud lost their internal section hierarchies upon being incorporated into Cumbal, although the smaller neighborhoods within which juntas de acción comunal operate sometimes retain the names of colonial parcialidades, such as Adgán in Cuaspud. Although the memory of the consolidation process is not a conscious element in the Cumbal historical repertoire, it effectively dictates the contemporary configuration of historical narrative.

The major protagonists of the mid-eighteenth-century disputes recorded in resguardo titles were the caciques of Quilismal, especially Pedro Alpala and the Mites family, and a group of brothers from Nazate whose surname was Tarapués.[14] Contemporary storytellers deploy these political leaders across time and space in very different ways than the historical documents do. For example, Moisés Tapie of Nazate identified the Mites caciques, who were father and son from Quilismal in the original titles, as brothers residing in Guan, where many families still bear the Mites surname. He placed Pedro Alpala in Cuaical instead of Quilismal, probably because the band of territory in which the two veredas are located is usually glossed as Cuaical. In keeping with the original document, Alpala was described as living in a later time period than the Mites caciques. But he transported the Tarapués brothers of Nazate from the colonial period to the nineteenth century, despite the fact that the documentary record describes them as being contemporaries of Alpala. Some older people in Nazate even claim that their parents knew them! Chronology is thus transformed by modern storytellers to conform to the rotational hierarchy.

The Shape of Time

Near the end of my stay in Cumbal I began to discuss the possibilities of ultimately sharing the fruits of my research with the community through a series of culturally sensitive materials following the section order. A number of ideas resulted from brainstorming sessions with Helí Valenzuela, Moisés Tapie, and others, ranging from a publication to the painting of historical murals in the cabildo office. Although a Spanish-language publication beared to a Cumbal readership—which I am currently working on—ultimately turned out to be more feasible than a mural, our discussions about the latter provided me with food for thought. We planned a series of five wall paintings (since Cuaical and Quilismal share a territory and a common history, they could occupy a single visual space). As I worked with a number of cabildo members and former cabildantes on the themes to be depicted in these murals, a clear pattern began to emerge in which historical chronology recapitulated geographic hierarchy. The themes also replicated the specific historical topics I had been able to collect in each of the veredas.

The result of these discussions was a group of central historical images, loosely connected with supporting events into a series of constellations associated with veredas and organized in section order. All of the central referents were associated with periods of struggle, depicting the history of the resguardo as a trajectory of ever more successful land claims. But while key events were arrayed in chronological order, the earliest in Guan and the most recent in Cuaspud, the supporting images were not arranged chronologically. In other words, although time proceeded forward from vereda to vereda, the events assigned to each section were not necessarily contained within a single historical period. These constellations of knowledge of the past were structured in the following manner:

1. *Guan:* Guan is framed by the personage of the cacique Cumbe, the colonial chief from whom Cumbal derives its name. He is associated

49

in the oral tradition with Guan, because the surname Cumbal predominates here; those bearing the surname are believed by some to be Cumbe's descendants. The Cumbales say that Cumbe was the founder of their resguardo, cementing his claim to traditional lands in the face of Spanish encroachment. Cumbe can be associated with the early colonial period, sometime before the mid-eighteenth century, when the resguardo titles were written.[15]

2. *Tasmag:* The next major event that was chosen was the repossession of Las Tolas, the upper part of Tasmag, by a Supreme Court decision in 1869.[16] Las Tolas had always been resguardo land, but it was temporarily ceded to the church to support a *cofradía* or religious brotherhood. In the nineteenth century, when church lands passed into the hands of the state, Las Tolas automatically became public land and was placed on auction. The cabildo successfully fought the expropriation, effectively demonstrating that Las Tolas had only been lent to the church and was still part of the resguardo. After a protracted legal battle, the Supreme Court declared that Las Tolas was resguardo property. Although the restoration of Las Tolas to the cabildo follows chronologically and geographically from the founding of the resguardo, the referent framing Guan, it is surrounded by a constellation of earlier events, including the memory of a number of sixteenth- and seventeenth-century decrees delimiting resguardo boundaries, which are listed in the original Supreme Court decision.[17] Although these decrees antedate the repossession of Las Tolas, the memory of them is associated with the later event, because it is by virtue of the cabildo's battle to reclaim the territory that the documents were incorporated into the historical memory.

3. *Cuaical and Quilismal:* The 1869 Las Tolas decision also provided for the return of an hacienda located in Cuaical and Quilismal, known as El Zapatero. Also leased to a cofradía, El Zapatero subsequently fell into the hands of a local mestizo politician, who refused to part with it after the Supreme Court ruled in the cabildo's favor. It was only in 1975 that El Zapatero was restored to Indian hands, when the inhabitants of Cuaical and Quilismal occupied the hacienda in the first of what was to become a long series of land occupations. Thus, the framing event for Cuaical and Quilismal occurred considerably later than the event ascribed to Tasmag. Nevertheless, it does not stand alone: it is supported by a number of earlier events dating back to the mid-nineteenth century, including the story of how the hacienda was lost to mestizos, a tale I will describe in considerable detail in chapter 6.

4. *Nazate:* Even more recent is the central image linked to Nazate.

The westernmost portion of Nazate, called Cuetial, was purchased in the eighteenth century by the hereditary chiefs of Nazate, who had been forcibly relocated there from Chiles. The eighteenth-century rein-corporation of Cuetial into the communal holdings is recorded in the Royal Provision. As a result of the purchase, land ownership in Cuetial generally took the form of private property, recorded in *escrituras* or deeds originating in the municipal notary's office. In contrast, most other property rights in Cumbal are communal in character; comun-eros can only claim usufruct rights, substantiated in legal briefs gener-ated by the cabildo, which are called *documentos* or "documents." In 1981 a militant cabildo repossessed El Laurel, a huge hacienda to the east, in concert with Chiles and Panán, thus reconstituting the late colonial unity of Gran Cumbal. Inspired by its victory, the cabildo flexed its muscles in Cuetial, declaring the deeds to private property null and void and reincorporating Cuetial into the resguardo structure. The year 1981 was chosen by my interlocutors as an anchor date for the history of Nazate, backed up by the memory of the eighteenth-century purchase of Cuetial.

5. *Cuaspud:* The final reference is associated with the history of Cuas-pud, the sixth vereda. Here the key date is 1985, when the hacienda of La Boyera was redistributed to comuneros after a protracted struggle. Many narrators conceptually link the repossessed hacienda to the 1863 war with Ecuador, when La Boyera became a major battlefield. The civil wars of the nineteenth century are frequently associated with land loss in the minds of Cumbales, and are therefore appropriate support-ing detail for the key image, which recounts the reincorporation of territory through political action.

Each of these focal images depicts a step in the continued process of the reconstitution of Cumbal's traditional political authority and land base, beginning with the founding of the resguardo and ending with recent land repossessions. The constellation of supporting details that antedate the images are generally events that created the condi-tions making the repossession strategy necessary; all are related im-plicitly or explicitly to land loss. Thus, the historical chronology is at once a representation of the past and a political appropriation of the organizing model used to correct it.

Making History

A kind of historical-geographical chronology emerges here in which time is not arranged in a strictly linear fashion but in a series of con-stellations of images whose key motifs are structured both chronologically and in accordance with the section hierarchy. In other words, the six-section model provides a blueprint for representing the past (a model *of* the past), but the section system is also a political vehicle for correcting the abuses of history (a model *for* the future).

In Quechua, when appropriate diacritic markers are used, the terms for "the past" and for "in front of the observer" are identical: *ñawpa.* In other words, in the Andean vision of the past, history is *in front of* the observer and moves *backward* toward the observer (Earls and Silverblatt 1978; Urbano 1978).[18] This spatiotemporal view of history contrasts with our own, in which the past is located *behind* the observer and historical process moves *forward,* always remaining behind our backs.

The Cumbales are monolingual Spanish speakers, but they have retained what was probably a feature of their ancestral Pasto language and have translated the same distinction into Spanish: in Cumbal, when one wants to refer to a past action, one says "adelante" ("forward" in time or in space): "The King confirmed [the resguardo title] on January 25, 1758, but before [*forward*], there had been other titles . . . in 1746 and in 1630" (Benjamín Cuaical, Vereda Cuaical).[19]

This feature of Cumbal Spanish is relevant to any understanding of the meaning of history: when the past is located in front of the observer, it confers a historical aura on the activities of the present. But in order for a linguistic feature to acquire significance, the people themselves must express the concept in some way. I am not making the argument that these linguistic structures determine modes of thought; rather, I wish to explore people's *conscious* exegesis and how it sheds light on modes of thinking about the past. Panán comunero Manuel Fueltala's explanation of this particular space-time frame centers on practice as opposed to fact: although events occurred in the past, we live their consequences today and must act upon them now. For this reason, what already occurred is in front of the observer because that is where it can be corrected. History, therefore, is most relevant to the present and is *of the present.*

What is significant here is that history can be *corrected,* since it lies in front of the observer. In this vision of the past, unlike our own, historical correction is not empirical in nature; it does not involve the revision of historical accounts on the basis of new data. Instead, it is founded on the use value of the past. Historical facts are not rewritten; rather, the conditions that arose out of the historical process are the elements of the past that must be corrected.[20]

The territorial structure of Cumbal is reproduced over and over as the cabildo reincorporates reclaimed lands into the communal regime of the resguardo, thereby "correcting" history. The process began in 1975 when a huge tract of land called the Llano de Piedras was wrested from mestizo control. The Llano de Piedras had been occupied by non-Indian townspeople in 1923, when Cumbal was destroyed in an earthquake. The ruins of pre-earthquake Cumbal can still be seen in Puebloviejo, today occupied by comuneros. Before 1923, the Llano provided communal grazing land for the resguardo, as it had since 1711, although it was in continuous dispute throughout the nineteenth century because it was prime valley land. Inspired by Hilarión Alpala, one of Cumbal's most renowned historians and governor of the resguardo in 1975, the comuneros occupied the Llano, living under siege from the police until the following year. When it was formally handed over to the cabildo, the Llano was divided into veredas and distributed to the six regidores, who in turn distributed plots to their constituents (see fig. 1). The process of land redistribution was described to me by the 1975 cabildo president:

> Well, it was by sections, with a surveyor.
> First he distributed it. He made the portions for the veredas and he made roads, entryways, exits, right? So that there would be somewhere to walk.
> And in the first place, each vereda drew up an act, so that each regidor worked under an act listing the affiliated people in each vereda.
> And then they made the distribution by meters, by however much they could. Afterwards the cabildo distributed what they could to each person by meters. (Efraín Chirán, Vereda Cuaical)[21]

The Llano reproduced the structure of the resguardo, creating a mirror image of it, with each vereda bordering its counterpart in the reclaimed territory. But the configuration of the Llano de Piedras is a more perfect representation of the organizing scheme of the resguardo itself, because the surveyor—under orders of the cabildo—carved six, not five, tracts across the valley, giving Cuaical and Quilismal their own distinct plots. A similar strategy was employed in 1981 when El Laurel was repossessed and distributed. The 1985 redistribution of the hacienda La Boyera produced similar results. This particular strategy for land distribution does not appear to be an option for other militant communities outside Nariño.[22]

The cabildo follows precise rules when it maps the veredas onto reclaimed lands. Ideally, according to former governor Alonso Valenzuela, who presided over the redistribution of El Laurel in 1981 and La Boyera in 1985, all repossessed haciendas should be oriented toward Mount Cumbal, with Guan on the right-hand side, thus reproducing the orientation of the original sections. A look at figure 1 indicates that this is not always the case; in fact, in El Laurel the opposite ensued. Guan is on the left-hand side of the volcano in El Laurel, the result of disputes following the original redistribution to veredas. Those who discussed the issue with me emphatically stated that El Laurel's section order was "wrong" and "reversed."

The logic of land distribution in the respossessed haciendas recapitulates the image that people have of how inhabited space is organized. Nonetheless, I could find no one who believed that the Llano de Piedras was divided into veredas before its expropriation by the mestizos; everyone thought it had been open grazing land. It is quite likely that there were no fences in the Llano, the kind of physical reminder that contemporary narrators would recollect from their childhood. But according to nineteenth-century sources, veredas have always staked individual claims to the valley.[23]

The creation of mirror images reproduces an important facet of Cumbal's territorial relationship with its neighbors. Guan, the first vereda, borders on the resguardo of Muellamués, which is itself organized in sections, the first of which is Guan, located immediately to the north of Guan/Cumbal. Similarly, the sixth and last section, Cuaspud, borders on the resguardo of Carlosama, whose alternate name is also Cuaspud. A comparable pair divides Chiles from Mayasquer, where both border veredas were once called Gritadero.[24]

The repossession of lands and the consequent correction of history through the incorporation of usurped territories into the resguardo is completed when the six-section scheme is reintroduced into these lands. In the Llano de Piedras, El Laurel, La Boyera, and the other haciendas repossessed since, it is only by reintroducing the past into reclaimed territory that they are reconstituted as resguardo property.

THREE

The History-Makers

O~N~ A WINDY AFTERNOON an old man leans on his cane as he makes his way across the patio to a field behind his Cuaical house, accompanied by the cabildo and by his sons, one of whom is himself a cabildante. Already in his late seventies, don Benjamín Cuaical is about to transfer his use rights to Ríonegro to one of his sons. Before the possession ceremony commences, standing still and straight with his hands resting quietly on his cane, don Benjamín lectures the gathering on his son's obligation to maintain him, now a landless old man, just as don Benjamín once sustained his son with the fruits of this field.

Don Benjamín knows the history of the ownership of Ríonegro all the way back to 1860, when a certain Braulio Quilismal enjoyed its usufruct in the days when it was called Santísimo. Quilismal was a carrier on the Camino de Barbacoas, the road that linked the Nariñense highlands to the riverine port of Barbacoas and the Pacific harbor of Tumaco and, thence, to the rest of the world. The Barbacoas road was so treacherous that until the late nineteenth century it would admit only foot traffic; goods and passengers were carried up and down the cordillera on Indians' backs (see Taussig 1987, 295–303). Braulio Quilismal met his downfall on the road to the sea:

> That man Braulio Quilismal, he drank a lot.
> Now that the road brought traffic for Barbacoas, around Piedra Ancha [Mallama] and those parts, they always sold a great deal of *guarapo* [fermented cane juice].
> There he was, for sure. He'd had his guarapos. He'd gotten

drunk. And he arrived in Barbacoas with that load, just
when the market was closing.

So he sold what he could. But now he sold at a lower
price.

Then he went to report to his boss. And the boss—don Ramón Revelo-just wrote it all down, that's all, the loss he'd suffered.

Then, with so many trips and such, don Braulio Quilismal
owed money, they say. And when he had no way to pay back
that money, well, since here he had the field, he turned it
over to don Ramón Revelo and to Dolores Revelo. (Benjamín
Cuaical, Vereda Cuaical)[1]

Revelo eventually sold the field to one Nicolás Ruíz, who passed it on
to his son, José Félix. The latter was friendly with Valentín Cuaical,
don Benjamín's father, and some time in the 1920s he sold don Valentín
the land. In 1980 don Benjamín converted his deed to Ríonegro into a
document, transforming the land from private into communal
property.

Benjamín Cuaical would not know the detailed history of this parcel
were it not for the fact that he had read the associated deed with
great interest:

That's what the deed said. Yes, I saw the deed from those
days. It had laid around. They'd kept it. I read the deed and
even Braulio Quilismal's document, which the cabildo gave
him. It had been made by a Valerio Quilismal, [who] had
been secretary in 1860. And the president had been don Manuel María Alpala, in those days, in 1860.

They'd had the papers around. I read them and the deed
as well. (Benjamín Cuaical, Vereda Cuaical)[2]

Here we have a perfect example of a *memorista* or community historian.
While others might have saved the original deed and document in a
safe place, such as between the leaves of the family Bible or in a plastic
bag of important papers kept at the bottom of a trunk, without reading
or remembering them, don Benjamín incorporated this bit of historical
evidence into his own historical repertoire, juxtaposing a story of the
Camino de Barbacoas with another of the workings of the mid-
nineteenth-century cabildo, ultimately grounding both within the history of the loss of territory to mestizo landlords.

Histories and Stories in Gran Cumbal

Memoristas are known for their command of local tradition, but the
lines dividing history and fiction, personal experience and history, are

fuzzy. A great deal of what history is depends upon the social context in which a story is told, the vereda in which its narrator lives, his or her personal experience, and the talent that he or she brings to the telling.

The cabildo, driven by the ever-present template of the section hierarchy, originally asked me to spend time in each of the six veredas, a request that I fulfilled in reverse order, beginning in Nazate where I already had a number of friends. I swiftly discovered that with the exception of such widely known topics as the 1923 earthquake, changes in seeds and agricultural technology, the Camino de Barbacoas, exchange relationships with warmer regions, or the history of prices, most subjects of historical interest were confined to one or two veredas.

The Guaneños and Cuaspudes are best at recounting the process of land loss in the valley, since it was largely from their territories that valley-bottom haciendas were carved, and they provided the bulk of the labor force for the dairy farms that grew up there. Guan and Tasmag follow the shore of the Laguna de Cumbal, the large lake next to the volcano, where the devil is said to have stolen a large pan with carved designs on it, ultimately used for cooking cane juice in the cane-producing village of Consacá; the devil stories are told most frequently in these two sections. The first two veredas are also the principal source of information regarding festive dance, since they provided Corpus Christi dancers for the other veredas into the 1950s.

Cuaical and Quilismal are, without doubt, the primary location for learning the history of the exploitation of Mount Cumbal for its sulphur and ice, given that they lie closest to the volcano. But they are also the most likely sections for uncovering cabildo history, ranging from the appearance of the first land titles in the colonial period to the duties and obligations of early twentieth-century cabildos. The reasons for Cuaical's monopoly on official cabildo history will be discussed later.

Nazates know a great deal about the dangers of the long trip across the mountains to Mayasquer, especially the story of the Moledora, a large rock that was used to grind the bones of unwitting travelers. Voyagers would protect themselves from Mama Graviela, the cannibalistic witch who lived there, by tying themselves together into long lines to avoid her predations. But she would short-circuit their moves by selecting those in the middle of the line as her victims. Although Mama Graviela was killed by trickery and her ashes turned into flies, most people still fear the Moledora and no one will tread on the rock. The story of the purchase of the hacienda Cuetial by the caciques of Nazate is another popular tale told in the fifth vereda.

Finally, anyone wishing to learn about the nineteenth-century civil wars that laid waste to the Nariñense countryside needs to visit Cuaspud, where a major civil war battle was fought and is still remembered. And for an entertaining yarn of the trials and tribulations of smugglers working the Colombia-Ecuador border, one must seek out a narrator in Cuaspud, since the vereda lies along the international boundary.

Of this broad range of accounts, I found that those that describe cabildo activity were generally the most highly valued. Included are the story of the creation of the resguardo, any information on colonial caciques, and the nature of the cabildo in the old days. The process of land loss and of subsequent cabildo efforts at land claims, whether through occupation, court appeals, or purchase, are all part of this communal past, bits of which are known in all of the veredas.

Cabildo history is perceived as providing a model for future activity, emanating principally from accounts of land claims of the past:

> This is a very pretty history, which leaves us with much to remember.
> And it is an example for others, for the youth soon to come, so that they realize how exactly the elders fought to reposess [lands] with clear thoughts, with new ideas. (Efraín Chirán, Vereda Cuaical)[3]

It is important to remember that although the narrator here is a middle-aged former cabildante, very different people, ranging from young men to older women, also consider cabildo history to be a fundamental source of inspiration. This does not mean that alternative historical voices are undervalued in Cumbal. The history of costume, of marriage customs, of prices, and of the suffering of sharecroppers provides background and foundations for cabildo history, and political history is most effective when set against the backdrop of everyday life.[4] The best memoristas are those most skillful at articulating evidence from diverse sources into an integrated account. This is precisely what don Benjamín Cuaical was able to do in his recounting of Braulio Quilismal's forfeiture of Ríonegro: integrate the recognition of the cabildantes of yesteryear into a framework provided by anecdotes detailing land loss and the experience of the Camino de Barbacoas.

Cumbal narrators thus make no firm distinction between communal history and narratives of personal experience. A contrast is drawn, however, between fabulous tales (*cuentos*) and accounts of real-life experience (*historias*):

> Well, the difference between historia and cuento . . . well, a cuento is made up. Most of the time it's a lie, right? I know

that when someone thinks I'm going to tell him a cuento, one takes it out of one's head. One lies to the other so he laughs a bit, or so that one is happy being with the other.

But historia is something that is true, what happened to our elders and what was done during repossessions, because we were witnesses. (Efraín Chirán, Vereda Cuaical)[5]

It is this very act of witnessing, of direct experience or of exposure to a piece of historical evidence, that distinguishes historia from cuento.[6] For Efraín Chirán, for example, the tale of the Moledora is merely a cuento, because he has never seen the ominous rock:

Because I would also go over there, but I didn't see any-thing.

They'd say "The Moledora, the Moledora," but where's the Moledora?

When we'd go there, they'd say there's a stone in the bush. But I want to see it.

No one says, "Come here, there it is. I'll show you, here it is."

Because you have to see to believe. Because otherwise, un-less you see it, it's like a cuento. (Efraín Chirán, Vereda Cuai-cal)[7]

Efraín Chirán's emphasis upon experience is shared by others I talked to, although two people might not necessarily agree upon whether a given tale is historia or a cuento. Moisés Tapie, unlike the more deci-sive don Efraín, had not made up his mind about the veracity of the story of the Moledora, since he never had visited the site; he neverthe-less agreed that personal experience or the experience of others with a piece of evidence lends truth-value to a tale. The primacy given to direct contact with historical evidence in evaluating the historicity of an account suggests that for the Cumbales history is inextricably bound up in the experiences of everyday life. More precisely, historical narratives are built upon those themes that do not appear to be directly concerned with the official cabildo past, such as the production of ele-ments of material culture, adventures during travel, or the vast expanse of natural history.

The veracity of historical evidence is also determined by tapping chains of transmission of such data. This is certainly the case in a com-munity that routinely cites written documents in its oral accounts, as will be analyzed in more detail later, but it is equally true for the Cum-bales' understanding of oral testimony. If trustworthy older people narrate a tale, then it is more probable that it is historia and not cuento:

The elders tell something that was truly certain, because if it had been a cuento, cuentos are told in a different way and are quickly forgotten.

And everything you believe, you can't forget like you would a cuento, so it's considered historia. That's it.

Because they're always recounting [tales], they're always re-counting.

If one asks them, "And might this not be a cuento?"

Then they say, "This is an historia told to me by such-and-such elder," they say.

And then if the other elder is alive, you say, "You told this in such-and-such a way."

He says, "If that old man told me that, then that's how it was." (Segundo Nazate, Vereda Panán Centro, Panán)[8]

What is interesting about this quotation, excerpted from a conversation I had with a young man who has taken it upon himself to learn the history of his resguardo from his elderly neighbors, is its attention to genre in distinguishing cuento from historia.[9] According to Segundo Nazate, cuentos are told in a nebulously unspecified "different way" from historias (which, unfortunately, I neglected to follow up) and are also forgotten more quickly. This reminds me of Efraín Chirán's comment on the beauty of a particular narrative ("this is a very pretty history . . ."), which suggests that there is also an aesthetic component involved in the evaluation of historical accounts. Although developed storytelling techniques are not necessarily required of good historians, the best memoristas are usually talented narrators who can spin a good yarn.

The Making of a Memorista

My original intent when I set off for southern Nariño was to record historians in all six veredas of Cumbal as well as in the other three resguardos of Gran Cumbal: Panán, Chiles, and Mayasquer. It quickly became apparent, though, that most people believed the best historians were from Cumbal, and in Cumbal it was generally accepted that the most important memoristas lived in Cuaical and Quilismal. This was borne out in the interviews my collaborators—Angélica Mamián, Helí Valenzuela, and Iván Villota—and I taped in the different resguardos and veredas. The most thorough and varied narratives were collected in Cuaical and Quilismal, especially from two memoristas, Benjamín Cuaical Alpala and Lastenia Alpala Tarapués. A look at the attributes of these two local intellectuals clarifies what distinguishes them as memoristas of high repute.[10]

Lastenia Alpala: Chains of Oral Transmission

One evening, as I entered the kitchen of the house where I lived in Cuaical, I was greeted by the commotion of a lively debate: Lastenia Alpala sat by the hearth, arguing with her grandchildren over which language Christ spoke. Almost a century old, her hands twisted by rheumatism, she alternately resides in the homes of her three daughters and granddaughter in Cuaical, Quilismal, and Tasmag. This diminutive but charismatic woman never learned to read and write, but she has a profound memory, exceptional storytelling abilities, and analytical skills that make her one of Cumbal's best memoristas (plate 2). From her I heard the most stirring renditions of the history of the land struggles of the colonial period and the nineteenth century, of commerce along the Camino de Barbacoas, and of numerous twentieth-century cabildo disputes. Seated at the hearth with doña Lastenia and her family, I heard about how a neighbor discovered cacique Cumbe's tomb, and about Mama Graviela and the Moledora. I listened to countless descriptions of her own personal experience, ranging from the first time an airplane landed in Cumbal to the excitement of accompanying a brother up Mount Cumbal to gather sulphur.

Doña Lastenia was profoundly influenced by her maternal grandfather, Manuel de Jesús Tarapués from Nazate, who in the late nineteenth century led the cabildo in reclaiming a number of haciendas through judicial means and purchase. Most of the official cabildo history that she knows she learned at her grandfather's knee: the first disputes over the Llano de Piedras in the nineteenth century, the loss of the hacienda El Zapatero to mestizo politicians, the purchase of the hacienda Cuetial and, later, of Cimarrones in Nazate. Manuel de Jesús Tarapués appears constantly in her tales, usually assuming the role of narrator, as he does, for example, in her recounting of the cabildo's trip to Quito in search of their resguardo title:

> They were going to walk.
> In those days, my grandfather would say, "From Tulcán south, from that country, those moors, there was scrub, right? And some very narrow roads."
> Sure, they traveled with the knowledge that the roads were like that, but anyhow, they were on foot.
> "Well, somehow we'll arrive south of Tulcán," he would say. "We went," he would say, "asking how to arrive quickest in Quito."
> That's what he'd say.
> "That's why," my grandfather would say.

> Then he would say, "I would say that the *puendos* [Ecuador-
> ians] are," he would say, "a wholesome and charitable
> people." (Lastenia Alpala, Vereda Quilismal)[11]

Such repeated emphasis on the source of a tale is characteristic of women's narrations. Men generally outline the chains of transmission whereby they acquired the story, but they do not belabor the point. What is most significant for the purposes of this chapter, though, is that narrators cite their oral sources, and that access to them determines who will become a memorista.

Lastenia Alpala also incorporates oral information acquired from literate relatives, treating their descriptions of colonial resguardo titles as though they were spoken accounts. Most of her knowledge of the earliest caciques, for example, comes from her brother, Hilarión Alpala, who had himself read eighteenth-century legal briefs.[12]

Clearly, a narrator with direct access to a powerful individual who figured in an important juncture in Cumbal's history, or who was able to obtain copies of relevant historical documents, will be able to interpret the past better than other comuneros. Generally these narrators are members of certain politically powerful families—the Cuaicales of Cuaical, the Alpalas of Quilismal, the Tarapueses of Nazate—descendants of the caciques of the titles. In effect, these families have supplied Cumbal's most important history-makers, both in the sense of those who bring historical events into being and those who recount them. Despite the fact that the governorship circulates from section to section, power ultimately remains in Cuaical and Quilismal, people from other veredas told me. And only the powerful have access to the evidence, whether experiential or documentary, of which cabildo history is made:

> Well, let us suppose that the elders had . . .—because long
> ago the elders knew history. The late Fernando Taimal was
> also a great historian, the late José Domingo Paguay likewise,
> among the old people from earlier on.
> But it must be that their children finished off those histor-
> ies, or how else could it be that we don't have any inclination
> at all?
> And those who maintained [the histories], they retain them
> and know them.
> Since we never were able to have those histories, no . . it's
> the same thing with Law 89. I don't know Law 89, you see.
> And when some of us join the cabildo leadership, some of
> us are lent [the documents] and others aren't lent them. Only

the governor, the president, hold on to them, and they don't
lend it to you so that you don't learn and don't progress.
    So you can have more experience, passing—just like some
of them say—they say, "You passed by the cabildo table, you
know the law."
    But how are we to know laws or history?
    Because they haven't been given to us. We haven't even
read them, even if we had the memory to retain them. (Julio
Paguay, Vereda Tasmag)[13]

According to some, it is indeed a vicious circle, because only those
who know the past can lead the struggles of the present and only
important cabildantes with access to the archives can learn history.[14]
    Lastenia Alpala's privileged position as a member of the Alpala and
the Tarapués families provides her with significant access to the kind
of historical information that a memorista must have. But notwithstanding some of the accidents of her birth, doña Lastenia's individual
attributes were also influential in her making as a memorista: she is
intuitive and knows how to use analytical skills and storytelling capa-
bilities to interpret the evidence she has been lucky enough to receive.
It is no accident, then, that in a region in which women hardly ever
assume public roles in community life, it was doña Lastenia who, citing the colonial titles she had heard so much about, dissuaded cabildos
of the 1940s from leasing rights to Mount Cumbal's sulphur beds to a
foreign company (see chapter 5).
    I will linger here a moment to contemplate doña Lastenia's storytell-
ing abilities. She, like other memoristas, is an excellent narrator who
mesmerizes her audience with her words, employing conventions also
used by non memorista storytellers. One mark of her talent is the rich
detail that she brings to her accounts. Note, for example, her description of the toad at cacique Cumbe's tomb:

    Suddenly, in a cave she was in, she saw some mud inside.
This deep. And the branches like a hut.
    She saw a toad, a frog seated, a frog seated there.
    Then she said, "And how in the world, that toad? There it
is. There is that toad."
    She looked at it.
    The more she looked at it—because the toad has some
black spots and some yellow ones, yes. Then, the yellow
ones, she saw them shining. She said she saw them.
    She'd look some more. Then she'd spend a little time col-
lecting firewood. She'd look again, and again she'd only see
it shining.

So suddenly she looked well.

"And those spots," she said, "how yellow they are! So why would that toad be like that?"

Then she saw it had a crown.

Then they say she thought, "Ah!" She said, "That's why I've heard it said that the flies and the animals have their king: the toads also have their king," they say she said. (Lastenia Alpala, Vereda Quilismal)[15]

Few other narrators would dwell with such precision upon the attributes of the toad or the mental process whereby the narrator realized the import of her discovery. The texture of doña Lastenia's narrative, moreover, is conveyed through direct quotations, that invite listeners to share in the woman's thoughts as she observes the toad, as it starts to shine, as the crown appears. And although the dialogue was composed by doña Lastenia herself, it conveys an impression of historical accuracy, as though she were citing evidence from the past.

But it is not only richness of detail and dialogue that make doña Lastenia's histories so gripping. It is also the emotion that she weaves into her accounts. Let us close with the story of how her brother, a sulphur collector, saw the sea from atop Mount Cumbal:

"Once we went, I don't remember with whom," he said, "to look. One day when there wasn't a cloud in the sky."

And they sat down to look.

"It's not far," my brother would say, "to the Pacific, because you can see it."

But he said he saw it in this way.

He found out when, he said, "we saw a group of small mountains, nothing else, all snow-capped. Now, where would all those mountains be? I've always read," he'd said, because he knew how to read.

"But no one has ever told me, nor have I seen in the history books and the geography that I've read. Where would all those dense mountains be, like a village, like a whole cordillera? I'll go ask."

The priests were friendly in those days.

He said he asked a father called Benjamín Arteaga, when he went to leave the first fruits, as was the custom.

My brother said, "Father, be so kind as to answer me a question I will ask you. Tell me, where is it that there are so many mountains so close together?"

"And where did you look from?"

"From here. From Mount Cumbal. On a clear day."

He said he told him how it had happened: "And we saw

an island with mountains, all snow-capped. That's what surprised me. Where is that place?"

And the father said, "Silly, those aren't mountains: that is the sea, that is the Pacific." (Lastenia Alpala, Vereda Quilismal)[16]

Doña Lastenia builds up suspense in this story, telling us bit by bit how her brother finally came to the realization that the distant sea was actually visible from Cumbal.

Benjamín Cuaical: Literacy and Leadership

When he was still a young boy, Benjamín Cuaical's father bought him a copy of the Colombian Constitution and Law 89 of 1890:

> When I was still in school, I was already a youth of some 14, almost 15 years, and it was the last year I spent in school; I had seven years of schooling from my father.
>
> Well, my father had a friend out there in Carlosama, called Manuel Cuaical. He'd been a cabildante, a governor. And he'd won a suit and was a kind of lawyer.
>
> Well, he was a good friend of my father's; my father would even rent him a team of oxen so he could work in Carlosama. And when he saw that I read, studied, he said to my father, "And why don't you buy him a law? I'll sell you a law. I have one," he said, "from the cabildo," he told him. "I have the Colombian Constitution."
>
> So I even studied the Constitution. I even copied out the Constitution. It was the Political Constitution of Colombia, the first Constitution from 1886, which was then reformed in 1910.
>
> So I even copied out the Constitution of '86, because it wasn't very long. The Constitution was short, that is, the mother of the law. Elay!
>
> Then that man sold my father a small notebook of Indian Law 89, and I studied that one. That's why since that time I know Law 89, the faculties of the cabildo and the lands, and that it protects the Indian race.
>
> That's how I learned. I found out about Law 89, and discovered what it meant to respect Indian people, what it says regarding the distribution of lands. (Benjamín Cuaical, Vereda Cuaical)[17]

Since he knew how to write well and had learned the law, at age seventeen don Benjamín was invited by the cabildo to assist them in preparing legal briefs destined for Bogotá. Older cabildantes provided training to the budding secretary, instructing him to keep notes and a diary. Although these diaries have since been lost, he did show me copies of poetry he has written over the years. In 1929, at age nineteen, don Benjamín was appointed cabildo secretary, a post he would occupy five times between 1929 and 1975, punctuated by a year as regidor and a stint as cabildo president (plate 3).

Other comuneros echo the value that don Benjamín places on literacy, especially as regards the utility of reading and writing for transmitting historical knowledge. With the exception of Lastenia Alpala, all of the other memoristas I heard of or spoke to were not only literate but regularly used these skills in everyday life. Nestor Tarapués of Nazate, for instance, ten-times cabildo secretary, ran a private school for children of the vereda for a number of years.

Fernando Mimalchí of Tasmag produced for me a beautifully written description of his reactions at the time of the 1923 earthquake, eloquently illustrating the fact that in Cumbal it is common for men to keep notes on what occurs around them. Don Fernando's diary records the destruction of the church and the death of the wife of townsman Floresmiro Guerrero, which occurred when a tower fell on her. He writes of the quakes that continued for the next eleven months; twenty-three tremors hit the town on the day of the largest earthquake, December 14, 1923. He even records the names of the priests who consoled the homeless. Earthquake relief, writes don Fernando, was not meant for all: "And other soldiers came. And others also came to donate food and clothes and money, people from the other towns that were not destroyed. But all of this came for the whites."[18]

In his notebook, don Fernando added that the mestizos moved from the ruins of their town to the Llano de Piedras, erecting their new town center on Indian lands.

Non historians value literacy as much as memoristas do. The late Alvina Chalparizán of Cuetial, doña Lastenia's first cousin, remembered her father lending copies of the resguardo title to interested parties:

A.C.: That's why my father used to keep those papers that were left.

J.R.: What kind of papers?

A.C.: The ones that had the demarcations from the first titles for Cuetial. They would look at them, or he would lend them so that other people who knew how could study them. (Alvina Chalparizán, Vereda Nazate)[19]

In order to keep alive the memory of a turning point in community experience, Diomedes Paguay of Guan prepared a lengthy written history of the repossession of the Llano de Piedras, as seen from his perspective.[20]

A great deal of memoristas' knowledge is acquired by reading or listening to the explanations of others who have done extensive reading. Many memoristas keep personal libraries in their homes: collections of ancient dog-eared school textbooks, one or two tattered number of literary magazines, perhaps a copy of a popular history book, the *Historia sagrada* (an anthology of biblical stories), or a few legal codes. Based largely upon his reading of Jesús María Henao and Gerardo Arrubla's (1938 [1910]) classic history text, don Benjamín shared with me his own vision of *historia patria* or national history.[21]

Although memoristas may be familiar with printed works, they often draw their historical examples from the documentation at hand in the cabildo archive. In fact, almost all of what could be called cabildo history derives from these written documents (as will be evident in later chapters, however, oral interpretations frequently display little resemblance to written sources). Benjamín Cuaical peppers his narratives with references to these legal briefs, only some of which still can be found in the cabildo archive. Many have been retained by the courts as legal evidence for the numerous lawsuits the cabildo has brought against hacendados; others have been borrowed by interested readers and never returned.

The archive is stored in a wooden cupboard kept in the casa de cabildo (plate 4), its contents occasionally consulted in the course of a dispute over use rights to a plot. Organized in seven sections, six contain the still valid usufruct documents of the veredas and one comprises the historical papers of the cabildo ("Asuntos Varios" or "Other Affairs").

Each year the archive is inventoried by the outgoing cabildantes (plate 5):

> Well, they also make an inventory of the archive.
> It was the regidor from each vereda who had to make an inventory of the documents that have existed, the old documents, the terminated documents that no longer were valid. These went in a separate volume. But so many terminated documents were recorded, now, so many documents that are actually still circulating.
> They went along reading them, year by year, what in which year, which documents, whose, of which people. They would name the individual, the plot, the vereda, and then

they would copy the number of documents into some books that are still there today.

That's it.

And then each regidor, using an inventory, an inventory or a volume of components, the president with the secretary would give this to the president of the new cabildo and the secretary of the new cabildo.

Also, that was the volume that listed the components, and there there would be so many briefs, suits, resolutions, circulars, from the government, about any number of civil affairs.

That's a large volume. It holds some documents from the past, like Deed 228. (Benjamín Cuaical, Vereda Cuaical)[22]

Don Benjamín makes it sound easier than it really is. On inventory day, clusters of men crouch in the corridors, taking turns at sounding out the names and plots listed in the documents they hold while one of them, with painful slowness, scratches out a record in an unskilled and sometimes illegible hand. These note-takers are not the memoristas, who write in an elegant and fluent hand.

These painstakingly prepared inventories are used only once. On the day the archive is transferred to the incoming cabildo, the two regidores for each vereda, accompanied by their followers, check the veredal archive against the inventory. The inventory prepared for "Asuntos Varios" is also checked.

The 1935 inventory of "Asuntos Varios," prepared by don Benjamín Cuaical, is still available for consultation.[23] Written in a clear script on four sheets of unlined legal-sized paper, the inventory includes fifty items. These items are arranged in three columns that incorporate (moving from left to right) the number of the item to be listed, a description of the item inventoried, and the page length of the item. A glimpse at the documents still extant in the archive shows that they are generally written on very large pieces of paper that are folded over like a notebook and sewn together into a kind of quarto, called a *cuadernillo* in the inventory.

Don Benjamín opens with some of the documentary items most significant for the cabildo, those that are frequently consulted or of great symbolic importance. Paramount among these are Law 89 of 1890, several cuadernillos of nineteenth-century court transcripts and land titles for the Llano de Piedras, a copy of the Royal Provision, copies of colonial documents originating with the Crown and found in judicial archives in Ipiales, and a cuadernillo documenting the expansion of mestizo townspeople onto the site of the modern town of Cumbal in the

Llano de Piedras—the creation of the *zona de población,* an area open for habitation by non-Indians. None of these documents is particularly old; the colonial originals that were once retained by Cumbal's caciques were employed as legal evidence during the judicial battles of the last three centuries and thus were lost to the cabildo.[24]

Following this list of the most significant items contained in the archives are some thirty-odd documents emanating from the government—copies of laws and resolutions sent to the cabildo as well as a number of censuses and other papers written by the cabildo for the municipal or national administration. The inventory ends with documentary materials produced by the cabildo for internal use: the libros de devoción listing festival sponsors, lists of community members who had done their obligatory week of labor for the municipal authorities (the story of the abolition of the hated *trabajo personal y vecinal* is an important theme in official cabildo history), and notebooks containing resolutions and copies of written communications by the cabildo. The overwhelming majority of these items were produced in the 1920s and 1930s, when the first generation of school-educated young men, like Benjamín Cuaical, became available for cabildo service and began generating the papers that are still stored, although hardly ever consulted, in the archive cupboard.

The order in which don Benjamín listed the contents of the archive in his inventory provides us with further information as to how he envisioned the history of his community. Of greatest importance are the voices of the distant past, whether indigenous or European, because the colonial documents legitimize Cumbal's claim to resguardo status. Not quite so important are early twentieth-century decrees and laws, which open windows onto the resguardo's relationship with the dominant society but are not valid as evidence in a lawsuit. Of least importance are the relatively recent voices of Indians, which are a source of evidence for a history of local political process as it is played out in internal land disputes or in festival sponsorship. But don Benjamín's ideal history is at odds with the realities of the scope of memoristas' knowledge. The usefulness and novelty of Benjamín Cuaical's histories stem precisely from his command of the sorts of information contained in the two less-favored categories.

The archive cupboard is closed to most comuneros. Until the cabildo office was built in the 1960s, the archive traveled from vereda to vereda and was stored in the home of the president or the secretary. It might be stored in a wooden chest, or it could be precariously stacked on a table cluttered with any number of other articles, including coffee cups and plates of food, well within the grasp of the sticky fingers of curious children. It is indeed a wonder that the archive survived these peregrinations.

Many cabildo secretaries were employed by the cabildo for five to ten years, frequently training their sons to take over the positiion. Two of don Benjamín Cuaical's sons, Valentín and Salomón, have served as secretary on several occasions. Because of the extended terms and practices of succession, only a very limited group of men has spent enough time with the cabildo to study its archives. The oldest of these men, like Benjamín Cuaical or Nestor Tarapués, are today's historians. Others, like fifty-year-old Salomón Cuaical, will be the memoristas of the future.

In the heat of contemporary land struggles and in response to the support that the Cumbales have received from non-Indian organizations, a new breed of memoristas has surfaced, people whose historical narrative takes artistic form. Their musical or theatrical renditions of the past will be considered in detail later. Here it is merely important to mention that two of them—Valentín Cuaical and Gilberto Valenzuela—have also served their time as secretary of the cabildo.

While access to documentation and to chains of oral transmission are the primary sources of historical evidence for memoristas, formulaic utterances and striking images form the basis of historical knowledge for other comuneros.[25] Their repertoire, while imperfect and much reduced in comparison to that of memoristas, draws upon the interpretations of the latter. The remainder of this chapter and chapter 4 explore the ways in which memorista history is interpreted by the broader Cumbal public.

Popular Historical Knowledge

During the past two decades, new strains of potato that can be planted and harvested virtually year-round have been introduced in Cumbal. In the old days there were just two plantings, in May or June and in December or January. March and November frequently brought nights of intense cold when frost fell on potato fields and harvests were lost. Such periods of *hambruna* or famine forced people to travel to the warmer valleys or *guaicos* in search of food and to climb Mount Cumbal to extract its ice and sulphur. These travelers were generally men; women stayed at home, trying to make ends meet with the few crops they could harvest. One such hambruna crop was turnips.[26] But sometimes even turnips were so scarce that they had to be guarded at night or they would be stolen. The guard, who generally watched over cattle,

slept in a small, mobile hut called a *choza*, where he was protected from the cold and could doze until the dogs alerted him with their barking. The broad range of experiences encompassed by the misery of the hambruna are expressed metaphorically in everyday speech, remembered not so much through narration as by a cliché: "We even had to guard the turnips in chozas" was a refrain I heard over and over again in all the veredas.

Those who do not have the storytelling talents and the privileged ear of a Lastenia Alpala or the access to written documentation of a Benjamín Cuaical—that is to say, the majority of Cumbales—remember history through similar recurrent images. These images serve, on the one hand, as mnemonics for the recollection of more extensive accounts; on the other, they recall the past through metaphor as opposed to the statement of experience. Turnips were probably not guarded in a choza all that frequently, but the image eloquently expresses people's desperation in the face of famine, when they were forced to consume such a lowly food as the turnip and to guard it as though it were as valuable as cattle.[27]

I will return to such recurring images throughout this book. I have already shown, for example, how the section order becomes a gloss for political history. Later chapters will show how the staffs of office carried by cabildantes fulfill a similar function, how the image of cacique Cumbe is a gloss for pre-Columbian autonomy, and how the symbols of the bull and the hitching post recall well-known stories of land loss. One such image of writing lies at the intersection of the literate and the oral transmission of history, of local and cabildo history, and of the history of memoristas and of the vast majority of Cumbales.

The Three Trunks of the Tarapueses

Perhaps the most common mnemonic to be found in Cumbal is the family nickname. I am speaking here not of apellations given to individuals in commemoration of some significant juncture in their personal history but of labels given to entire families, the descendants of particular noted individuals, who all share a common surname. Such nicknames recall the past or provide evidence of it, and are a frequent subject of discussion and joking. One example is the name given to don Benjamín Cuaical's family, "Chima," which recalls Chimag, an extensive piece of land, since divided and subdivided, that belonged to don Benjamín's ancestors. The Chimas descend from don Benjamín's great-grandfather, don Agustín Cuaical, the first owner of Chimag and the first to be called "don Agustín Chima." Another nickname, whose documentation has escaped the notice of its owners, is "Chuca," used for a branch of the Chinguad family from Tasmag. Unbeknownst to the twentieth-century Chucas, Chinguad-Chuca was the title of the caciques of Cuaspud.[28] Finally, the "Chulde" wing of the Valenzuela family was so named because four generations ago a woman from Ecuador, where Chulde is a common surname among the descendants of the Pastos, married a Valenzuela, who subsequently gave his surname to the children she brought to the marriage. The Chuldes provided me with a detailed genealogy of this woman's descendants.

A complex and multilayered example of the historicity of nicknames is provided by the series of epithets given to members of the Tarapués family of Nazate. Divided into the "Eugenios," "Ursulos," and "Alcántares" (the last is doña Lastenia's grandfather's family), the Tarapueses live for the most part in Cuetial, the hacienda purchased in the colonial period by their ancestors, the caciques of Nazate. Listen to memorista Nestor Tarapués on the origin of these names:

> This hacienda was bought by Messrs. Miguel Tarapués, Bernardo Tarapués, and Manuel Tarapués, the two brothers and the other unrelated, but all of them Tarapueses. The two brothers were Miguel and Bernardo, the other one was Tarapués, but unrelated, as I am telling you: we are unrelated but we're Tarapués.
>
> For example, as I told you, I am Tarapués with all the Ursulos, as they have told you, Tarapués Ursulo, because Bernardo Tarapués had a daughter named Ursulina, and we come from that line, up to today: that's why we are called the Tarapueses Ursulos, because our great-grandmother-mother was called Ursulina, daughter of Bernardo.
>
> And from Miguel come the other Tarapueses; the Eugenios are from Manuel [sic].
>
> There is a thick notebook recording the descent lines, in which they'd drawn something like trees; they'd made three trees of the three Tarapueses, and they descended from those, right? The lines ran from one, from the other, and from the other, the children, the grandchildren, and the generations . . .
>
> I belong to the first tree, of don Bernardo and from him, doña Ursulina, and from Miguel come the Eugenios, from Manuel the Alcántares, but they're three Tarapueses. (Nestor Tarapués, Vereda Nazate)[29]

For many, the mention of the three nicknames brings to mind forgotten family rivalries: they symbolize a family divided. Most of those who did not know how to explain the three "trunks," as the lines are commonly called, did express their preference for one or the other, generally the Alcántares or the Eugenios. Some knew nothing of the source of the nicknames but grew angry when my collaborators or I referred to them, reminding us of the fact that *suppressed* memories can be as potent as official ones (Cohen 1986; Lapierre 1989). In one interview in particular, the sons of memorista Pastor Colimba would not permit Angélica Mamián to proceed with her questions. It is said that in the distant past the Colimbas of Cuetial were brought there from Guan to work as peons and, therefore, might be construed as interlopers in Tarapués territory.

For others who choose to remember a bit of family lore, the nicknames refer to the three lines of the family who came into conflict over the high mountains of Cuetial, where the Ursulos built a gate keeping the other Tarapueses out of their territory. María Isabel Tarapués maintains that the Eugenios, the group to which she belongs, contributed the bulk of the funds used to purchase the lands but were denied entry to them. Here the recurrent images of the Ursulos, Eugenios, and Alcántares are rooted in an orally transmitted tale of what must have been a nineteenth-century dispute.

A further layer is added to this story when we consider the fact that the Tarapueses actually kept written genealogies. Although I was told repeatedly of these written sources, neither I nor Angélica Mamián ever saw them. Significantly, we were told that they were owned by Pastor Colimba, the very man whose sons attempted to surpress their memory. The hidden notebooks lend an aura of veracity to the nicknames; at the same time, they deprive them of legitimacy as oral sources. It is not difficult to imagine what these genealogies might look like. Colonial-era documents frequently contained chiefly genealogies written in prose, beginning with a contemporary figure and working back in time to his or her ancestors. A good example is the genealogy of don Nicolás García Paspuel Tusa, eighteenth-century cacique of Tusa, in what is today Ecuador:

> Don Nicolas Garcia Paspuel Tusa principal cacique of the towns of Tusa, Puntal, and Angel, jurisdiction of the Villa of San Miguel de Ybarra, legitimate son and heir of don Thomas Garcia Paspuel Tusa who was principal cacique of the stated towns and legitimate grandson of don Sebastian Garcia Paspuel Tusa and legitimate great-grandson of don Xptobal Garcia Paspuel Tusa and of doña Francisca Tusa, who were principal caciques of the stated towns, now dead.[30]

The cuadernillos in Cuetial may be eighteenth-century records of disputes over hereditary chiefdoms that were retained as "kitchen-archives" (Behar 1986) by the descendants of the caciques.

The Cumbales describe these notebooks in metaphoric language, much as they describe their family nicknames. In an untaped discussion with María Isabel Tarapués, these formulaic utterances were developed in considerable detail. She spoke of the genealogies as "trees." The Eugenios, Ursulos, and Alcántares were the "roots," which were said to be "reborn" from the original Tarapués "trunk." Doña Isabel used the verb *reformar,* to reform or to correct, to describe the written tracing of genealogical ties. As later chapters illustrate, the notion of the "reborn" is a common metaphor for establishing links to the historical past. Likewise, the concept of history as a process that can be re-formed or corrected is central to the very practical vision of the past that fuels the contemporary Indian movement. Such symbolically loaded formulaic utterances are an oral alternative to memorista citations of the documentary record, not so much for the information they convey as for the associations they evoke.

I must return briefly to the memorista Nestor Tarapués, who is one of the few who connects the Alcántares, Eugenios, and Ursulos to the three great caciques, Bernardo, Miguel, and Manuel, eighteenth-century purchasers of Cuetial. The memory of the three caciques is alive in the oral tradition of Nazate, although most people cautioned me that the three "trunks" came at a period considerably later than that of the three chiefs. Nevertheless, storytellers such as María Isabel Tarapués were careful to supply me with the name of the Spanish landowner from whom Cuetial was purchased. Gertrudes de Erazo, the hacendada, was not a historical figure, but it was indeed the Erazo family that owned Cuetial in the eighteenth century.

Only a handful of memoristas diverge from the truncated chronology of most oral narrators. When Nestor Tarapués, ten-times secretary of the cabildo and teacher to many of those who told me the oral lore of the brothers Tarapués, makes reference to the purchase of Cuetial, he is not so much drawing upon the oral tradition as he is citing the archival document from which the story was first extracted, the Royal Provision. It is to this *written* source that the *oral* story of the integration of Cuetial into the resguardo can ultimately be traced, a lengthy document read by few other than a handful of more diligent cabildo secretaries. The oral tale provides little information beyond that contained in the written evidence: the names of the caciques and of the Spanish parties to the transaction, the price they paid for the hacienda.

Elaborate oral narratives, insults, suppressed notebooks, and colonial documentation: all must be considered together to understand the meaning of the three Tarapués nicknames. Each provides an angle on the significance of these sobriquets, a series of cross sections of reality, each originating in a different form of transmission of knowledge, each drawing upon the others for legitimacy at the same time that it disavows their veracity. As novelist Salman Rushdie explains with regard to the relationship between fiction and reality, these different worlds exist at angles to one another:

> The country in this story is not Pakistan, or not quite. There are two countries, real and fictional, occupying the same space, or almost the same space. My story, my fictional country exist, like myself, at a slight angle to reality. (Rushdie 1983: 29)

In later chapters we will see how such various expressive worlds build reciprocally upon each other, forming narrative constellations that are continuously transformed with the flow of time.

FOUR

History and Everyday Life

THE ACT OF HISTORICAL analysis, according to Marc Bloch, takes its color from the present and gives life to the past:

> In the last analysis, whether consciously or no, it is always by borrowing from our daily experiences and by shading them, where necessary, with new tints that we derive the elements which help us to restore the past. (Bloch 1953,44)

In Cumbal, I discovered that Bloch's words could be taken quite literally: the past is most fully experienced through everyday life in the present. Throughout my stay, I was struck by how people perceived many current practices, agricultural and political, ritual and interpersonal, as being the stuff of which history is made. As they construct historical narratives and as they compose plays and songs about the past, they draw heavily upon activities of the present, almost to the exclusion of references to historical events. As we have already seen, in Cumbal there are men and women with fine memories and profound life experiences who are considered to be historians, or memoristas. But notwithstanding their considerable influence, history, for the most part, is expressed through activities of the present. Representations of present-as-past are centered around those aspects of life that appear most indigenous to comuneros and are thus perceived as constituting historical evidence.

The present-as-past in Cumbal is most effectively represented through non-narrative genres of expression, such as ritual and elements of material culture, that recall the past without enumerating it.

In these genres, historical interpretation works at various levels. For some, they simply establish a link with the past, although the nature of that relationship is unimportant. For others, key names and events are associated with these everyday expressions of history. And for a few, exegesis unearths the historical detail embedded in these practices. There is an enormous power inherent in non-narrative genres of historical expression.[1] This is evident when we consider that memoristas, who frequently deploy their evidence in accordance with the images that their listeners expect to hear, must incorporate the framework provided by non-narrative genres into their own narrations.

The Historicity of Possessions and of Work

Our examination begins with that is closest to the life of Cumbal's residents: the tangible evidence of the past that the Cumbales see, touch, or walk day after day. Undoubtedly, many elements of material culture—from houses and fields to looms and cooking pots—provide historical evidence for individual pasts in Cumbal. Nevertheless, here I wish to address a very specific group within this broader array of historical evidence, those elements that encode highly charged symbols relating to the communal past. Within this more exclusive group, the most important are cabildo staffs of office and boundary ditches.

Staffs of Office

All cabildo members carry staffs of office to official functions (plate 6). An inheritance from Spanish colonial councils, the staffs function as symbols of autonomous indigenous authority (Rasnake 1988). Nevertheless, in the early colonial period other objects served as insignia of chiefly rule. Late sixteenth- and early seventeenth-century Pasto caciques included in their testaments silver and lacquered *keros* or drinking vessels as symbols of their political power. Early colonial caciques were presented with textiles when they assumed political office, as we can see in the following quotation from the 1693 investiture of the cacique of Cumbal:

> And in virtue of the decree from this other party and chiefly title with which he required the said justice don Ambrosio de Prado y Sayalpud cacique of the parcialidad of Cumbal, [he] took by the hand said don Ambrosio de Prado and he seated him in a small wooden stool in the presence of the male and female Indians of said parcialidad of Cumbal and he removed the mantles of the principal Indians of said parcialidad and placed them on the ground and ordered that they stand and

that each one gave him a bow and he embraced all of them as a sign of possession and true possession [of the cacicazgo] which was given him really, actually, corporeally with almost no contradiction on the part of anyone and with no prejudice on the part of another third party who had a firmer right.[2]

It is not until the mid-eighteenth century that staffs of office appear in the documentary record for the Pastos.[3] Today they constitute the principal symbol of political authority for the resguardos of Nariño. Although in other parts of Colombia cabildos maintain a complete set of staffs that are issued to officeholders each year, most Nariñense councils do not control the insignia they carry. Instead, they are the property of individual community members who lend them to cabildo officers for their yearly terms.

Each of these staffs has its own history. Don Benjamín Cuaical owns the original staff that belonged to the early nineteenth-century governor, don Agustín Cuaical:

B.C.:   The staff that is kept at Mr. Benjamín Cuaical's is more than two hundred years old. Its first owner was Juan Agustín Cuaical. As a youth, he danced with it [at Corpus Christi celebrations] for twelve consecutive years.
   Then it passed to the power of Fidel Cuaical.
   After Fidel Cuaical, the staff passed to the power of Valentín Cuaical, who was my father.
   Since then and to the present, I, Benjamín Cuaical, own it, and with this staff, Juan Agustín Cuaical completed a year as governor in Túquerres.

J.R.:   And [as you mentioned before,] this staff saved don Agustín's life. . .

B.C.:   Yes ma'am. This one saved his life. When they were going to kill him by firing squad in the time of the Revolution—but I don't know what year the Revolution was in, possibly in the time of the war of Tomás Cipriano de Mosquera. No, it wasn't in Mosquera's time. I can't give you that fact, because I don't know which Revolution that was, [because] in those days there were so many revolutions, and they made revolutions to win power.
   But they discovered in those days, during one of those wars, that they were to execute don Agustín Cuaical. He was, as I already said, an old man, and they were to take him and execute him.
   And then, when the firing squad was ready, there appeared a commander from the Armed Forces. And that's

when he shouted, "Halt!" he'd said, "That Indian was governor in Túquerres, spare him!"

That's what happened, yes!

And so, he carried that staff as governor of Túquerres. (Benjamín Cuaical, Vereda Cuaical)[4]

The conversation illustrates that the staff of office, which represents
the cabildo, stimulates historical memory: both genealogical memory
and the broader communal memory of relations between the resguardo and the dominant society, in this particular case, the history of
nineteenth-century civil wars.[5]

Don Benjamín's reminiscences of the history lodged in his staff of
office are similar to the memories of countless staff owners, who can
easily repeat the history of their insignia, tracing them back to illustri-
ous nineteenth-century ancestors. And, in fact, cabildantes routinely
share information on the history of their insignia with their colleagues.
The staffs do not only represent individual genealogies but a communal one as well, since the most famous staffs were once the possessions
of celebrated governors.

The "Royal Crown," a symbol used to refer to contemporary objects
like the staff of office as well as to historical evidence, links history-as-
activity to the more formal narrative history of Cumbal's memoristas.
A number of places, documents, and objects are called "the Royal
Crown," including Deed 228. Contemporary theater represents history
by referring to the resguardo title, without any necessity of recounting
past events. This is clear in an excerpt from *Historia de los grandes curan-
deros y desencantadores que existieron en nuestras tierras indígenas, que a hoy
se encuentran descansando* (History of the Great Curers and Disenchant-
ers who Lived in Our Indian Lands and Today Are at Rest), a play
produced in 1986 by a group of young people from Cuaical and
Tasmag:

> Indian brothers: one day early in the morning I left to find
> fortune for my household. But one day I climbed the high riv-
> erbanks of Gran Cumbal and was taken prisoner out of bad
> blood. First, I want to tell you this: In dreams I called for help.
> When I found help, I collided with a rope tied to a *frailejón*
> and I fell next to a box. When I was very close, there was a
> thieving jaguar, sitting on that box. And when he saw that I
> was frightened and about to flee, that great thief tried to catch
> me with his claws. And I was so frightened that I didn't know
> what to say, [so I said] he should return those things that be-
> long to us. And so he said: Indians, your things are yours. I
> took them in my hand and looked at them. I saw marvelous

and beautiful things. Then all of a sudden, as I looked at those things, I heard a voice that said: count the 228 claws on the jaguar, because from there comes the Royal Deed 228 of 1906, because there you will find your salvation for all your obligations, that is, Law 89. (Grupo Artístico "Los Cumbes," Vereda Cuaical)[6]

The speech, written by Miguel Angel Alpala, compresses the past into a number of key symbols: the number 228, the beautiful contents of the box, the frailejón, all of which refer to the history of the marking of Cumbal's borders. The frontiers of the resguardo lie in the *páramo*, the high and swampy grassland of the northern Andes, abounding in frailejones (*Espeletia sp.*), a high altitude plant that looks like a man wearing feathers on his head. Hence the reference to the páramo plant: the narrator is in the páramo, on the boundary, and is reenacting the laying of boundaries as he recounts his experience. His actions include the perusal of the beautiful contents of the box, most likely the contents of the cabildo archive, where Deed 228 is kept. Deed 228 is represented as a number: the claws on the jaguar's paws. By counting the claws the narrator will find his salvation, re-creating Deed 228 and the more encompassing Law 89. Finally, the playwright pointed out to me that the jaguar represents the white landlord; by reclaiming the box from the cat, the narrator repossesses stolen lands.[7] In essence, then, the passage links past and future and demonstrates that history is something to be transformed or corrected.

Deed 228 is one of several referents for the Royal Crown. In a song of the Indian movement composed by Valentín Cuaical, the Crown is said to have been left by cacique Cumbe, the chief from whom Cumbal derives its name:

Largo tiempo estuvieron tus tierras	For a long time your lands
En las manos de un hombre tirano.	Were in the hands of a tyrant.
Hoy tu raza reclama esa tierra	Today your people demand that land
Porque escrito dejaste un papel.	Because you left a paper written.
¡El cacique Cumbe tendrá que venir!	Cacique Cumbe will have to come!
Porque es de San Pedro,	Because he is from San Pedro,
De nuestro Cumbal,	From our Cumbal,
Donde dejó escrito	Where he left in writing
La Corona Real.	The Royal Crown.

One of Cumbal's best-known singers, Gilberto Valenzuela, explained the song to me:

The record is called the "Cacique Cumbe." Cacique Cumbe means that he was the ancient one from here, he who fought and administered this territory or *parcialidad* called Gran Cumbal, under the Royal Provision or Deed 228.

The record reads, at least: "Cacique Cumbe will have to come! Because he is from San Pedro, from our Cumbal." The municipality of Cumbal used to be called San Pedro.

And so, the record says: "Because he is from San Pedro, from our Cumbal, where he left in writing, the Royal Crown." That is, the Royal Crown is Deed 228, issued in the Royal Court in the Viceroyalties of Ferdinand VI in Quito. (Gilberto Valenzuela, Vereda Cuaical)[8]

The song associates Deed 288 with the cacique Cumbe, although his name does not appear in the document. Other stories compare Cumbe himself with the crown by describing his grave as being inhabited by a toad wearing a crown, as Lastenia Alpala related in the previous chapter.

But the Royal Crown is not just Deed 228 and the cacique Cumbe; it is also an alternate name for the Llano de Piedras, the first extensive landholding repossessed by the cabildo in 1975. The cabildo that reclaimed the Llano carried in its hands staffs of office that were crowned (see figure 2), as was so clearly explained to me when I pondered the repetition of the Royal Crown symbol across so many domains:

G.V.:   Of what exists in the indigenous communities, at least on the staffs, there are crowns.

That is, it is the sacred crown of the viceroyalty from over there. And he took the crown and kissed it, and sent Mauricio Muñóz de Ayala, in the eyes of the Royal Crown or the Royal Court in Quito, to do the same and to fulfill the obligation or the order as an authority, or as the Alcalde Mayor of the Pastos, because we belong to the Cacique of the Pastos.

J.R.:   Which is the crown on the staff?

G.V.:   There is a crown, a ring, it looks like one. We call it a ring, but it's not a ring, it represents things: it's a crown.

M.J.T.:   They're cut out like a crown.

G.V.:   Yes. So that is the crown. That is, it represents the Royal Crown of Ferdinand VI. So I say it's not a ring, but a crown, and that gives us Indians from Gran Cumbal more credibility, for what is written, what is said in the Royal Decree or the Royal Crown.

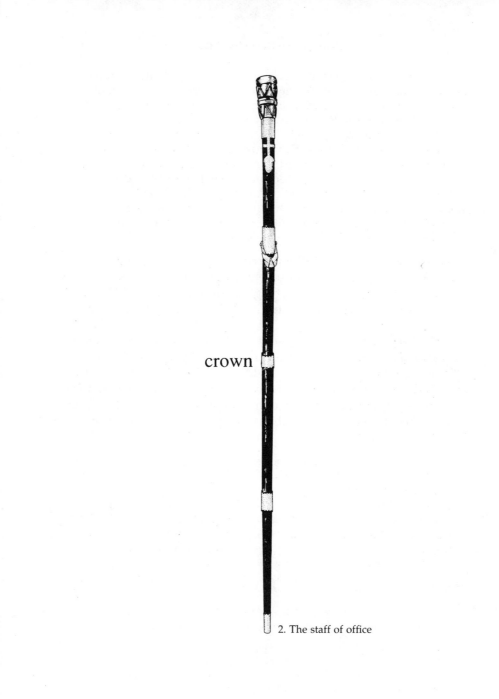

crown

2. The staff of office

And our grandfathers, our caciques, also believed in that,
and for that reason it is a staff. They put the crown on it, and
there it is. (Gilberto Valenzuela, Vereda Cuaical, and Manuel
Jesús Tarapués, Vereda Nazate)[9]

Thus each time the cabildo member carries his staff or passes it to his
successor, he carries with him the Royal Crown: the condensed memory of the cacique Cumbe, the creation of the resguardo, the inception
of Deed 228, and the history of the Llano de Piedras. The historicity
of place, object, and document is indeed activated in a multiplicity
of forms, each articulating common images and drawing upon their
potency to produce history.

Zanjas

In light of the above discussion of the historicity of discourse surrounding staffs of office, it is interesting to consider another component of material culture, boundary ditches, whose presence also reaffirms the historicity of the land (de Certeau 1984; Halbwachs 1980) and
whose construction lends history to a territory that has been robbed
of its past.

One of the most striking features of the Nariñense landscape is its
complex web of ditches, called *zanjas* (plate 7). These ditches line fields
and paths, continuously forcing the pedestrian to cross small bridges.
Zanjas vary in size: some are a mile long, ten feet deep, and six feet
wide while others are twenty or thirty feet long, two feet deep, and
only a foot wide. Some are new and well kept; others are old, over-
grown with weeds, and filled with water. They are an immense bother
to officials and technicians, who complain that Nariñense Indians use
up too much space, digging ditch after ditch to surround even the
smallest plots of land. However, the Indians say the zanjas are wonder-
ful and necessary boundary markers because they are permanent,
keep neighbors' animals off their plots, and make it more difficult for
thieves to pass cattle from one pasture to another. In the bargain, they
are good roads and even latrines.

Zanjas and other man-made features of the landscape, such as *gradas*
or steps—remnants of pre-Columbian terraces—also appear as
boundaries in colonial-era documents. Authors frequently specify that
these are "old" features of the landscape, which they are reusing to
mark new borders:

Item. I declare that on the upper slopes of said hill I have another block of lands that I bought from Ana Ytaman, that borders on one side and the other with two old zanjas, on the one

side Cuesaca stream, and above, with the lands of my brother, don Juan . . [10]

The archaeology of a zanja would thus provide a wealth of information regarding the history of a typical family, documenting from generation to generation the nature of land tenure and the passage from large holdings to the *minifundia,* or smallholdings, of today. Zanja history is especially fascinating when it is elicited from an older person who remembers four or five generations of his or her ancestors and who, many times, still possesses adjudication documents from a grandparent or great-grandparent to complement oral claims.

Such is the case of don Benjamín Cuaical, whose great-grandfather, Agustín Cuaical, acquired usufruct rights to the lands of Totoral and Carcuel in the early nineteenth century. As a history of land tenure in Totoral and Carcuel would be unnecessarily lengthy, I will instead point out some of the major highlights of zanja-building over the years. Figures 3, 3a, and 3b illustrate how rights to these lands were transferred and consolidated by don Agustín's descendants.

In approximately 1835, Agustín Cuaical (1 in figure 3) acquired usufruct rights from the cabildo to the lands of Carcuel and Totoral. The date of acquisition is known to some of the current owners because his great-great-grandson, Salomón Cuaical, used to have a copy of the original document, since lost. As can be seen in the figures, Carcuel was bounded to the north and to the west by gradas (figure 3a). To the south was a canal and a path running from Mount Cumbal to town. Don Agustín dug two zanjas to the north and the east to outline his property. Totoral, to the northwest of Carcuel, was bounded to the south by the same canal (figure 3b). Don Agustín dug zanjas to the east and the west with his neighbors.

After Agustín Cuaical's death, his lands passed in 1872 to his son, Fidel (2). An 1872 adjudication document for the lands of Chendé, which also had belonged to don Agustín, is kept by Salomón Cuaical. The document indicates that the properties were adjudicated to don Fidel but were to be used by his mother, Anselma Tarapués, until her death. As we read the document, we note that boundaries were a complex series of markers, some permanent, like zanjas, and some more temporary, like plants:

> From the starting point, they meet with the lands of Mateo Taramuel, via a central zanja, until they meet in a semicircle with the lands of Julio Guadir, running along the side until they meet in a corner with the lands of the aforementioned Guadir, [where they] continue until the lands of Agustin

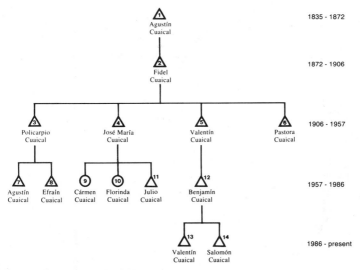

3. Genealogy of a zanja, 1835–1986

Poso, until they meet up with a stone boundary marker planted there with a *guamuco* plant at the lip of the zanja dividing [the lands] from [those of] the aforementioned Poso; at the foot, running from the aforementioned rock or guamuco, with central boundary markers, they limit with the lands of Crisanto Acpala until they meet another planted rock and "chilco" plant that is found at the lip of the zanja and entrance to [the lands of] Balentin Cuaycal; and on the final side, they continue bordering upward with the same entryway and zanja, until they meet the first boundary stated at the beginning.[11]

Although boundary markers included references to neighboring landowners as well as plants and zanjas, only the most permanent—the zanjas—survive.

When Fidel Cuaical passed his lands on to his heirs in 1906, a number of zanjas were dug in acknowledgment of the new ownership. In the 1940s, the same owners dug a zanja to the north of Carcuel to delimit other lands; as Carcuel was divided and sold among Fidel Cuaical's descendants, neighboring lands were also acquired, converting this zanja into the outer boundary of the plot. Significantly, although such features as paths were erased over the course of 150 years, zanjas remain as testimonies to the family's past.

The memory of the digging of all the zanjas is central to claims that

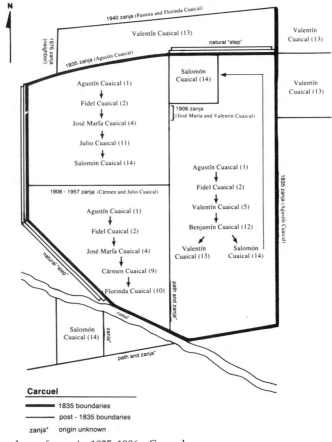

3a. Genealogy of a zanja, 1835–1986—Carcuel

might be pressed at any point by any of the owners or their descendants. For this reason, I suspect, old zanjas are not erased even when the same individual acquires property on either side of the ditch, as Valentín Cuaical did in the northeast corner of Carcuel. Nevertheless, the origins of a few zanjas are unknown; they are marked by asterisks in figure 3a.

Certainly, the zanjas that crosscut Cumbal are part of the family memory, their origins unknown to all but descendants of the original owners and their neighbors. Significantly, they also place limitations on who can know the past, since in order to unlock the historical evidence encoded in the zanjas, one must possess the lands in which they are

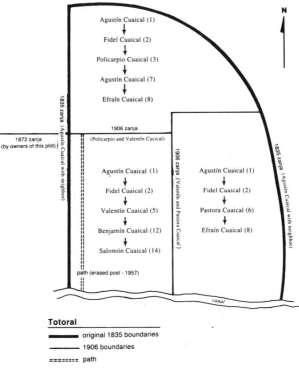

3b. Genealogy of a zanja, 1835–1986—Totoral

located or which they border; the landless and the land-poor thus have less access to this form of historical interpretation.

Nevertheless, zanjas are in many ways part of the communal memory. The multiple divisions of land that they mark, all recorded in the cabildo archive, are evidence that Cumbal is a resguardo and that non-Indians have no legal claim to its territory. When each of the lands marked by a zanja was distributed, the cabildo recognized the claims of its owner through a formal ceremony, itself full of historical referents, which I will describe later. Moreover, zanjas are dug by communal labor parties called mingas. The minga is slowly being replaced by wage labor. Where it once was central to all agricultural labor, it is now employed only for zanja-digging and for house-building. Even today, the act of digging a zanja is a communal reaffirmation of a collective history of usufruct rights.

Clearly, there is a complex process operating in Cumbal: history is recorded both in written documents and in the oral memory of the terrain, and comuneros consider both to be valid legal evidence. Historical knowledge is embedded within a complex fabric intertwining contemporary customary law with its colonial and nineteenth-century counterparts, and colonial means of delimiting territory with twentieth century law.[12] In part, this mix of the oral and the literate and of layers of law is the product of Colombia's unique Indian legislation. According to Law 89 of 1890, the cabildo is an autonomous juridical unit with respect to the settlement of internal land disputes; its existence is legitimized by colonial title. Colombian courts are not called upon to settle internal questions of resguardo land tenure. Indeed, the Division of Indigenous Affairs can only make suggestions to the cabildo, which is the ultimate authority in these matters. This has provided an opening for resguardo members to combine both national and local forms of documentation in their construction of a local history. In daily life written evidence is normally not consulted, and oral tradition provides fertile ground for elaborations upon the contents of the written historical record, allowing such material forms of historical evidence as zanjas to structure the comuneros' model of the past. But history is ultimately validated in the cabildo by written documents, and elaborate ceremony surrounds the inventory and transfer of the cabildo archive, whose contents are consulted when the need arises. In this case, zanja evidence provides a guide and framework for the selection of written records to be presented in support of a particular claim.

Although most zanjas are remembered only for the lands they delimit, many larger ditches mark major historical events. For example, many zanjas in the repossessed hacienda of La Boyera and in the resguardo of Panán are remembered as the mass graves of soldiers from nineteenth-century civil wars. A huge zanja, extending from the southern boundary of Cumbal and Panán all the way to Mount Cumbal, was dug in the 1940s by Indian labor contracted by a white hacendado who had usurped all the land in the extreme western portion of Cumbal.[13]

Zanjas evidently serve as historical markers in other cases as well. Nestor Alpala told me once that there were pre-Columbian zanjas in Güel, to the northwest of Mount Cumbal. When I visited Güel, though, I found no zanjas; instead, there were a large number of pre-Columbian habitation sites, an aqueduct and canal system, and numerous pre-Columbian agricultural terraces. The interpretation given me leads me to believe that anything old, anything deemed historical in any way, is represented as containing zanjas, since they are examples par excellence of tangible history lived from day to day.

Zanja history transcends family history in another way, acquiring a communal significance through political action. As was mentioned in chapter 2, in 1975 the cabildo repossessed the Llano de Piedras, which had been under continuous dispute with mestizo townspeople since the 1830s. After a 1923 earthquake that destroyed the town of Cumbal, the mestizos had resettled there. In their 1975 entry into and repossession of the Llano de Piedras the cabildo reincorporated these lands within the traditional resguardo structure by digging zanjas to delimit vereda boundaries. By dividing the repossessed lands into sections marked by zanjas, the cabildo returned historical referents to a terrain that had been robbed of its own history by non-Indian invaders. Here is a clear expression of how history should be corrected: not by adding more or better facts to a body of knowledge but by acting upon the consequences of the past, in this case by putting zanjas where they should have been had the lands been occupied continuously by Indians.

Note that the construction of zanjas does not simply *reconfirm* history but *reestablishes* historical process in lands that have been outside of the flow of resguardo time, so to speak, because they were usurped by non-Indians. As chapter 1 demonstrated, resguardo legislation giving the cabildo authority in matters of land tenure is also called "history." When the cabildo redistributes reclaimed land it is, in a sense, reintroducing history in the valley—history here is both a body of legislation legitimizing historical relationships to the land and the memory of those past forms of land tenure. Zanjas are reconstituted historical evidence that cement the Cumbales' historic claims as confirmed in written documents. The zanja, then, does not simply encode history; the process of digging a zanja is itself a historical activity.

History and Ceremony

Zanjas and staffs of office are the tangible products of other everyday activities, principally rituals and other practices related to the inheritance of land. The historicity of symbolically charged objects is reaffirmed, moreover, in daily activities, including family ritual, that mirror cabildo ceremony concerning inheritance, insofar as they deploy common symbolic elements. Family ritual is, in essence, a signpost directing the observer to another, communal historical marker; it calls people's attention to cabildo ceremony, which is felt to constitute historical evidence. Family ceremony is thus historical only inasmuch as it is linked through images to other referents that are more historical in nature.

The Reborn

The Cumbales draw a link between themselves and their forebears, built upon a moral continuity originating in the family, which is a fundamental vehicle for historical expression. As I have already illustrated, for example, cabildo history is remembered through the genealogy of the owners of a particular staff of office while local history is recalled through tracing the owners of a particular plot of land or the diggers of a particular boundary ditch; indigenous identity is validated through the comparison of contemporary surnames with chiefly names appearing in colonial documents.

The power of the family as a symbol of the past was made clear to me in the theatrical presentations of Epiphany Carnival in Panán, held on January fifth and sixth. Small groups, or *comparsas*, come together to prepare tableaux of their own past or of biblical history. In 1987 the winning comparsa was entitled "The Caciques and Their Descendants." A man and a woman, dressed in tunics decorated with Pasto iconographic motifs and dancing to flute music, portrayed Cumbe, the colonial cacique of Cumbal, and María Panana, the female ruler of Panán. With them danced two children, dressed somewhat incongruously as Guambiano and Otavaleño Indians, perhaps to denote "true Indianness," since these communities have distinctive costumes. Although neither written documents nor the oral tradition state that Cumbe and María Panana were married, or that they had children, the comparsa represented the four as a family, expressing the notion that the family is a fundamental symbol of the past. In fact, there was little "historical" about this presentation beyond the names of the caciques. It was their *image,* a dance with descendants who could have been any one of the spectators, that forged a link with the communal past.

This presentation has a double meaning. Historical knowledge in Gran Cumbal is transmitted within families, from one generation to the next. Documentary references are acquired from the cabildo archive, the cabildo being a broader family. But families do not only transmit history; they create it. In Nariñense Spanish, descendants are called *renacientes,* or reborn, a direct reference to the valued relationship between the contemporary Cumbales and their ancestors: contemporary comuneros are twentieth-century manifestations of Cumbe and María Panana. The high value placed upon genealogical continu-

4. Cumbe coat of arms

ity is represented in the coat of arms adopted by the cabildo, which carries the motto "Cumbe vive en los renacientes," or "Cumbe lives in the reborn" (see figure 4; also Rappaport 1992). Rebirth occurs within families, whether the biological family or the political cabildo family.

The notion of the reborn revolves around the regeneration of a stock. The birth of children adds membership to the broad groupings of relatives who cannot always trace their relationships to one another, but who call each other *familia* or family on the basis of common surnames and vereda residence (see Allen 1988). Obviously, veredal endogamy plays a key role in maintaining such groups, within which members enjoy multiple affinal and consanguineal ties with their neighbors. While I heard numerous stories of parents who opposed their children's marriages to people from other veredas—especially to the Cuaicales, who are believed to be thieves, or to the Valenzuelas, who are said to be corrupt and untrustworthy—even within a single section there are clear preferences that are repeated, generation after generation. The genealogies I collected from the Alpalas and Cuaicales in Cuaical and Tasmag, for example, indicated that almost no one married neighbors bearing the Chinguad or Quilismal surnames.

Occasionally, as in the example of Nestor Tarapués's "notebooks," the descent lines of branches of a family are recorded in writing, providing a material record of the reborn. The Alpalas and Tapies of Cuetial know who belongs to their stock because they own a family Bible in which, over three generations, significant life crises have been recorded haphazardly in the margins of its yellowing pages.

The concept of the reborn can also be understood within its broader territorial and political context. The renacientes carry distinguishable surnames, setting them apart as Cumbales from mestizos and from the comuneros of neighboring resguardos. But at various points in recent history non-Indians have been recognized as resguardo members by virtue of a cabildo vote and the taking of an oath in the presence of community members. While in the case of mestizo townspeople with no affinal ties to comuneros, renaciente status is perhaps debatable, it is more acceptable in the case of Aura Rodríguez, the mestiza wife of Helí Valenzuela, whose daughter, Milena, is certainly of "Chulde" stock. How one enters into the ranks of the reborn is especially ambiguous in the case of the children of Cumbal, Panán, and Chileno colonists born in Mayasquer. With ties to two resguardos and houses in both, they might be considered twice-over renacientes. But in many parts of Mayasquer, colonists' children have virtually replaced native Mayasqueres, the latter having migrated as colonists to the Putumayo. Cumbal colonists frequently dominate community affairs, over the feeble protests of the few remaining Mayasqueres. In all these cases, however, it is a kind of fictive descent validated by cabildo ceremony that allows for rebirth to occur.

Rebirth through Blessing

Both the nuclear family and the cabildo periodically reaffirm the status of the reborn through a ceremony charged with historical symbols. Essentially a Christian ritual, the blessing of family and community members bestows rights to resguardo lands, privileges that originated in the past and are codified in written documents, law, staffs of office, and boundary ditches. The same images that arise in these historical representations crop up in blessings, reinforcing the moral bond between past and present.[14]

Throughout Nariño, the inhabitants of the countryside maintain the once-widespread Christian custom of blessing their children in the morning, in the evening, and upon meeting them on the road. In most cases, the child simply asks the parent for a blessing and the parent responds by saying, "May God bless you," and by making the sign of the cross on the child's head. But in some families the older and longer version of the blessing is enacted numerous times every day. In these cases the child kneels before the parent, intoning, "Blessed and praised is the Lord, the holy sacrament of the altar. Good morning/good afternoon, Mother/Father." A good child will always remember to ask for the blessing, because to forget would mean to risk a beating. Although Cumbal children are only infrequently punished, negligence in asking for a parent's blessing is one cause for punishment; a whipping is sometimes also given to ensure good performance in weaving or other work.

Cabildo ceremony replicates family rituals, raising them to a higher communal and historical level. Elements of family ceremony that are also present in cabildo ritual find their prototypes in the documents that legitimize resguardo boundaries and cabildo authority. The cabildo ritual that concerns us most here is the granting of usufruct rights to a new landholder, a ceremony of European origin.

The granting of such rights comes after a series of legal procedures that begin with an appeal at the cabildo meeting. If there is no opposition within the family to the transfer of land rights, the cabildo ceremoniously names the individual to the plot. The secretary of the cabildo draws up a document and the family prepares itself for the possession ceremony and festive meal. When the day arrives, the cabildo and family members meet on the plot for which usufruct will be granted. The cabildo opens the meeting, as it does in its office, by placing staffs of office in a vertical position and declaring the session open. The secretary reads the adjudication document to the gathering. This is a ceremonial reading, for he frequently recites the words so quickly that no one can understand what he is saying. When the secretary is finished, the new usufruct holders kneel before the president of the cabildo (plate 8), who says:

> Administering justice in the name of the Republic of Colombia and by authority of law, I grant you real, formal, and material possession to this plot, so that you may work it and use it during your life, and afterward it will pass to your legitimate descendants, by virtue of which the cabildo orders you to roll on the ground, to pull out grass, and to throw it in the air, as a sign of true possesion, that the cabildo by merit of justice, grants you.[15]

The new usufruct holders then fall to the ground, pull up weeds, and throw them in the air while the governor's lieutenant whips them, shouting: "Work hard! Do not sell, rent or mortgage your land!" The new owners kneel in front of the president, ask for his blessing, and kiss his staff of office.

In many respects, the possession ceremony is identical to family ritual, using the same prayers, the same action of kneeling, the same preventive punishment. In other words, as Salomón Cuaical commented to me, cabildantes oblige new landholders to treat them as though they were parents. The image of the cabildo as a communal family is also expressed in the terms used for its officers, who are frequently addressed as the fathers of their veredas: Taita Guan, Taita Tasmag, etc.

But the possession ceremony is not identical to the blessing of children, because it raises the level of social integration of the activity from that of everyday family relationships and personal history to the broader history of the resguardo and its founders, much as the digging of zanjas in reclaimed land transforms markers of family history into a reaffirmation of the communal past. This is accomplished in various ways: (1) The Cumbales maintain that the possession ceremony was dictated by Law 89, which they gloss as "history." (2) They read and sign an adjudication document that will be filed in the cabildo archive, becoming part of the corpus of communal history. (3) The usufruct holders solicit the blessing of the president's staff of office, repeating the ceremonies of childhood before a symbol that represents various generations of political rule. (4) The president's words are reenactments of the granting of resguardo title, appearing in Deed 228, the Royal Provision, and similar documents.

In fact, when community historians are asked about the original granting of resguardo title, they always repeat the president's words in their narrations:

> And [Mauricio Muñóz de Ayala, High Magistrate of the Pastos] came for an inspection lasting two weeks in this same year of 1758, and traced the boundaries with Juan Tapie, the same Tapie family native to here.
>
> And within the two weeks he granted possession, which means that to the present, our cabildo, or myself as president, I must declare the act open to grant possession of the land in usufruct to the Indians.
>
> And Mauricio Muñóz de Ayala said: In the name of the Republic of Colombia and by authority of law I grant you real, formal and material possession to the Indians, male and female, girls and boys, of Gran Cumbal. (Gilberto Valenzuela, Vereda Cuaical)[16]

Clearly, the man whose words I reproduce was profoundly influenced by contemporary practice in his recounting of the past. Although the final words in which he specifies the sex and age of the Indians are reminiscent of colonial documents, the bulk of his narration is derived from contemporary experience. The narrative of the creation of the resguardo hinges on audience recognition of the ongoing presence of the Tapie family in Quilismal and in cabildo office. Moreover, the narrator uses an example from contemporary cabildo practice to construct the climax of his tale, drawing in his listeners by quoting the Spanish official Munóz de Ayala as having said, "In the name of the Republic of Colombia .. " more than a half-century before Colombia won its independence from Spain.

These rituals are the most tangible examples of historical evidence that an average Cumbal resident will experience during the course of a lifetime. Many resguardo members rarely attend community-wide political meetings, much less serve as cabildo officials. Memoristas are generally not sought out to share their knowledge, except by family members or political leaders. Therefore, the blessing, occurring daily in the family and several times a year when nuclear family members or close relatives transmit property rights to others, is a continuous reminder of links to the communal past. While the average comunero may not consciously make the link between family and communal ceremony, or between ceremony and history, it is certainly a priority for political leaders. In the course of land occupations and through widely disseminated songs and theater, both of which will be described in more detail later, some of this exegesis is transmitted to the general public.

A History of the Present

On the surface, Cumbal notions of history as expressed in everyday life are contradictory. In the beginning of this chapter I noted that history is lodged in the present and is expressed primarily through those aspects of everyday activity that the Cumbales see as distinguishing them from their non-Indian neighbors. But with the exception of zanjas, most of the historical elements that the Cumbales have incorporated into everyday activity are of European origin, although they have passed from common usage among the members of the dominant Colombian society: staffs of office were first carried the cabildos of the Spanish colonizers; the Royal Crown refers specifically to the Spanish monarchy; the possession ceremony was introduced by the Spanish administration and its manifestation in Cumbal is similar to colonial land-granting rituals in other areas; the blessing of children is a standard Colombian Catholic practice; the sources for most historical images are colonial documents of Spanish origin. Why do the Cumbales look toward clearly European practices to reaffirm their Indianness?

Indigenous experience is by necessity interpreted within the framework of the dominant Colombian society, a clear statement that those Spanish institutions that have permitted the maintenance of an autonomous identity are a fundamental part of history. Without the territorial protection afforded by the resguardo and the political autonomy implicit in the cabildo, there would be no Cumbales. For this reason, they are selective in their choice of historical evidence, displaying a bias toward sources that document their legitimacy as a group and provide a guide to action for assuring their continued survival. Their principal evidence is drawn from the European institutions under which they have been forced to defend their distinctiveness. Over the years, Cumbal identity has merged so thoroughly with the institutions that ensure it (and that endangered the Cumbales autonomy in the first place) that today those institutions, and ritual reminders of them in everyday activity, supply the Cumbales with a definition of who they are and why they continue to exist.

Notwithstanding the Europeanness of individual elements of Cumbal Indian identity, however, such features contrast sharply with the usages of local mestizos, insofar as they are articulated within the six-section structure of the resguardo. The strategies the Cumbales use to refer to history in everyday practice also strengthen the unity of the six sections, both because they sustain the authority of the cabildo on already-occupied lands and because the structure is replicated through political organizing, ritual, and land distribution each time a new hacienda is repossessed. Although the staff of office, the blessing, and the possession ceremony were introduced from Europe, they stimulate comuneros to draw connections to their past and to their future by alluding to, strengthening, and continuously reconstructing the distinctive mode by which their community is organized.[17]

What is recalled in material culture, in ritual, and in territorial organization is a history of the present. It has already been noted that the most talented memoristas regularly insert the scanty references they cull from colonial-era and nineteenth-century documentation into a narrative framework recalling experiences of the recent past. Objects and ceremony in everyday life likewise constitute a nonverbal intertext in relation to the narratives of colonial caciques, carrying the distant past forward to the immediacy of contemporary experience, where it can be most meaningfully recalled, interpreted, and acted upon.

FIVE

Writing History

THE NATIONAL ARCHIVE OF ECUA-
DOR occupies the upper stories of a downtown Quito government
building located across a broad avenue from a large park. Its public
offices are housed in a series of rooms on the second floor, including
a waiting room for those who need copies of recent notary records and
the *sala de investigadores* or reading room, which is filled with nine or
ten small desks at which readers scan documents under the watchful
eye of an archive employee. From time to time, however, the denizens
of the sala—academics and their hired assistants—give way to a new
reading public. Colombian Indians—Guambianos in blue kilts or Páez
in long ponchos—cluster in groups, gathered around desks or assembled in the hallways surrounded by piles of the cardboard boxes in
which documents are stored, combing the archives for evidence of
their past.

The cabildo of Cumbal has not visited Quito for years. In 1944 they
were lucky enough to find the Royal Provision much closer to home,
in the notary archives of Ipiales. In the 1970s, they discovered Deed
228 in the notarial offices in Pasto. The cabildo's typescript copy of the
Royal Provision acknowledges their 1944 acquisition of the document
on its introductory page.

These vignettes are more the rule than the exception in Colombia
and have been for centuries. Since the colonial period, Indians have
consulted legal documents as justification for their claims to lands and
to authority. Yet, while Andeanist ethnohistorians have always paid
close attention to written evidence, particularly to the colonial sources
from which ethnographic data can be mined, and have engaged in

textual analysis of seventeenth century chronicles by indigenous authors, most ethnographic studies of contemporary Andean society remain curiously silent on the influence of the written word within indigenous communities.[1] Scholars have virtually ignored indigenous literacy, despite the fact that for the past 450 years Indians have participated in the literate conventions of the dominant society, employed the written word as a bridge between community and state, and looked to the archive as a window onto the struggles of their forebears.

Writing as Dialogue

Recent anthropological writing has emphasized the need for ethnographers to explore the multiplicity of voices encountered in the course of fieldwork (Clifford 1988; Clifford and Marcus 1986; Price 1990, among others). In their pursuit of a theoretical framework, many draw heavily upon the work of literary critic Mikhail Bakhtin (1981), particularly upon his concept of polyphony, or the process by which an author reports the words of others. Yet the anthropological espousal of polyphony is largely confined to the oral domain. James Clifford insists that in contradistinction to the limitations imposed upon historians by their reliance on the textual record, ethnography is singularly rooted in orality, experience, observation, and the present (Clifford 1988, 340). However, if we ignore the impact of literacy in communities traditionally studied by anthropologists, many of the alternative voices we seek will be obscured, because they speak to us exclusively through the written channel (see Boyarin 1989).

The multiplicity of voices in Latin America and the dynamics of polyphony are clearly manifest in the written dialogues that unfold in the legal arena between indigenous communities and the state. There is more at stake here than a command of the technology of writing. Infinitely more significant are the ways in which power is consolidated through the written word. Of particular significance is the degree to which political and administrative control is exercised through exclusionary legal language and rules of acceptable evidence. We must also remain aware of the culturally specific strategies subaltern authors employ to wrest control of written channels from their adversaries. Finally, written communication needs to be interpreted within its historical context, which includes more than the time and place in which it is produced; we must take care to explore how writings are read across time and across cultural boundaries. In addition to the multiplicity of voices that characterize contemporary written communication between subordinated groups and the state, then, we must also consider the polyphony of the historical record from which evidence is extracted for the contemporary dialogue (Comaroff and Comaroff 1992, 35).

In a masterful analysis of antagonistic perceptions of the indigenous and the Euroamerican Other as they are expressed in written dialogue between Mayas and North American archaeologists in the first half of this century, Paul Sullivan adopted the metaphor of the conversation. In this example, however, conversation does not necessarily imply the effective exchange of ideas; instead, it is a kind of a "double monologue":

> In my metaphorical long conversation, we must be less confident that there *are* answers. Each encounter between Maya and foreigner was an extraordinary experiment in cross-cultural communication. Many a Maya and foreigner had never met individuals of the other kind. They did not speak each other's language very well (if at all); were guided by very different motives; had different ideas about speaking and writing and the kinds of beings who can use language; had different senses of place, time, causality, and different knowledge of what had gone on before. They could not share one set of answers to questions about their dialogues. Each side, in fact, would have quite different questions to ask about what had and was transpiring between them. (Sullivan 1989, xxvi)

The terms upon which such a conversation is constructed are subverted by its long duration, in the course of which the interlocutors, their objectives, and the context in which they operate are all in a continual state of flux:

> On top of that, time can corrupt our ability to speak accurately about what we have done, despite our belief that objectivity is enhanced by the waning of a moment's passion and interest. Imagine a conversation that lasts much, much too long—so long, that is, that even as interlocutors converse, refusing to let go of some evidently engrossing topic, they age perceptibly. Some die, and suitable onlookers step in to pick up the thread. As time passes, the pronunciation, syntax, and vocabulary of the speakers drift away from those of their predecessors, whose remembered utterances now seem subtly out of date, their references to the world obscure. The place where the speakers meet and the landscape about them are modified by human hand or natural forces, and to them attach new sentiments and meanings for the things that have happened there during this long conversation. . . . This conversation goes on so

long, in fact, that all significant features of personal and collective identity shift—all the standard experiences and doings of
an ordinary life, all the shared communicative means of our
avid conversationalists, and the wider world context that
shapes the motives for their speaking and the meaning and
effect of what is said. (Ibid.)

Sullivan's metaphor is appropriate to indigenous communities
across Latin America and in Nariño in particular, where such intercultural exchanges have continued over four centuries. These eternal conversations commonly take the form of double monologues unfolding
in the written briefs of lawsuits and letters, in oral testimony, and
through the deployment of written evidence in land titles and in wills.
They are ultimately interrupted by the use of force. At times, the
paired interlocutors are Spanish colonial administrators and hereditary chiefs. Later, post-independence cabildos appropriate eighteenth-
century voices in their own dialogue with the state (Izko 1992). Copies
of colonial briefs—now interspersed with nineteenth-century papers
and peppered with the early twentieth-century names of those who
have requested copies of the documentation—lay the basis for contemporary communication with the national bureaucracy as well as for
forays into the world of written communication among Indians themselves. As Michel de Certeau has shown, the double monologue of
community and state fosters a similar exchange between the living and
the dead: the words of the departed constitute a medium of conversation for the living, a discourse expressed in the third person (de Certeau 1988, 46).

Each time documentary exchanges are appropriated, they are interpreted in conjunction with the intertexts of contemporary oral tradition, historical knowledge as it is manifested in material culture and
in ritual, historically informed political rhetoric, and militant action.
Thus, the oral histories of Cumbal's memoristas are products of a long
and sometimes unfruitful conversation that has taken place across time
in a variety of media. While on the surface these histories appear to
belong to the realm of orality, in fact they are created at the interface
of written, non-written, and even nonverbal forms of communication.

While literate communication remains the medium of Cumbal's relations with the state, most people are not equipped to participate fully
in this written conversation. The educational system in the resguardo,
consisting of poorly staffed public schools established during the past
two decades and private vereda-based schools before that, has never
been particularly sympathetic to the needs of Indians. Many prefer
schools in town to nearby country schoolhouses. However, both Ben-

jamín Cuaical and Nestor Tarapués studied in mestizo schools in Puebloviejo some seventy years ago and still remember how their teachers, afraid that Indians would excel over mestizo pupils, refused to promote them to fourth grade. Most teachers today are mestizo townspeople who are overwhelmingly opposed to the ethnic rights movement and refuse to recognize the Cumbales as indigenous people. Thus, there is much working against the young Cumbal student.

Reading, moreover, is by no means a favored pastime. Some memoristas maintain personal libraries in their homes. Before his eyesight betrayed him, don Benjamín was an avid reader of periodicals, even going so far as to memorize poems he particularly enjoyed. But most are slow and painful readers, preferring to spend their free time in more pleasant pursuits, such as conversing with family members or watching television.[2]

The majority of Cumbales thus participate only vicariously in the literate mode of communication. Literacy in Cumbal is not so much the ability to read and write as the acquisition of information that has been stored in the written channel but transmitted orally by the few who read well. Written documents, carefully stored in wooden chests, their folded edges caked with years of grime, are spoken about more than they are read, just as they were during the colonial period:

> With the necessary solemnities [Don Simon Mainbas, cacique of Tuza and Puntal] submits some ancient instruments belonging to some lands that he owns, so that Your Honor will order that the present scribe copy over what he finds legible, because with the ravages of time they are being consumed and are in need of repair.[3]

Given these conditions, the memorista becomes the bridge between community and state as well as between the oral and written records. Conventions of legal writing fashion the contours of memoristas' oral discourse while the rules of oral historiography determine the shape of indigenous written communication, as we will see in the following mid-twentieth-century double monologue I discovered in the cabildo archives.

An Andean Reading of the Documentary Record

Conflicting Discourses

The following letter was written on June 16, 1950 by the cabildo of Cumbal in defense of its sulphur deposits on Mount Cumbal, which were in danger of being leased by the Colombian Ministry of Mines and Petroleum:

> REFERENCE: Community of Cumbal regarding its sulphur deposits whose exploitation-extraction and mining of the mineral date from the ROYAL COURT OF SAN FRANCISCO DE QUITO—June 9, 1758—52 years before the call for INDEPENDENCE of July 20, 1810.
>
> —The rights acquired through the observance of the laws of the king of SPAIN were declared by the FIRST CONSTITUTION of the REPUBLIC, to be recognized, protected, and by no means violated by the new AUTHORITIES.
>
> —And one and another time, the Spanish Infantry Captain and Magistrate of HIGH JUSTICE OF THE PASTOS, don MAURICIO Muñoz de Ayala—by commission of the ROYAL COURT OF SAN FRANCISCO DE QUITO—legalized the possession, he made it good, and he also made good the dominion of the four hereditary chiefs—TAPIES—over the expanse of land in whose center the volcano named CUMBAL stood out like a pyramid. For a week the Infantry Captain had to identify, one by one, the natural boundaries within which the expanse of land granted to the Indian masses, with their chiefs at their head, was encompassed by boundary markers. ACCOMPLISHED the patient tracing of boundaries, to which chiefs from other towns were invited, the Spanish Infantry Captain knelt on the plain, and then, assuming the gold crown of his king, his natural lord, in a loud voice handed over the land in its tenancy, its possession, and its very dominion to the chiefs, the genuine representatives of the peoples of CUMBAL. And at the same time, the expanse of land was cleansed of blacks, of Spaniards, and of all interlopers.[4] THEN as now came the accessory to the principal: the land was of utmost importance, without equal, given that the Indian masses were given their sustenance from it, albeit with their own work, and the daily pastures provided for their cattle were theirs spontaneously and in abundance.
>
> —THIS is how tenancy, possession, and ownership was acquired, in front of all the people, in the presence of the King, his ROYAL COURT OF SAN FRANCISCO DE QUITO, his Infantry Captains and his Magistrates of High Justice.
>
> —WITH great intelligence law 35 of 1943 advised that the NATION, through its technicians, would do the work of EXPLORATION. It is rational, first, to look, to find the deposits that produce nothing, that no one benefits from, that no one reaps nor has reaped advantage. (Art. 2 of the cited law 35). SO that in the second article it is forseen that it will be necessary to explore, to find what has not at any time been worked, made

productive by work. OUR elders, from time immemorial, of which one does not know for sure when was the first day, have exploited, extracted, to have a livelihood, the snow [glacial ice], in blocks, and the sulphur. THEY have carried on their backs, on those slopes down Cumbal, blocks of snow and quantities of sulphur. Below at the place called LIADERO is where the load is then put onto their beasts of burden to go to the markets of Colombia and Ecuador. It CANNOT be denied that it is a favor, a gift of the KING. And that today the REPUBLIC pretends to seize it by force, that which first is work, even life-threatening, on those slopes, where the hides of many of us have remained, and that which is, afterward, still at a great cost and effort, traded in the towns of Colombia and Ecuador —IN the office of the First Notary of Pasto, on June 9, 1908, the titles we use to distinguish ourselves were registered, and they are worth as much to us as a LIFESAVER. WE are the race that dearly requires a new redeemer, of the stature of SIMON BOLIVAR.

—IN the post office of Cumbal they never deliver our mail. We hope that it will be sent to Pasto, where we have a person whom we have given the power to withdraw it from the OFFICES OF AVIANCA [the airmail postal service] or from the National Post Office.

On May eleventh (11) we sent our first brief, in defense of what we have to work with and, consequently, to live by.

Others have unexplored deposits, and therefore unexploited ones, benefiting no one, [yet] no one has thought up a business with them nor could do so, even with much technical knowhow.

Why is it that the apple from the other orchard always has to be more tasty??? (signed, VICE-PRESIDENT, Amiliano Álpala. CABILDANTE OF CUMBAL: 1950; Agustín Colimba, SECRETARY OF THE CABILDO OF CUMBAL)[5]

The government's attorney responded with the following note:

Please be advised I am in receipt of your petition of June 2 of this year addressed to the Minister of Mines and Petroleum.

In view of the fact that this is a matter concerning a community of indigenous people who, perhaps, are not familiar with the laws and decrees concerning mining concessions, I am obliged to inform you that if you consider the requested concession to be an infringement of legitimate rights of the indigenous community of whose Council you are yourselves members, you must present your written objections to the Governor of the Department at the time the proposed contract is considered—along with the documents that verify your rights. The Governor will forward the documentation to this Ministry, which will take the matter into consideration and, if the objection is formally presented, it will be sent to the Superior Court of Pasto for a ruling.

Inasmuch as the objection is not formulated legally, this Office can do nothing regarding the above-referenced petition.

I am at your service (signed, Gonzalo Pérez Castro, General Secretary)[6]

The Filter of Everyday Life

Here is a written exchange involving two completely different types of discourse. The issue is simple: indigenous control of mineral resources on resguardo lands. The authors of the petition could simply have made reference to specific legal precedents granting Indians control over the territory, presenting evidence of the legality of the boundaries of the resguardo. Instead, they do something quite different.

The first letter begins, as shrewd minority discourses often do, with an implicit acknowledgment of the majority form of the codification of power, in this case, the law. The first paragraph refers to colonial legislation granting Cumbal the right to exploit its mineral beds; the second paragraph refers to the continuation of that right under Republican law, a theme returned to in a later paragraph with the reference to Simón Bolívar, father of Colombian independence. The two paragraphs recognize legal codes as the dominant discourse of Colombian society. In effect, by opening the letter with these two paragraphs (and by closing it with a plea for a response to a previous unanswered letter and a complaint that they have trouble receiving their mail in the mestizo-operated post office), the cabildo implicitly acknowledges the subordinate relationship into which it has entered with the state by virtue of being forced to communicate in a written mode over which the authors have little control.

But in the third paragraph the letter erupts into something quite different: an apparently irrelevant but detailed description of a ceremony granting the community possession to its lands, one that is vaguely anchored in time, witnessed by local and neighboring chiefs, and repeated at unknown intervals. Why is such information included in a legal brief demanding that the government grant the cabildo autonomy in its control of natural resources?

The document to which the cabildo—more precisely, the memorista/secretary Agustín Colimba—refers in this confusing paragraph is the Royal Provision that was acquired in typescript form from the First Circuit Notary of Ipiales in 1944 and in a shorter version, called Deed 228, from the First Notary of Pasto.[7] The typed version is over two hundred pages long. Considerably longer in its colonial-era manuscript original, it presents a daunting task to memoristas who attempt to read it, as I discovered in a session with the cabildo of Panán. People regard the original manuscript with an almost mystical sense of awe:

> In the cabildo now they have so many copies. There are photocopies; the real one is in the cabildo, the real Royal Provision.
>
> I know it, I saw it, I looked for it: it exists in the First Circuit Notary of Pasto [sic]. There is the Royal Provision.
>
> I saw it, only I couldn't read it. There were the names of the caciques. It even had some seals. It's on parchment, the Royal Provision in Pasto.
>
> And when it's needed in quarrels, in lawsuits, the cabildo requests it. They request it there, but it's very hard to copy. The scribes copy it, they copy it when there's sun, with a lens: then it appears, then it appears clearly.
>
> Because they showed it to us, when we were in the office to know the Royal Provision, the mother of the others. It was sunny and the secretary took us out to a patio, a little plaza, and he said, "Come see, see if you can read it." And we read it.
>
> It said, "From Mallorca, the King who was from Spain, from Cursia [sic], from Corsica." We also could read it there in the sun. (Benjamín Cuaical, Vereda Cuaical)[8]

The original, the "mother" of later copies, such as the typescript in the cabildo archives, is thought to be impenetrable except when read in the sun, with special instruments, and, most important, when its decipherment is mediated by the non-Indian notary. The best description I encountered of the difficulties of reading colonial script is the following: "I went to talk with so-and-so, who was named Fernando Cuesta, and he has a deed [in] which the caciques used to make the writing in reverse" (Rosario Malte, Chiles).[9]

But it is not only the colonial handwriting that is indecipherable in these documents. Even the typescript of Deed 228, a much briefer document, is highly intimidating, with its seemingly-endless array of legal briefs condensed into so few pages, marking the multiple steps in the legal process by which the caciques of Cumbal and Nazate attempted to claim their rights to the hacienda of Guamialamag, then in the hands of Spaniards. To read a colonial title is to enter a maze in which only a few details are visible: the names of the caciques and the Spanish authorities, the boundaries of chiefly landholdings, the ritual legitimation of land tenure.

It is not accidental that Agustín Colimba focused in on the possession ceremony encoded in the Royal Provision, since the ritual is still enacted repeatedly today to legitimize the transfer of usufruct rights to resguardo lands. As we have already seen, the ceremony qualifies as a vehicle for historical remembering. From the point of view of a cabildante it would be obvious that this ceremony, even more than the abstract delineation of boundaries, should constitute the central piece of evidence for indigenous landownership.

But the cabildo was probably also operating on the basis of previous experience with local mestizo authorities. Although usufruct rights are legitimized through the registration of documents at the mayor's office, even Cumbaleños (as mestizos are called, to distinguish them from the indigenous Cumbales) recognize the possession ceremony as the moment in which land rights are really transferred. This fact was brought home to me when I witnessed a dispute over a plot of land whose usufruct was granted to a comunero by the 1986 cabildo, but which the municipal mayor had claimed as his private property. When the cabildo and community gathered to grant ritual possession of the land, the mayor arrived and violently broke up the meeting, sending a number of comuneros to the hospital.[10] If ritual constitutes the moment at which the transfer of land rights is recognized by local mestizos, the retrieval of such a context from a colonial document would also be perceived by the cabildo as appropriate evidence for the authorities in Bogotá. But why do they have Mauricio Muñóz de Ayala enacting the possesion ceremony over and over again?

The Polyphony of Documents

As in any lengthy lawsuit, judicial decisions in eighteenth century Cumbal were rendered, later withdrawn, and, after a long appeals process, delivered again; as a result, the caciques were repeatedly granted ritual possession of their lands. Although the Spanish colonial administration was fueled by an overelaboration of the written word, its laws and statutes were validated, enacted, and experienced by most people through ritual practice. And although these rituals are encoded in written form in legal titles and other documents, their description is more properly a product of oral than of written communication: they do not demonstrate the economy of expression that characterizes literacy, but duplicate in written form, repetitively, the words spoken at

these ceremonies.[11] The ambiguous relationship between eighteenth-century literary conventions and modern writing is manipulated by twentieth-century readers, who perceive such repetition as inherently meaningful, even when it was not initially meant to be understood this way: "And one and another time, the Spanish Infantry Captain . . . legalized the possession, he made it good. . . . "

Colonial documentation is polyphonic in its very construction. The legal papers with which we are concerned are amalgams of a number of documents hailing from a variety of time periods:

> The notion of "title" in the colonial Spanish world went be-yond the concept of a simple deed. Full title—whether to land, territory, or jurisdiction—involved not only an original grant or sale, but also an investigation on the spot to consult third parties and see if the situation was as described, and finally formal acts of giving and taking possession. Only then did the grant or sale, until that point merely virtual or hypothetical, enter into force. A Spanish notary would keep a running re-cord of the whole proceeding, repeatedly signed by officials and witnesses; this record, appended to the original grant, or-der, or the like, constituted the title (Lockhart 1982, 371)

Cumbal's titles contain a variety of records spanning some forty-six years, from 1712 to 1758, including multiple testimonies of local chiefs and non-Indians residing in the area; written records of ceremonies granting land rights to any of a number of parties to the dispute; docu-mentation of the numerous requests for testimony, judicial consider-ation or investigations that kept the lawsuit going for more than four decades; copies—and occasional originals—of earlier documents, es-pecially royal decrees granting Indians territorial autonomy in the sev-enteenth century. A perusal of Deed 228, in the typescript form in which it is kept in the cabildo archives, elucidates the nature of the multilayered legal brief.[12]

Deed 228 is transcribed onto modern *papel sellado,* official paper bearing a seal in the upper left-hand corner, which is used for legal briefs. The purchase of papel sellado is a form of taxation, a require-ment that was only recently suspended for indigenous litigators. The transcribed document is dated June 9, 1908, the day on which the title was registered as required by Law 89 of 1890. On the first page, the cabildo is noted as presenting in twenty folios a copy of the commu-nity title; land boundaries are provided, followed by reference to an 1871 provincial ordinance.

The two following pages are transcriptions of communiqués regard-ing various cabildo requests for authenticated copies of the title, in this case, in 1908, 1869, and 1865. The nineteenth century request, it is noted in the text, supplied the cabildo with legal evidence of its claim to the Llano de Piedras. In the original, these documents would stand out from among the older briefs, distinguishable by handwriting and paper quality.

It is only on the back of the third page that the original title begins, with a *real provisión de proclama*, a royal decree announcing the initiation of an investigation into the ownership of the lands. The record of the investigation includes the testimony of twelve witnesses, six named by the authorities and six by don Pedro Alpala, cacique. This document is followed by a *real provisión de amparo*, granting royal protection to the Indians; handwritten marginal notes indicate that the words "real provisón de amparo" are of importance to contemporary cabildo readers. The document opens with a long list of the king's titles and contains the various documents written in support of the community's claims:

1. A January 22, 1758 report by the Indians' legal council, the *fiscal protector general de los naturales del distrito*, introducing don Pedro Alpala's petition (ff. 3v–4r).

2. Don Pedro Alpala's request, which opens with genealogical information tracing his descent back to his great-grandparents. He cites three *amparos*, or royal grants of protection, prepared in 1633, 1678, and 1692; a handwritten note in the margin reads "amparos." Alpala states that according to the amparos, no Spaniard, mestizo, black, or mulatto can live on the land; the sentence is highlighted in pencil (ff. 4r–5r).

3. Official receipt and issuance of the real provisión de amparo, dated January 25, 1758 (ff. 5r–v).

4. A copy of the 1678 amparo of don Diego de Inclán y Valdés. Little crosses are marked in pencil next to caciques' names (ff. 5v–6r).

5. Alpala's formal request for the amparo, now that the evidence has been submitted (ff. 6r–v).

6. Documentation of the provision of protection by Mauricio Muñóz de Ayala, all underlined in pencil, and announcement of the coming *vista de ojos*, or measuring of the land (ff. 6v–7r).

7. A copy of the June 9, 1758 subpoena of the cacique and governor of Cumbal, don José Cumbal, requiring that he present himself at the possession ceremony (f. 7r).

8. Documents notifying various other caciques from neighboring Muellamués of the proceedings (f. 7v).

9. A report of the June 12, 1758 possession ceremony, including a list of the boundaries of the community and a verbatim account of the possession ritual. Both have been highlighted in pencil by contemporary readers (ff. 7v–8r).

The last two pages of the transcript acknowledge receipt of copies of the title in 1826 and in 1957, and the registry of the title in 1908.

The title thus exhibits a considerable layering of documentation, a unique sort of intertextuality and multivocality characteristic of legal writing (Vining 1991). A correct reading of these briefs presupposes a competence that includes an understanding of the arrangement of varied forms of documentation within a single record. The fact that the titles were produced by multiple authors over several centuries is frequently obscured, because these documents were commonly copied into the record by a small number of scribes, and hence are written in only one or two distinguishable hands.[13]

A look at the marginal notes in pencil indicates that only particular items were singled out by contemporary readers: boundary markers, the names of the caciques and of Mauricio Muñóz de Ayala, the word "amparo," the possession ceremony, the exclusion of non-Indians from the lands. In effect, these are the data that are taken up by memoristas in their recounting of the colonial history of Cumbal.

Misreadings of Documents

Such documents prove confusing to twentieth-century indigenous readers, generally men with extensive political experience and a deep knowledge of community oral tradition, but with only two to four years of formal schooling. Note, for example, Panán memorista don Nazario Cuásquer's description of his community's title:

> And then they lodged a complaint. The communities of Muellamués, Cumbal, Carlosama, Guachucal, Panán, Mayasquer, Chiles came and they made the complaint to the Royal Court of Quito.
> The Royal Court of Quito then sent their brief, principally the complaint, to the Antilles, to Turman [sic], to Count, and in turn, to everyone, and in the end, to the Spanish King Crown.
> Then the King Crown ordered, it says, that a commission from the Royal Court of Quito go there to force them to re-

spect these lands. (Nazario Cuásquer, Vereda Panán Centro, Panán)[14]

Don Nazario misreads the multiple titles of the Spanish King that open all royal decrees, listing them as though they were distinct individuals to whom the complaint was sent. This is clear when his account is compared to the following excerpt from one of the decrees included in the title to Cumbal:

> Don Felipe, by the grace of God, King of Castile, of Leon, of Aragon, of the two Sicilies, of Jerusalem, of Navarra, of Granada, of Toledo, of Valencia, of Galicia, of Mallorca, of Seville, of Sardinia, of Cordoba, of Murcia, of Jaen, of the Algares and Algeria, of Gibraltar, of the Canary Islands, of the East and West Indies and of the Main Land of the Ocean, Archduke of Syria, Duke of Burgundy, Count of Naples, of Flanders, of Tirol, of Barcelona, Lord of Viscaya and of Molina, etc., etc.[15]

Similar errors are inherent in the cabildo's letter to the Minister of Mines, demonstrating that the titles were not all that transparent to the 1950 letter writers. For example, note the jumbled chronology of the last paragraph of the letter:
> —IN the office of the First Notary of Pasto, on June 9, 1908, the titles we use to distinguish ourselves were registered, and they are worth as much to us as a LIFESAVER. WE are the race that dearly requires a new redeemer, of the stature of SIMON BOLIVAR.

The cabildo dates its title to the 1908 registry of the colonial copy instead of pointing to its eighteenth-century origin, which is, ultimately, what validates the document.

In another instance, the authors create their own layering by jumping from the colonial period to the early nineteenth century, presumably seeking validation of their claim by associating the title with Simón Bolívar:
> REFERENCE: Community of Cumbal regarding its sulphur deposits whose exploitation-extraction and mining of the mineral date from the ROYAL COURT OF SAN FRANCISCO DE QUITO— June 9, 1758—52 years before the call for INDEPENDENCE of July 20, 1810.

Bolívar is said to have authorized a version of the resguardo title, but it has never been found.

A second type of layering is inherent in indigenous readings of colonial documents. Although the titles contain multiple references to ceremonies outwardly similar to those performed today, the rituals have undergone slight alterations in content over time, given that they have been played out in widely divergent social contexts. Twentieth-century Indians reinterpret modern typescript transcriptions of the titles through the filter of these rituals and transmit this knowledge in oral form to other community members. The memory of the existence of the colonial document has been maintained by oral means as well as by reference to symbols, such as the "Royal Crown," that bring together such disparate items as lands, markers of political authority and even written documents around a common metaphor. In the end, we are confronted with a written interpretation, most probably prepared by individuals who never read the document in question.

A good example of this type of layering is, once again, don Nazario Cuásquer's reading of the Panán title:

> Then the Captain took their hands and gave them possession, the four hereditary chiefs who arrived, Sebastián Tarapués, Hilario Nazate, Gabriel Nazate, Bernardo Tarapués.
> And they were given possession in the name of the Republic of Colombia, under authority of the law, they should roll. So they rolled. Then they threw grass, sod, [symbolizing] true possession.
> The decree ended and those others there listening were told to take care not to fool the Indians, that whoever did would be fined a hundred *patacones*. (Nazario Cuásquer, Vereda Panán Centro, Panán)[16]

Don Nazario's references to the Republic of Colombia are, clearly, a product of the post-independence period, despite the fact that he concerns himself with colonial-era chiefs. Colonial caciques, although they understood Spanish, were also competent in the Pasto language, which disappeared some time in the early nineteenth century. Thus, their linguistic understanding of the ceremony and the way in which they shared their impressions with their subjects contrasts with that of post-independence cabildos. Moreover, the colonial example involves hereditary chiefs, recognized as such by the Spanish administration and permitted certain trappings of nobility, such as the title "don." Nowadays cabildos are elected for a year's term and individuals hold no permanent claim to political authority. Finally, during the nineteenth-century consolidation of the Colombian Republic, cabildos lost much of their authority as they were transformed from semiautonomous political leaders to intermediaries between state and citizen. Within this context, the texts of the two possession ceremonies, while similar, carry highly different meanings.

Finally, there is a third form of layering that characterizes any contemporary reading of these documents. The cabildo's understanding of the contents of the titles is conditioned by the nature of the Colombian legal system. The competence necessary to read or produce these documents, even in the colonial period, was founded upon a familiarity with legal discourse more than with an expertise in alphabetic literacy. Those who read the titles today, moreover, operate under multiple legal systems simultaneously: the colonial, the Republican, and the contemporary legal codes, each of which builds upon the others but can be comprehended only within its own social and historical context (Moore 1986, 1989). So, for example, the indigenous letter writers must refer to colonial, independence, and contemporary legislation in one breath, creating a highly confusing juxtaposition of dates and legal codes in order to establish their claim to the sulphur beds of Mount Cumbal.

Memorista History and Written History

The cabildo's 1950 letter to the Ministry of Mines finally jumps from the eighteenth century to 1943, with a recitation of the contents of a law regarding ownership of natural resources. This citation is as reasonable from the legal standpoint of the dominant society as it is for the cabildo, but for entirely different reasons. While the bureaucrats understand legislation as a charter for action in the present, for Cumbales it is historical evidence and, as has already been mentioned, is conflated with colonial documents and glossed as "history."

But the cabildo's use of legislation and historical evidence in this paragraph is more complex than that, because in support of their citation of Law 35 of 1943 the Indian authors offer evidence in the form of a description of sulphur and glacial ice exploitation on Mount Cumbal. They emphasize the difficulties they encounter in carrying these materials on their backs, the loading of their animals at the Liadero (the end of the bridle path), and their commerce in ice and sulphur in surrounding cities. In another draft I discovered in the same file, perhaps the first letter the cabildo sent to the ministry, the authors add that ice was extracted with axes and that sulphur was used in the fabrication of straw hats.[17]

During the course of my stay in Cumbal I collected countless personal reminiscences of the exploitation of the resources of Mount Cumbal, especially from poor or landless comuneros from Cuaical and Quilismal. Don Alejandro Chirán, for example, recounted his experience of carrying sulfur down to the Liadero:

For sulfur, it was necessary to take a basket, a good long
one.
When the basket was full, what we call a cape was put on
the head, the forehead.
And then from there we carried it on our backs, with a
good walking stick to steady us, so we didn't fall.
And that's how we'd descend to the Liadero, as far as the
droves of mares could go. And there we'd load the animal
and make our delivery in town. (Alejandro Chirán, Vereda
Cuaical)[18]

According to Alonso Tarapués of Mayasquer, the loads of sulfur, dug
out with a pick axe, diminished over time:

At first you carried a *bulto* [100 pounds]. Then the loads
got lighter, because when I first went they were heavy loads
of four *arrobas* [25 pounds each], a bulto. So each person carried just a bulto. Then the loads got lighter.
We were accustomed to carrying an entire *carga* [250
pounds], but the cargas weren't heavy, they weighed five or
six arrobas at the most. (Alonso Tarapués, Vereda Tiúquer,
Mayasquer)[19]

Don Alejandro also remembers the labor-intensive process of ex-
tracting ice from the glacier:

The snow is taken out with an axe, making little trenches,
making it a square, on all four sides, you hear?
Then, when the trenches in the snow on the mountain are
very deep, then you give it two hard strokes with the axe on
each side.
Then you make the trench through the middle and attach a
rope with a halter and there we go, pulling and dragging it,
you hear?
Until you reach level ground, and then you carry it on
your back. And on level ground you go ahead, you hear?
You must go ahead, carrying it in back, and sometimes it has
a strength of its own and can get the better of you, you hear?
Then you arrive at a place we call the Liadero. There we
would have straw cut and ready, and frailejón and some
hemp ropes to tie it up. And then the straw, then the frailejón, and it's packed up, all pretty.
And then you load the animals and deliver it to Tulcán, Ipiales, to Túquerres. You send it to Sandoná, Cumbitara, Tumaco, everywhere. (Alejandro Chirán, Vereda Cuaical)[20]

None of these narratives transcends personal reminiscence to consider the historical roots of sulphur and ice exploitation, except for

Benjamín Cuaical's brief mention of the name of the first man to extract ice from the mountain. Although those who seek ice (*nieveros*) and those who dig sulphur (*azufreros*) are generally different individuals, their activities are always grouped together. Despite the fact that only the sulphur beds were at issue in the cabildo's letter, the missive also includes reference to the exploitation of glacial ice, a nod to the narrative genre in which the evidence originates.

The fact that personal experience is used to justify the citation of contemporary legislation and is juxtaposed with historical evidence from the colonial era indicates that cabildo secretary Colimba wrote his letter from the standpoint of a memorista. As we have seen in the narratives of Benjamín Cuaical, historical analysis in Cumbal involves the juxtaposition of historical data with descriptions of everyday life and material culture in the present or in the very recent past. The past is meaningful only insofar as it is framed by the present. This is brought home further by the cabildo's mention of the Liadero, which, like other toponyms on the mountain, serves as a mnemonic for recalling the recent history of the exploitation of Mount Cumbal. Autobiographical narratives always contain lists of these sites, so that history acquires the aspect of an itinerary of the physical operations necessary for moving from place to place (de Certeau 1984).[21]

Historical Writings by Indian Militants

With the advent of the Indian movement, Cumbal's ethnic activists began to contribute their own written accounts of their struggles to the national Indian newspaper, *Unidad Indígena*, as well as to emulate their Guambiano and Páez allies from the Autoridades Indígenas del Sur Occidente (AISO) by producing mimeographed pamphlets delineating their political philosophy (AISO 1985). This marks a new stage on the influence of literacy in rural Nariño: the written word is now a vehicle of intercourse among Indians as opposed to as a channel of communication with the dominant society. Nevertheless, the following appraisal of various attempts at writing history in Cumbal and Panán demonstrates that the nature of historical description and the use of evidence from the past remain similar to the practices of the cabildo letter writers and to the oral narratives of memoristas.

Delfín Canacuán: History and Legal Writing

On Christmas Day 1986, I was invited to the home of José Delfín Canacuán in El Placer, a vereda overlooking the town of Panán. I had already met don Delfín on a number of occasions. He is an ardent supporter of Panán's cabildo, being a former cabildo president and secretary. Now in his mid-fifties and an influential member of the community, don Delfín's passion is the revitalization of herbal lore, which he learned some years ago from a shaman from the Putumayo. He is now sharing this lore with his compatriots through the creation of a cabildo-sponsored herb garden in the repossessed lands of La Libertad (Laurel). Seated on a bed in a room that alternates as workroom and sleeping quarters, guinea pigs scurrying underfoot, that Christmas afternoon I was shown a manuscript copy of a history of Panán that would contribute, its memorista and *curandero* author hoped, to the revitalization of historical knowledge.

Don Delfín's history follows the model of the legal brief, interspersing political demands with citations of historical documentation. But unlike the briefs, which are addressed to Colombian legal authorities, he told me that his manuscript was prepared for his own community:

> It was written with the intention of contributing to medicine, history, education, culture.
>
> For me, we lack everything, all of us must search for everything, not only for the understanding of the group, but that everyone should know about everything.
>
> And we must make a textbook of everyone things, a textbook or a large notebook. (José Delfín Canacuán, Vereda El Placer, Panán)[22]

Don Delfín's political philosophy, then, is oriented toward educating his readers; this is not a list of demands to be submitted to a government authority in the style of a traditional legal brief. In contrast to legal writing, which demands action on the part of the state, his historical citations are meant to stimulate indigenous political action that will correct the errors of the past. As the last paragraph of his text declares, this is a history for the future:

> And so compañeros, let us recognize who are positive and who are enemies. Let us begin to walk our path, surer day by day. And if we are detoured by something, we must tread slowly, but sure of our way, until we find our path, as an example and a history of the future of our children, who will say, "This is how my parents were, once, in those days when they struggled." Because it is a right that they have usurped from us, which goes back many years and centuries. (José Delfín Canacuán, *Historia de Panán*)[23]

An attempt at cultural revitalization, don Delfín's manuscript nevertheless is organized according to the only model of written history with which he is fully familiar—the legal brief.

The baseline of don Delfín's history is 1492, described as a moment of rupture and loss, which he compares to the repression unleashed upon the cabildo since it began to espouse militant land-claims tactics in the 1980s. Don Delfín has been influenced by the growing movement to commemorate the quincentenary of Indian resistance (as opposed to the five centuries of European domination); he calls 1992 a "birthday" of suffering and struggle, and frames his history by this reference to the discourse of the wider Indian movement.[24]

But when he turns to the history of Gran Cumbal, the Panán author takes up the mantle of the cabildo secretary, outlining the process by which the boundaries of Gran Cumbal were legitimized in Deed 228. He lists the dates of major struggles—1633, the first amparo, followed by 1757–58, the granting of title—and describes the transfer of land rights by Mauricio Muñóz de Ayala to the caciques. In essense, he cites the same evidence from the titles as the authors of the 1950 letter did. And like that legal brief does, he jumps from the colonial period to Law 89 of 1890, which he perceives as establishing a basis for the rights that were bestowed upon the Indians by Bolívar, rights that were made a reality through the cabildo of Panán's repossession of a series of haciendas in the 1980s: the Llano de Piedras, El Laurel, Laurel Chiquito, La Poma, Puscuelán.

Don Delfín then departs from legal discourse, assuming the role of memorista as he recounts recent experience. He gives a detailed description of the struggles over the lands of El Tambillo, which took place in Panán from 1915 to 1955:

> In those years we, the community, entered, clearing part of the brush. The enemies, from Mengambis Hill, shot at us constantly in the brush. The next day they caught up with us on the same hill, to stop us from entering to work. With fifteen long-range guns, they fired constantly, and we, the Indians, surrounded them. On the second day we built a large hut to continue working and not leave again, and a commission went to the landowner's house to tell him to abandon the farm. He begged for three days' space. In those days they grabbed a potato field with the people from Chiles. We didn't encounter the landowner, but his foreman, telling him that this land was the Indians', and immediately we dug zanjas. (José Delfín Canacuán, *Historia de Panán*)[25]

The narrative supplies the names of *terratenientes,* or landlords, and compares the struggle for Tambillo to other more recent land occupations. It emphasizes community unity and the power of Indian legislation, and lists the sufferings of the militants in the face of repression.

It ends with a call for the community to deepen its commitment to the struggle, to educate itself, and to unify into a single strong organization, echoing the mimeographed leaflets prepared by the contemporary Indian movement.

This is the discourse of a man long familiar with the written procedures of the cabildo, with the historical evidence employed by cabildantes, and with the mode of documentary citation used in legal briefs. Operating within the framework of the legal brief, don Delfín has sought to expand upon the traditional model of historical discourse, offering additional evidence culled from his own experience in mid-century land-claims mobilizations and incorporating a list of political demands found in contemporary broadsides.

Chasqui Cumbe: *History and Everyday Life*

During the winter of 1986–87, a group of young men appeared at cabildo meetings in Cumbal, selling a mimeographed magazine called the *Chasqui Cumbe—Boletín Educativo* or *Cumbe Post—Educational Bulletin* (see figure 5).[26] The *Chasqui Cumbe* was written by a collective of activists from Cumbal, then typed and mimeographed by the Committee in Solidarity with the Indian Struggle in Pasto. Its authors include Efrén Tarapués and my collaborator in the collection of oral histories, Helí Valenzuela, both from Vereda Nazate. Efrén and Helí are in their early forties, militants who frequently have been at loggerheads with cabildantes allied to traditional Colombian political parties.[27] Efrén completed several years of high school, has published poems in regional magazines, and is currently an employee of Corponariño, a local development agency. Helí, who never completed primary school, is a tailor married to a mestiza. Virtually landless except for small plots in the repossessed lands of La Boyera, both live in the mestizo town center.

The authors of the *Chasqui Cumbe* employ different narrative models than Delfín Canacuán, insofar as they pattern their written discourse after the oral narratives of memoristas and the political rhetoric of contemporary cabildos rather than frame their history in the discourse of the legal brief. That is, although they make mention of the caciques, the resguardo, and the titles, they are most concerned with elucidating the realities of everyday life in the recent past. Note how they explain the political contours of Cumbal's history.

Like Delfín Canacuán, the *Chasqui Cumbe* collective's aim is public education, in particular, the elucidation of historical data hidden in archives:

5. Cover illustration from *Chasqui Cumbe*

For much time the good customs of our elders, the laws, the experiences of struggle, culture, traditional medicine, beliefs and the good lifeways have been forgotten; likewise, the forced sufferings, domination, racial discrimination and economic and social humilation.

For that reason it is worthwhile to make known to the Great Cumbe Family its hidden experiences, guarded in its archives, which have been the fundamental basis for demanding [our] rights and following [our] historical process as autonomous people with the right to live and develop as human beings in our motherland inherited from our GREAT CACIQUE CUMBE. *Chasqui Cumbe, (p. 1)*[28]

The *Chasqui Cumbe*'s proposal to open the archives is a challenge to memorista hegemony, insofar as it subverts existing controls over historical information that confines its use to a narrow and powerful sector of the community.

Unlike don Delfín's legalistic treatise, the *Chasqui* provides a more conceptual treatment of the history of the resguardo. Instead of listing the names of caciques and the dates of documents, the *Chasqui* authors choose to analyze the social organization of the resguardo, concentrating on aboriginal agency rather than European legal conventions:

Cumbe territory was delimited with boundary markers, such as neolithic rocks with holes or hollows, rivers, streams, hills, volcanos, lakes and mountains. This delimitation was done, perhaps, many centuries before the Spanish colonizers arrived. The boundaries were agreed upon and sometimes struggled over by neighboring cacicazgos; to thus conform a free and sovereign territory, to work it in a COMMUNAL manner benefiting all the inhabitants that make up the cacicazgo. *Chasqui Cumbe*, (p. 5)[29]

The language used here is clearly that of the dominant society, a discourse with which the authors are acquainted as a result of their formal education, their extensive (and frequently anthropological) reading, and their experience in a variety of political movements.

Heavily cultural in emphasis, but almost generically so, these and other excerpts from the *Chasqui Cumbe* have much in common with politically inspired indigenous writings throughout Latin America. They emphasize certain standard features of the pre-Columbian era, including communal economic organization, sun worship, and territorial sovereignty, whether or not they paint an accurate picture of the pre-Columbian Pasto. Key words, such as domination, humiliation, oblivion or forgetfulness, and struggle paint an image of post-invasion society. These are all part of a broader indigenist discourse that values aboriginal cultural purity and employs familiar political terms that are broadly acceptable and universally legitimate (Diskin 1991; Ramos 1988). Ethnographically accurate description is not characteristic of this discourse, which emphasizes unity over diversity (Jackson 1989, 1991; see Landsman and Ciborski 1992). The ethnic political idiom is widespread, and can be noted in the writings of indigenous people throughout the hemisphere (Moody 1988). In fact, it is almost certain that this discourse was diffused through the written channel in the first place (Ramón Valarezo 1992).

Notwithstanding the political nature of its discourse, the themes expounded upon in the *Chasqui Cumbe* are those taken up by oral narrators: historical referents evoked by places, natural and man-made. For example, the authors mention rocks with holes (*piedras con agujeros*), bringing to mind the stones encoded in Deed 228 and visited in 1982 when the cabildo and its supporters—including Efrén and Helí—traced its boundaries. In essence, then, the authors draw a mental map of the territory, a space of social practice made meaningful through walking or political processional. This discourse is not so very different from that of the 1950 cabildo letter, which describes the exploitation of sulphur in terms of the geography of Mount Cumbal.

An emphasis on autonomous practice in the present, as opposed to European papers in the past, is manifest in the *Chasqui's* delineation of the lifeways of the ancestors. They highlight subsistence practices, toolmaking, ceramics, and barter in a series of brief paragraphs that tell us more about the lives of the authors' grandparents than those of the pre-Columbian Pastos. These descriptions are made more immediate by the drawings of Oligario Valenzuela, Helí's brother, which transport the reader back into a pure and untouched past of fierce caciques and smoking volcanos (see figure 5).

The *Chasqui's* authors convey the immediacy of their historical interpretations through a variety of genres. In addition to prose description, a poem by Efrén Tarapués entitled "Dios sol y paz" (God the Sun and Peace) is printed to evoke rather than to represent a feeling for aboriginal religion. A long passage, accompanied by an illustration (figure 4), proposes a coat of arms for the resguardo:

> The structure of the coat of arms has its foundations in the Sun of the Pastos, carried by two monkeys. Its upper part is covered by two branches representing autochthonous vegetation. In the sun, indigenous tools and arms are intertwined with staffs of office and justice. In the center of the sun is an anthro-

pomorphic figure, just as our ancestors represented it. The motto is "CUMBE LIVES IN THE REBORN."

According to our ancestors, the Sun of the Pastos represents "the supreme God," the god who illuminates life and bestows good light to he who worships and adores him with great happiness and joy. Even today, he is the center of our lives. Without Him, the world would be covered in a blanket of death.

Within the sun lie the arms, the tools, the staffs of office, with which our Indian ancestors struggled to live, to make the land produce, to organize themselves as a sovereign people in a free territory, with their own worldview.

The monkeys are considered to be a symbol of fertility, the progenitors of the living race, the TOTEMIC gods worshipped in sacred sites. The branches represent the fertility of the land when united with man's hands; man and nature are related in the autochthonous cultivation of potatoes and of wild plants, which were the bases of traditional medicine, art, and industry.

With its motto, "CUMBE LIVES IN THE REBORN," we are trying to identify ourselves, the contemporary Indians, with the thought left us by our elders. We strive to revive and strengthen this constellation of social experiences that, in the course of time, has been diluted by law and by government, awash in a sea of forgetfulness and ignorance, creating a crisis of autonomy and driving the Indian to reject his race, his past, and his system of thought, to become marginalized in a capitalist world and a consumer society, where man is not a pillar of the community but only a lost and disoriented statistic. *Chasqui Cumbe* (p. 11–13)[30]

As the description of resguardo boundaries does, the proposal draws an image of ritual practice, depicting the importance of material culture as expressed in staffs of office instead of in political process. It also refers to physical reminders of the past as evinced in petroglyphs. The relationship between the distant past and the living present is expressed through the proposed emblem, "Cumbe vive en los renacientes" (Cumbe lives in the reborn), which brings to mind the ritual practice of contemporary cabildos.

Writing History in Cumbal

In Cumbal, as in other contemporary societies, once the written word becomes an acceptable means of communication it is difficult to contrast orality and literacy as opposing orders. Instead, as Brian Stock has commented, they become conscious mental categories that reciprocally influence each other, the oral molding the appreciation of literary genres while the written is nourished by oral discourse (Stock 1990, 7; see Goody 1987). The historical memory is indeed a palimpsest in which the oral and the written overlap, fuse, and are reinterpreted by new actors, over and over again. It is only by grasping this world of hundreds of voices, those of the dead and those of the living, those written or heard and those experienced in all their physical immediacy, those of the powerful and those of the powerless, that we can begin to discern the contours of historical expression in southern Nariño.

1. Recuperación: preparation of datura as a fumigant

2. Lastenia Alpala Tarapués

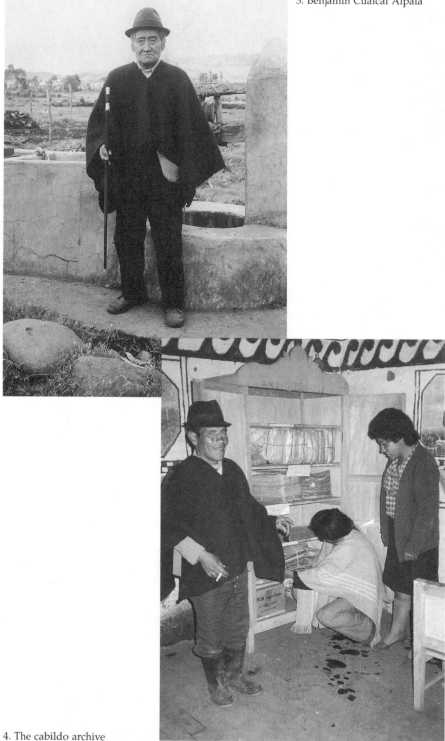

3. Benjamín Cuaical Alpala

4. The cabildo archive

5. Taking inventory of the cabildo archive

6. Cumbal's 1987 cabildo with its staffs of office

7. A recently dug zanja

8. A possession ceremony in Cuaical

9. A Muellamués image of the past: ceramics

10. A Muellamués image of the past: weaving

11. Correcting conquest history in Muellamués theater

Inside the sign:

CACICA MARIA PANANA
Vivió y Vivirá por siempre
EN
TODA MUJER INDIGENA!
Organiza: Padres de flia - Profesores

12. Caciques Cumbe and María Panana at the Panán Carnival

13. Portraying Muellamués's past in the tropical forest

14. Dramatic portrayals of caciques in Muellamués

15. Stereotypes of non-Indians: the priest

16. Sampson in Panán's Good Friday procession

SIX

Bulls and Hitching Posts

In EARLY 1975, the comuneros of Cuaical occupied the hacienda El Zapatero with an eye to reclaiming it, thus introducing a program of militant land claims that has continued to guide political action to the present day. Their claims were based in part on Deed 228, within whose boundaries El Zapatero clearly lies. But they also grounded their demands in an 1869 Supreme Court decision that restored communal tenancy to the hacienda, which had been usurped shortly before by a mestizo politician. Knowledge of this nineteenth-century battle between mestizo and Indian, which began in Cumbal and ended in Bogotá, was derived in part from the retrieval of documentation related to the case, located in the circuit court archive in the nearby city of Ipiales. But the Cumbales' claims were almost certainly driven to a greater degree by oral tradition, which paints quite a different picture of the loss of El Zapatero than that which can be derived from the judicial records of the period.[1]

This chapter will explore the logic that lies behind these two very different but intersecting cultural visions of the past of the hacienda El Zapatero. I am not so much interested in teasing history out of the oral account by identifying the mythic elements or clichés that mask historical fact (Miller 1980; Vansina 1985) as I am in examining how, in situations of intercultural contact, conflicting histories are negotiated, shared, usurped, negated, and acted upon in the interests of the various parties to a dispute (Cohen 1989; Orlove 1991a). The way Cumbales, mestizos, and the Colombian state negotiate the history of El Zapatero is mediated by a number of factors. Among them, key to the process of the creation of these different histories, are the images that each of the parties embraces regarding its own role in the dispute and that of its opponent. Historical evidence is frequently anchored by the traditions invented by the parties at different points during the century-long disagreement. The nature of the historical knowledge of the disputants and the sources they draw upon to stake and defend their claims are useful in comparing conflicting reports. Their differing political and cultural experiences also weigh heavily upon the historical memory. Finally, each manipulates the interface between oral and written modes of expression in its own way; approaches to literacy will thus also determine the relative ease with which the different parties employ the legal idiom that frames all claims and, consequently, all histories.

History, as it is created by the Cumbales, is by no means a monolith, nor is it divorced from similar and parallel actions on the part of opponents. Although the contemporary oral tradition of the loss of El Zapatero deploys a number of symbolic motifs that are pan-Andean in nature, these same symbols acquire further meaning within the context of practices imposed upon the community by the dominant society and the state. And they are interpreted by native narrators working through the filter of the written word. But access to the written word is not uniform among community members: the relationship between written evidence and oral interpretation is mediated by differential literacy skills (especially pronounced between men and women, but also between more affluent and poorer families), by a sufficient knowledge of the state bureaucracy necessary for gaining access to judicial archives, and by relative access to documents retrieved by community leaders. Such differences have existed since the colonial period, when the first documents to be referred to in the El Zapatero dispute were written. The contemporary oral account is the result of a complex process of interpretation of written documents at different historical junctures by a limited number of individuals whose access to and interpretation of written evidence were themselves mediated by an oral knowledge of the existence and contents of the documents. These individuals, in turn, transmitted their interpretations in oral form to other community members. The oral record is indeed multilayered, and it must be interpreted as such.

The written record is not a fixed and homogeneous entity either, as the previous chapter demonstrated. Like the resguardo title, the various archival holdings relating to the Zapatero dispute are themselves polyphonic in their very construction, amalgams of a number of documents hailing from a variety of time periods, which were inserted as evidence in support of cases that went to trial a century or more after they were written. In order to comprehend the importance of such holdings, whether for the nineteenth-century political actors who compiled them or for the late twentieth-century Cumbal militants who consulted them, we must distinguish among the various meanings that have been attached to these documents at different points in their existence.

In other words, if we are to contrast the written record and oral tradition, we must take into account the process by which each of these accounts was created, used, and re-created through repeated consultation over the decades. We cannot expect to be able to draw simple comparisons between written and oral forms of recording history, because each mode reflects and impinges upon the construction of its counterpart.

To study literacy in the post-conquest Andes is to study law, one of the prime vehicles used to incorporate Indians into the sphere of influence of the state. Contemporary visions of the history of El Zapatero are influenced by Colombian laws regarding land tenure in general and Indian landownership in particular, two conflicting bodies of legislation that must be negotiated simultaneously. Accepted forms of legal evidence for land claims become historical evidence for storytellers. In this way, law determines the sources and contents of historical narratives.[2] As earlier chapters have shown, legally inspired evidence is also interpreted through the filters of the rituals legitimizing land ownership and the symbols of indigenous authority that have come to define Indian identity in the Colombian highlands over the past three and a half centuries. These are invented traditions, initially created by the colonial and Republican states as a means of prescribing and codifying native customs through an overlay of European symbols and practices (Hobsbawm and Ranger 1983). But in the space of 350 years, they have been "reinvented" on repeated occasions and articulated within a local body of historical knowledge. Legislation and local politics have transformed these "reinvented traditions" over time, producing changing contexts within which indigenous notions of tradition have been continually redefined. We cannot simply point to a tradition as "invented," then, but must remain conscious of who invented it, how it has been used since its invention, who is using it now, and why. As I explained in chapter 4, for instance, for many comuneros such seemingly ancient customs take the place of written documentation, serving as evidence of a link with the distant past. As multilayered as the legal documents are, reinvented traditions are frequently interchangeable with them.

In this chapter I will review the conflicting stories of land tenure in

El Zapatero, beginning with contemporary oral tradition and working back through time in the documentary record, distinguishing Andean symbols from their European counterparts and inquiring into the invention and appropriation of parallel and intersecting traditions by parties to the dispute at different points in its course. Finally, I will return to reconsider the ambiguities inherent in the construction of native accounts of the dispute, in the course of which the Cumbales were forced to validate their rights, identity, and, ultimately, their existence as native people through recourse to Colombian law and European legal writing. In the process, these rights were denied by the very procedures that legitimized them.

El Zapatero: Two Conflicting Visions

Contemporary Oral Tradition

The story of how the Cumbales won and then lost the hacienda El Zapatero is well known among memoristas and laypersons, especially in Cuaical, where the farm is located. According to oral tradition, the hacienda had been usurped from the resguardo at some unspecified point in the distant past and ultimately passed into the hands of a local mestizo politician, Segundo Sánchez. José Manuel Alpala, a literate comunero, assisted the cabildo in bringing the case to the Supreme Court: "That man had copies of legal codes. And he was the one who used to lead, rule, and struggle" (Benjamín Cuaical, Vereda Cuaical).[3] The cabildo's case was based on documentation retrieved from provincial archives in Popayán and the archives of the former Royal Court of Quito. Lengthy oral accounts emphasize in painstaking detail the events that transpired on the monthlong treks to those cities (see chapter 3). Such accounts dwell upon the kinds of food that travelers were offered along the road, the people they met, the dog that accompanied them to Popayán, was lost there, and returned on his own.[4] Eventually the case was won, although most narrators have little to say about the court proceedings.

It is not at all surprising that oral narrators have little to offer regarding what actually transpired in the Supreme Court. This information is not included in the published decision or in court records. Available documentation registers the presentation of written communications, evidence, and other briefs, and should not be thought of as a transcript of what went on in court. Indigenous participants in the dispute, moreover, probably missed the point of much of the legal discussion, depending upon non-Indian lawyers to plead and defend their case.

The oral memory then jumps to the period after the Supreme Court decision. All narrators agree that the cabildo decided not to distribute El Zapatero to those comuneros who had supported the suit, but to work it communally until legal fees and other expenditures had been recuperated. But they committed the grave error of neglecting to thoroughly evict Segundo Sánchez from the land, which, it is implied, would have been accomplished if they had redistributed the land. Sánchez left behind a young bull and a hitching post, which went unnoticed for quite some time. When an older man found the stray bull, he visited Sánchez, asking him to remove his property. But the hacendado responded that he had left the animal and the hitching post as evidence of his continuing ownership of El Zapatero. Lastenia Alpala, granddaughter of Manuel de Jesús Tarapués, one of the original disputants, embellishes her account with dialogue that vividly conveys the hierarchical relationship between hacendado and community member:

> Well, one of the old men from our junta woke up early and left to take the cattle. He woke up and left without telling anyone, saying he'd tell the owner to come to get the calf, the bull.
> Oh no!
> When he got there he said, "Don Segundo, good morning."
> "Good morning, my son, come in."
> "I came to tell you that you should go get your little bull that was left behind there. We were going to pasture our own cattle there, but your bull was left behind."
> "It was left behind?" he said, finally, "It wasn't left behind."
> He said, "I left it there, and for that reason I haven't given up possession. That was there to mark my ownership, and that's why I left it there. I was careful. And for that reason, I'm going to take my cattle." (Lastenia Alpala, Vereda Quilismal)[5]

With that, the hacienda was lost again.

El Zapatero was won back in 1975, when Hilarión Alpala, then governor of Cumbal, applied his historical knowledge in the political arena, combining orally derived lore with a search for the pertinent documentation in the Ipiales archives as the basis for his repossession of the hacienda.[6] Don Hilarión's awareness of the existence of the amparos that validated the cabildo's claim to the land is lauded and emulated by most politically active people today. In the words of his sister:

> That's why my grandfather used to say, "My children, I won't last forever. I'm old already. I might die tomorrow, but my descendants, perhaps, if I tell them, will reclaim El Zapa-

tero. They should inquire, they should judge those papers.
Those sentences will never get lost," he'd say.
"There they are, sitting in the offices. They should find
them," he'd say.
"And then, perhaps, one of my descendants will turn out
more or less capable," he'd say.
And my brother made the commitment and won El Zapat-
ero, my brother Hilarión. (Lastenia Alpala, Vereda Quilismal)[7]

Knowledge of the El Zapatero dispute is distributed unequally
among the residents of Cumbal. The most detail is provided by narrators who are related to participants in the dispute or hail from the
powerful families that control access to community archives; the dual
relationship linking oral transmission to control of written records derives from the fact that both those who read documents and those
who tell stories are from the same politically powerful families. That
Hilarión Alpala shared the El Zapatero story with his fellow comuneros, selecting it as significant out of a mass of other narratives or
documents of disputes is, moreover, a matter of political savvy. History
is created in order to further legal claims, and, for various reasons, El
Zapatero was chosen from among any number of similar cases as a
more accessible target.[8] Most people, nevertheless, remember only a
few details of the El Zapatero story, making only fleeting references to
the bull and the hitching post, assuming a more complete knowledge
of the story on the part of their listeners. But even among these people,
historical knowledge varies in its profundity, depending upon the narrator's place of residence.

The scope of historical memory is governed by the section hierarchy
that pervades all of Cumbal's life. Comuneros from Tasmag remember
the successful recovery of the hacienda Las Tolas, which was won
through the same Supreme Court sentence that granted El Zapatero to
the community. Both haciendas had been leased for many years to
cofradías or church brotherhoods. The Cuaical narrators quoted above
know little of the history of Las Tolas while those from Tasmag remember only key images regarding the loss of El Zapatero:

Here was the Fathers' cofradía, here in Las Tolas. That's
why it was called the Paridero. It's in the documents. Because
it was only a cofradía for the Fathers' cattle, they say.
It extended all the way up to here, all of it.
And the Regidor at that time when they won, the Regidor
from this vereda of Tasmag, divided it up. He was a Chirán.
I don't know the name of that Chirán, but he was related to
all the Chiranes. That's how it seems to me. They say he was
Alvaro, Alvaro Chirán.

He divided it up, all of Las Tolas, for Tasmag, and the part [corresponding to] El Zapatero, they didn't divide it, saying that the Regidor from [Cuaical] said they should enter it, that's all.

"Later on we'll have to divide it. It's ours now, anyhow. Now we've won it. Later on, when we want to, we'll. . . . "

That's when he who had lived there came, for the bull, he said, and the hitching post. (Rosa Elena Aza, Vereda Tasmag)[9]

Historical knowledge is thus determined in part by family and vereda membership. Some details are known only by residents of specific territorial divisions: (1) El Zapatero was granted to the cabildo in the same judicial proceeding that granted access to Las Tolas in Tasmag. (2) Both El Zapatero and Las Tolas had been cofradía lands. (3) While Las Tolas was distributed to comuneros, El Zapatero was not; for this reason, it was ultimately lost to Segundo Sánchez.

In general, however, most adults know the following regarding El Zapatero: (1) El Zapatero was in the hands of Segundo Sánchez until the cabildo won it back by virtue of a judicial decision. (2) The cabildo decided to work El Zapatero communally instead of distributing plots to individuals. (3) Segundo Sánchez left behind a bull and a hitching post when he vacated El Zapatero. (4) Because of the bull and the hitching post, Segundo Sánchez was able to retain his claim to the hacienda.

Access to other information is determined largely by a combination of gender and political power. Men, rather than women, are generally literate and overwhelmingly control the political process and the archives. Only such men as Benjamín Cuaical, Hilarión Alpala, and younger cabildantes such as Gilberto Valenzuela—all former secretaries—enjoy access to documentation. This reduced circle is aware of a series of facts: (1) El Zapatero was won on the basis of a series of named and dated colonial decrees legitimizing resguardo boundaries. (2) These documents were acquired by the cabildo on visits to various archives and government offices. (3) Certain community leaders, including José Manuel Alpala and Manuel de Jesús Tarapués, were instrumental in assisting the community in winning its suit. (4) After losing El Zapatero a second time, the cabildo was forced to return to the court to press its demands.

Documentary Evidence for the Zapatero Dispute

The documentary record paints a very different picture of the fight over the hacienda El Zapatero. According to archival holdings, Las

Tolas and El Zapatero were among several portions of land that the cabildo leased to cofradías in the early eighteenth century. These agreements were documented in written contracts between the cabildo and the religious brotherhoods, and were remembered in the oral tradition. Andean Indians embraced cofradías as a means of defending from hacienda exploitation community lands and plots dedicated to pre-Columbian religious cults; they also served as sources of revenue for sponsoring fiestas for Catholic saints linked to Andean deities (Celestino 1982; Celestino and Meyers 1981). In the Pasto area, cofradía lands provided a buffer zone in which cattle could be raised and funds for tribute payment amassed; they also served as a source of revenue for maintaining the Roman Catholic cult. But they were also holding mechanisms for hereditary chiefs intent upon expanding their lands through deceitful means.[10] Along with all Church holdings, cofradías were subject to confiscation by the state during the nineteenth century, and on September 14, 1865, El Zapatero and Las Tolas were expropriated and brought into the public domain. During the following years, El Zapatero was sold twice to local mestizos, including Segundo Sánchez, a political strongman with considerable influence on the municipal level.[11]

When the cabildo realized that the two haciendas had been expropriated, it complained to the appropriate authorities, the Junta Suprema Directiva del Crédito Nacional, which rejected its claim to the lands, forcing the resguardo council to appeal to judicial authorities. In October 1866, the cabildo brought its case to the Circuit Court of Obando in Ipiales, using the eighteenth-century amparos as evidence of the fact that the haciendas lay within resguardo boundaries. The case was decided favorably for the cabildo in 1867 and brought to the Supreme Court for consultation in the same year. The Supreme Court upheld the lower court's decision, but it provided local authorities with a space of sixteen months within which they could demonstrate that El Zapatero and Las Tolas were not resguardo but cofradía lands. By June 1869, no contradictory evidence had been offered, and the decision was subsequently published.[12]

Although the comuneros had won their claim, they were not able to gain access to their lands. The local authorities, including the *jefe político* or cantonal administrative officer, Segundo Sánchez, refused to carry out the ruling. The cabildo's attorney, Joaquín Miranda, was forced to appeal to the provincial government in Popayán, which was dragging its feet in ordering local officials to carry out the sentence:

> Mr. President, the question you must resolve is of the highest importance. The citizens want to know if you support your

Jefe Municipal Segundo Sánchez to the degree that your orders and those of the Federal Court have been mocked ... in a country with a Constitution that guarantees property ownership.[13]

He thus provoked an official order from Popayán requiring that possession be granted the Indians.

A possession ceremony was held in Las Tolas on November 24, 1870, the cabildo thereby gaining control of the hacienda (ff. 18r–v). But when the ceremony was initiated at El Zapatero, Segundo Sánchez brought it to an abrupt halt:

> The Mayor proceeded to grant [the Indians] possession. In this state, Mr. Segundo Sánchez presented himself, opposing the granting of possession of the indicated farm "Zapatero," manifesting that he was its owner and that he was in possession of it, and that, besides, he enjoyed precarious possession by virtue of a sentence dictated by the Circuit Judge working in his National capacity. He accompanied his statement by an authenticated copy consisting of two pages of the sentence, the same that was ordered to be included within the record. In light of this, the Mayor suspended the possesory act. ... (f. 19r)[14]

Despite the fact that in February 1871 the President of the State of Cauca had resolved that the cabildo be granted possession to the hacienda and that Sánchez be levied a fine of fifty pesos (f. 25r), Sánchez continued to enjoy possession of El Zapatero. His influence as Jefe Municipal afforded him control over local authorities, and in March the cabildo's attorney was imprisoned in Cumbal on trumped-up charges (f. 29r). The local mayor consistently refused to obey the orders of the provincial government:

> The Mayor of Cumbal declared that he does not care if the President of the State fines him, because he will not pay the fine, nor carry out the sentence. The Jefe Municipal Sánchez also declared that we [the Indians] would first take possession of hell before [taking possession of] Zapatero. (f. 48r)[15]

In 1875, Sánchez and the state appealed the case to the Circuit Court of Ipiales, which upheld the 1869 Supreme Court ruling in favor of the cabildo, basing their decision in part upon the fact that Sánchez had never even paid for the land:

> The collaborating party, Segundo Sánchez, claims to be the buyer of the lands, although the purchase was never made effective and he never paid the sum to the State; and, abusing

the naïveté and weakness of the Indians, has made himself owner and possessor of them.[16]

The decision to uphold the 1869 ruling was also founded in specific legal strictures, including the fact that in both Spanish and Colombian law it would be impossible to overturn a Supreme Court decision.[17]

On the basis of the 1875 ruling, in 1877 the Indians requested and were granted permission to take possession of the land. They specifically asked "that at the same time all of the alien livestock pastured on the land be removed to avoid future controversy" (f. 14r).[18]

Sánchez continued to push his claims, basing his actions on the fact that the evidence used by the Indians consisted of illegitimate and unauthenticated copies of documents that were acquired from local, and thus inappropriate, offices (f. 20r). When governmental and community authorities congregated at El Zapatero on October 4, 1877 to ceremoniously grant possession to the Indians, Sánchez once again brought a halt to the ceremony, just as he had done in 1870 (f. 24v).

From 1877 through the 1890s, the case continued in circuit court, and I have found no documents summarizing its conclusions. Court records specify the methods by which Sánchez attempted to prove his right to the lands of El Zapatero. His basic argument over those sixteen-odd years was that (1) the lands had always belonged to the Church, and were thus subject to confiscation and subsequent sale; (2) he had purchased them from the state, and was now the legitimate owner; (3) the state had no business in the court proceedings, given that they no longer had any claim to the lands; and (4) the Indians' evidence to the contrary was inappropriately acquired and hence inadmissible in court.

The evidence upon which he based his case were culled from an array of sources, including: (1) colonial documentation of the 1703 contract whereby the cabildo ceded its ownership of a plot called Chalchagues to the cofradía of the Holy Sacrament;[19] (2) colonial documentation of a 1756 inspection conducted in the neighboring hacienda of Guamialamag, illustrating that the cofradía lands lay at the site called El Zapatero (ff. 106r–111r); (3) registry in 1865 of the expropriation from the Church of the lands of El Zapatero and Las Tolas (ff. 28v–29r);[20] (4) documentation of his purchase of El Zapatero and copies of his deeds to the land (ff. 26v–27r, 30r–v); (5) testimony from local mestizos and from cabildo members regarding the oral memory of cofradía lands in Cumbal and details concerning their ownership (ff. 82r–118v); and (6) records of an 1878 inspection of the lands, containing a map to provide geographic evidence of the information contained in documents (ff. 137r–138r).

Unfortunately for Sánchez, many of his assertions contradicted one another. He confused the cofradía plot Chalchagues (later called Santísimo) with El Zapatero, as a number of witnesses pointed out and as the map accompanying the documentation of the case clearly illustrates. Some of his Indian witnesses supported his claim that El Zapatero was owned by the Church while others claimed that it had only been leased to the cofradía. The deeds he produced as evidence of his ownership of the hacienda appear to have been drawn up for other lands. The case wore on until the turn of the century.

Of Bulls and Hitching Posts

Documentation of the Zapatero dispute and oral histories of the conflict coincide on a number of issues. Using varying amounts of detail, both clearly outline the parties to the dispute and the nature of the lands in question. Both emphasize the inconclusive termination of the case. The general outlines of the oral account are based in part on the court records, acquired in the 1870s and at some point after 1950. Where the two accounts differ is in their chronological treatment of the dispute and in the description of methods by which the antagonist gained control over the hacienda. While the documentary record is a series of judicial encounters spanning some forty years, including as evidence copies of documents from as early as 1703, the oral tradition compresses the multiple encounters into a relatively short period that is not marked chronologically. It also makes reference to colonial-era documents by creating an image of them rather than by outlining their contents. While the court proceedings demonstrate that Sánchez supported his claim with written and oral evidence, and effectively maintained possession through coercion and procrastination, the climax of the oral account is his use of the bull and the hitching post to win back his land.

Evidence and Its Uses

As we consult the documents pertaining to the El Zapatero case, we note that the attorneys for both parties used the same sorts of evidence—sometimes identical documents—to support their claims. Both, for example, questioned witnesses about information that their parents and grandparents had passed down to them orally. Both consulted colonial titles to ascertain boundaries. Both referred to nineteenth-century registries containing evidence of the expropriation of the hacienda.

Nevertheless, the two parties to the dispute used this evidence in culturally specific ways. Their references to the colonial title to Cumbal present a case in point. Sánchez's attorneys and the representatives of the cabildo brought into evidence the 1758 document that the Cumbales call the Royal Provision, the record of a lengthy dispute between local Spanish landholders of the Erazo family and the caciques of Nazate. At the time, Nazate was a semiautonomous political entity and sometime ally of Cumbal. Significantly, Sánchez's reading of the Royal Provision emphasized the Cumbal-Nazate chiefdom boundary, which by the mid-nineteenth century delimited the sections of Cuaical and Nazate as constituent units of Cumbal. The cabildo, in contrast, used the title as evidence that El Zapatero was communal land because it fell within the global boundaries of the decentralized resguardo encompassing the four colonial chiefdoms of Cumbal, Chiles, Panán, and Mayasquer. That is, they disregarded cacicazgo boundaries, preferring to emphasize the broader contours of their resguardo.

Differing uses of the Royal Provision by the two sides of the El Zapatero dispute point to the ambiguities inherent in the written mode of communication. When written sources are recontextualized in a different historical period, their contents become ambiguous and subject to a variety of interpretations. Far from being fixed, the written idiom provides fertile ground for oral elaborations whose structures are determined by contemporary concerns.

While we can ascertain some of the choices the parties made in their selection of evidence from colonial documents, the documentary record provides us with little information about how the titles were understood by the nineteenth-century cabildo (see Rafael 1988). Contemporary ethnography fills in some of these gaps by providing analytic entry points into the Republican written record. Chapter 2 described how contemporary Cumbales organize their historical vision and redistribute reclaimed lands according to the template of their six-section hierarchy. Similarly, the cabildos of a century ago emphasized the decentralized and hierarchical nature of their resguardo. It is probable that the nineteenth-century cabildo that used the Royal Provision as evidence of its claim over El Zapatero understood the document much as its twentieth-century counterpart does.

For the Cumbales, history is not so much an interpretation of detailed evidence as a series of striking images articulated in the course of political organizing. Colonial documents are retained in cabildo archives but are rarely consulted. Elaboration in the oral domain concentrates on key symbols, such as the chiefly participants in the 1758 dispute, that link contemporary families to their colonial-era forebears. The progress of the El Zapatero dispute is crystallized into a series of images, culminating with the discovery that Sánchez left behind his bull and his hitching post. The cabildo archives contain a copy of the 1869 Supreme Court sentence, which I gave to the council in early 1987 to replace an older copy that had been lost, but this document is not consulted for its contents as much as for validation of the community's own interpretations of the event.[21]

The mestizo townspeople are as insistent upon images as the Indians are. Although it would be fairly simple for townspeople to consult colonial titles in notarial offices (as the attorneys for Segundo Sánchez clearly did), they prefer to deny the existence of such evidence. This alleged vacuum in the documentary record serves as a justification for mestizo opposition to cabildo repossession activities. Also, many townspeople have embraced a stereotype that relegates Indians to the distant past, negating their existence in the modern world and, hence, denying their claim to historical documents. During the 1975 occupation of the Llano, the cabildo was forced to confront such attitudes at their initial encounters with the municipal mayor:

> The mayor asked me what I was talking about. I told him
> that in the first place there was a title, Deed number 228,
> given by the Spanish colony to the Indian resguardo of Cum-
> bal, and that we were the legal owners.
> And Mr. Mayor said, "And who told you that?"
> He said, "Those old papers you have, they're just an old
> story not worth anything anymore. According to government
> law, that land [the Llano] is common land belonging to the
> municipality." (Efraín Chirán, Vereda Cuaical)[22]

This quotation is interesting because it illustrates how Indians and local non-Indians appeal to contradictory bodies of Colombian law to assert their claims, a topic I will discuss further below. Of immediate significance here is the mestizo refusal to recognize resguardo titles. Similarly, Segundo Sánchez pursued his suit against the cabildo of Cumbal, even after repeated rulings in the Indians' favor, by claiming that the Cumbales had brought illegitimate and unauthenticated copies of documents into evidence. He attempted to deny the very existence of the legal papers substantiating the cabildo's claim, much as local mestizos did in the 1930s and 1940s to liquidate the Quillacinga resguardos.[23]

Law and Image

At center stage are the images deployed by twentieth-century indigenous storytellers, namely, the bull and hitching post. What role could the presence of livestock possibly play in cementing Segundo Sánchez's claim to El Zapatero? Although not directly referred to in the documentation, it is clear from both the written and the oral record that both the Indians and Sánchez organized their cases by appealing to Colombian property law, which defined possession of a piece of land by virtue of evidence of occupation for the space of a year. This could be proved easily through the testimony of three witnesses, an option Sánchez chose in the documentary record, or through proof of the presence of physical artifacts, as the Indians suggest in oral tradition. The possibility of Sánchez retaining his claim through an appeal to property law was of concern to the nineteenth-century Indians, who asked that the authorities remove all alien livestock "to avoid future controversy." Their request implies that, on the one hand, this is what they expected Sánchez to do and, on the other, that the tactic had already been employed by their adversary. In fact, moves of this sort, called "possesory actions" (*juicios de posesión*) in Colombian law, were frequently used by large landowners as illegal means of expanding their holdings (LeGrand 1986, 81). Nevertheless, there is no evidence that Sánchez had in fact staked his claim by virtue of the bull and hitching post, nor could he have asserted his right to the land through the presence of a single animal or a solitary post; in contrast, his case was based on documentary proof of ownership corroborated by oral testimony, and his presence at El Zapatero was assured by the lengthiness of the legal process and by his coercive behavior.

A story making use of similar interpretations of property law is told in Mayasquer, where in the early twentieth century the cabildo, with support from the Cumbal vereda of Nazate, reclaimed the hacienda Gritadero (today San Felipe) by judicial means. The mestizo owners of Gritadero had been the Arellano family, who, it is told, left behind a cock when they vacated the farm. They, too, were able to regain ownership by recourse to the stray animal that remained to stake their claim to the land. Early twentieth-century Mayasqueres perceived the presence of the possessions of former owners as evidence of a continuing claim, as is clear from the activities that followed the final and successful appropriation of Gritadero. As soon as the cabildo was granted possession, it destroyed a great many wooden planks left behind by the Arellanos, thus erasing all evidence of their presence.[24] In modern-day land repossessions, Indians frequently destroy former hacendados' houses for the same reasons, although recent cabildos have attempted to dissuade them from this practice.

Such interpretations of Colombian law, filtered through narrative and through political action, provide a complex and contradictory context within which the key images of the El Zapatero story acquire yet further significance. Nevertheless, although an understanding of the Colombian legal code explains the order of episodes in the oral tradition, it does not resolve the problem of why the particular symbols of the bull and the hitching post are central to the narrative at all.

Andean Images

Bulls and hitching posts surface in other Andean narratives about land rights. Quechua myth speaks of bulls whose presence on the land stakes a claim for their owners (Ortiz Rescaniere 1973, 35–37). High-altitude puna lands can be represented by a bull skin (Zuidema 1983). Colonial and contemporary Andean myth also associates the founding of population centers with the practice of throwing or planting staffs at sites and waiting until morning to see if they have been left standing, thus staking a claim to territory by implanting a vertical symbol much like a hitching post (Rappaport 1982; Rostworowski de Diez Canseco 1978; Garcilaso de la Vega 1960–65 [1609] and Sarmiento de Gamboa 1965 [1572] in MacCormack 1991). Former cabildante Mesías Puerres of Cuaspud told Helí Valenzuela that in Cumbal, the whip used to beat prospective smallholders in the possession ceremony was formerly made from the skin of an ox, an animal related to the bull.

Bulls used to mark territorial claims are also associated with riches in other Andean communities (Arguedas 1985, 14). Some are held on gold chains (Ortiz Rescaniere 1973, 73); others are killed in order to acquire more gold (R. Tom Zuidema, personal communication). In highland Bolivia, Aymara speakers perceive a close relationship between land fertility and the fertility of cattle, on the one hand, and the mining of metals, on the other (Harris 1987, 261).

Lastenia Alpala's grandfather told her that in the hacienda of Cimarrones, located in Nazate and purchased by comuneros in the nineteenth century, a bull, gutted and loaded with silver, stood on the lands formerly owned by the mestizo Urbano López:

> And so he said, "Caray! My money won't fit in a pot. Better, I'll gut my bull."
> And so he killed his bull and gutted it, and starting at the head, he turned the skin inside out. He took everything out. And he left the hooves, that's all, from the knees. And the rest of the meat, he removed all of it, and he left the skin.
> Then, he filled it up—with anything—and he let it dry. Since the bull's head was intact, I don't know how, he removed it. He left the horns. He painted them gold. And the eyes, he put in yellow eyes. And he covered the hooves with gold. And he left him standing up.

And then he filled him a little with silver, and he kept filling, filling.

And there stood the bull.

And in the mornings he would wake up and go see it. (Lastenia Alpala, Vereda Quilismal)[25]

That is, until one day, when the bull came to life and ran away.

Many years later, after old Urbano was long dead and buried, passersby noted other wondrous occurrences where the bull had stood:

It was a moonlit night, the full moon.

[Victor Tarapués] passed by the garden of the house that had belonged to old Urbano, when he says that he saw something shining in the garden, reflected by the full moon.

But that's what my cousin said, that they'd told him, although he hadn't seen it.

But he saw something shining.

When he saw the reflection, he asked, "What is shining over there?"

It was like a staff, and it got closer and closer and shined more and more. And when he was close and could see it more clearly, it was a snake, he says. When he went closer, the snake jumped and disappeared into the ditch, toward El Zapatero, and it was lost from sight.

"I didn't go any further, it frightened me," he said.

It had been a snake that shined there, a yellow one. "And when I got close, it jumped and burned and ran away and was lost." (Lastenia Alpala, Vereda Quilismal)[26]

In the same location, he also saw a cat:

"And so I came by there, where there are stones that used to be the hearth of the old house, which belonged to that owner," he said.

"And from above I saw something that moved there. What could it be? What could it be that moved over there?"

"So, when I came closer," he said, "I could see it by the light of the moon. I could see it: it was a cat. That's right, a red cat. By the light of the moon I could see that it was a cat."

But, he said, "I couldn't see the cat clearly. When I could clearly see it was a cat, close up, I saw a tremendous cat. Yes, a cat, but a deformed one. And when I got closer, it jumped and ran away," he said.

And it fell into the same Chilcas zanja, that zanja, that goes to the right of El Zapatero, where the fence of the garden of that house had been. (Lastenia Alpala, Vereda Quilismal)[27]

Here is a bull filled with money, associated by proximity with a golden staff that was transformed into a snake. In the same place there lived a huge, deformed cat that frightened passersby. The same constellation of images served historically as a metaphor for representing the social organization of the Incaic body politic; these animal metaphors also appeared in Inca ritual as expressions of the defense of political borders (Zuidema 1983, 46; see also Arguedas 1985).[28] In Quechua thought the same group of symbols also marks periods of transition between parts of the calendar year, stages of the human life cycle, and even eras of historical time (Ortíz Rescaniere 1973, 167); colonial Quechua iconography portrays felines and snakes as portals for movement between worlds (Allen n.d.a.).

In Cumbal, the same group of animals and objects is also associated with boundaries or transitional states. For example, the people of Cumbal, Panán, and Chiles perceive their montaña neighbors in Mayasquer as being capable of transforming themselves into jaguars or snakes to defend their possessions against outsiders; here the animals mark the boundary between highlands and coast, constituted by the intermediate slopes of the montaña. This boundary, I was told by Lastenia Chinguad of Mayasquer, was routinely crossed in the course of interzone barter. The paths were so muddy, though, that trade goods had to be carried from the montaña to the highlands on the backs of bulls.

The bull, staff, snake, and cat at Cimarrones indicate yet another sort of transition. The hacienda is located on the boundary between the sections of Cuaical and Nazate. This is not only a territorial boundary but a distinction between life-styles as well, since Cuaical is infamous throughout the region for its residents' habit of cattle rustling. The bull, object of the rustlers' attention, marks the boundary between what is perceived as the "healthy" section of Nazate and the thieves of Cuaical.[29] Significantly, the bull also functions as a symbol of Indian-mestizo rivalries over land, since the thieves of Cuaical are said to have developed their calling in response to the growth of mestizo-owned haciendas in their midst (Doumier Mamián, personal communication).[30] In the El Zapatero story, as in the history of Cimarrones, the animals mark land rights and transitional phases between mestizo and indigenous control over land. Clearly, these are highly meaningful symbols that articulate a broad array of concepts in the minds of Cumbal listeners. They are quite appropriately included as the climax of the El Zapatero tale.

Invented Traditions

The oral narrative obviously encounters some of its roots in Andean tradition. Yet many of its focal images are simultaneously "invented traditions," either introduced by Europeans and reinvented by Indians, or the inverse—aboriginal traditions reappropriated by mestizos. They are recast in daily activity, in political action, and in other narratives, bringing enhanced meaning to any retelling of the story of the El Zapatero dispute.

One of the traditions most central to modern-day Indian identity throughout the Colombian highlands is the staff of office, which, we have already seen, encompasses a broad array of historical referents, ranging from the family history it encodes, through its association with the symbol of the Royal Crown, to its use in the possession ceremony as a mnemonic for the resguardo title. Like the staffs themselves, the rituals in which staffs are used are European traditions that have been given local meaning by the Cumbales. While the staffs are most clearly significant in their ritual context, they also surface in political rhetoric, where a proper cabildo is said to be "vertical," just like its staffs of office.

It seems to me that the hitching post provides a climax to the oral tale of the loss of El Zapatero precisely because it reproduces a vertical staff of office whose point is buried in the ground during a possession ceremony. It is the clearest way that anyone in Cumbal can stake a claim to a piece of land. The vertical hitching post to which cattle are tied when they are in the corral similarly stakes Sánchez's claim in the narrative. The presence of the hitching post, which finds its roots in the distant Andean past, reproducing elements of pan-Andean cosmology, is also a reinvented tradition used to define indigenous identity and authority today.

Ambivalent Histories

Behind the hitching post lies a complex fabric of contradictory symbols and legal interpretations that, on the one hand, ground the actions of Segundo Sánchez in native categories, thus tacitly accepting his usurpation of the land, and, on the other hand, reject mestizo claims to resguardo territory. This double-edged objective is accomplished through appeals to legal authority and through the manipulation and contextualization of the hitching post as a symbol.

As we have seen in chapter 1, Colombia's indigenous population enjoys a special status, thanks to a body of Indian legislation that survived the Liberal attacks on native communities in the nineteenth century. Laws defining the communal regime of the resguardo system—especially Law 89 of 1890, but also many of the federal and state laws preceding it—establish the right to repossess lands lying within the boundaries contained within colonial titles, the same documents that provide native historians with evidence of their past. The existence of such colonial documentation should preclude non-Indians' appeals to other forms of law in their attempts to usurp land. Colombian property law, then, cannot have provided Segundo Sánchez with any firm title to El Zapatero. And, in effect, it did not: Sánchez retained the hacienda through sheer physical force and blatant procrastination.

But Cumbal storytellers appeal to property law in their accounts of the loss of El Zapatero: if they had only removed the bull and the hitching post, they lament, they never would have lost the farm; if they only had distributed the land and farmed it, Sánchez never could have gained a foothold in the hacienda. By giving property law priority over indigenous legislation, it is almost as though the narrators admitted to having lost what was never really theirs. Perhaps in a sense they have, since a great number of Cumbales transformed their use rights into individual property rights in the nineteenth century by acquiring deeds to landholdings that should have remained communal resguardo property.[31]

The presence of the hitching post at the climax of the tale represents a tacit acceptance of defeat at the hands of the mestizo. As I have already demonstrated, the post is a kind of a staff of office, legitimizing Sánchez's claim to El Zapatero. In this sense, the hitching post functions as a metaphor for the mestizo appropriation of native history that non-Indian townspeople use to validate their claims to resguardo lands. Included here might be the boundary ditches that carve out a multiplicity of tiny plots and serve as material reminders of the history of individual landholdings. These ditches are frequently dug by mestizo hacienda owners to keep Indians out of and cattle in the tracts they have usurped from the resguardo as well as to create a sense of their own legitimacy in the region, as Benjamín Cuaical so clearly explains with reference to the hacienda of Mundo Nuevo, between Cuetial and Mayasquer:

> That zanja, well, I can't give you information on how long
> it has existed.

> That zanja must have existed since the days of the rich
> men, since the time of Mosquera [mid-nineteenth century],
> because that's what the ancestors recounted, that that zanja
> was made by them, in the olden days, when they tried to di-
> vide up [the hacienda] Mundo Nuevo.
> The first rich men who entered there, the whites. That's not
> made by Indians, that zanja, no. That's made by the whites,
> trying to divide [it].
> That's why there are zanjas. (Benjamín Cuaical, Vereda Cu-
> aical)[32]

Although, on the one hand, the narrators of the El Zapatero story appear to accept defeat at the hands of the mestizo politician, on the other hand, they also deny the very basis of mestizo power by implying that their history cannot be appropriated by anyone other than themselves. This is accomplished through their focus on the hitching post. While the hitching post is *like* a staff of office, it is *not* a staff of office: it does not carry the historical load associated with the cabildo insignia and is therefore not a representation of a family; it has no "crowns," and therefore is not linked in any way to other important symbols of Cumbal land and authority, such as cacique Cumbe, Deed 228, or the Llano de Piedras.

The meaning of the staffs comes from a web of historical experience, not just from their usage in an isolated ritual context. In a similar narrative from contemporary Chiles, which Francisco Salazar told to Angélica Mamián, a woman named Graciana inserted herself into the possession ceremony that granted usufruct rights to some hot springs to the cabildo, but she was unable to gain control of the plot by virtue of such a fraudulent appropriation of ceremony. Luckily, they say, she was so far from the site of the ritual when she threw herself to the ground and uprooted grass that her possession of the site was not legitimized:

> It was called the Frailejonal. It used to be called that and it
> still is.
> That's the place where they were to give possession.
> And it was necessary to go via the peak of the volcano.
> You had to pass by there. And it's cold there, damn it. And
> from there down it is all downhill.
> When the woman got there, the cabildo was down in Fraile-
> jonal, receiving possession. So she also fell from her horse
> and rolled on the ground, thinking how far she was from the
> point where possession was being given.
> But for that reason it wasn't worth it and since then until
> now, they fought that struggle, the cabildo of Chiles. (Fran-
> cisco Salazar, Chiles)[33]

Both here and at El Zapatero, the stories recast mestizo or contrario behavior within native frameworks that should legitimize the antagonists' claims but instead demonstrate their essential fraudulence.[34] The hitching post is a valuable descriptive vehicle because it simultaneously appeals to deep-rooted Andean symbols, to invented colonial traditions, and to this peculiar sort of double negation that denies its very appeal.

Since the early colonial period European law has provided Andean Indians with an arm in their struggle to defend their lands and their community structure. Nevertheless, in colonial Peru, recourse to the European legal tradition forced Indians to relinquish control over their own structures of authority and to continue to play by European rules, even in the face of opposition from their own communities. Similarly, in nineteenth-century Otavalo, Ecuador, authorities appropriated Andean customs and colonial invented traditions and subsumed them under the authority of the state in an effort to entice Indians to appeal their problems to the state judiciary system instead of to their own authorities. As a result, the indigenous community structure was weakened (Guerrero 1989; Stern 1982).

In their struggle for El Zapatero, the nineteenth-century Cumbales were obliged to justify their cultural identity and their territorial autonomy by submitting legal evidence in the form of the Royal Provision, Deed 228, and other similar decrees, which, in essence, negated their claims both to a distinct identity and to an autonomous territory. The problem is that the Royal Provision does not provide Cumbal with clear title to its land: like other colonial titles, it is essentially a document of land loss, not a charter for territorial autonomy. True, it confers land rights upon the cabildo, which had been lost at the time of the Spanish invasion. But it returns these rights in pieces via titles, stipulating which lands will remain in Spanish hands, which will be claimed by Indians, and which are still under dispute.[35] For this reason, both Segundo Sánchez and the cabildo could use the Royal Provision as evidence; it is a document amenable to piecemeal use, and thus can back many contradictory claims. In short, the title forces the Indians to play ball with the Europeans according to Spanish rules and to envisage their autonomy as something to be claimed, bit by bit, within the Spanish legal system.

The oral tale, although it is based upon written documents and accepts them as valid, attempts to transcend this dilemma precisely by appealing to property law. In their recounting of the history of El Zapatero, the Cumbales assert that the reason for their claim is beyond litigation: Sánchez stole the land from them by fraudulently leaving a bull and a hitching post; thus, they must also transcend litigation by occupying and repossessing the hacienda. Ultimately, the ambiguities of the oral account are solved not in the narrative but in militant political action, which transcends law by refusing to play according to the state's rules.

In another way, indigenous use of colonial titles represents a solution to the dilemma of capitulation to European forms of argument and recording information. The titles are written documents, stored in archives, appropriate as legal evidence in Colombian courts. Ironically, the Indians perceive them as being sources for their oral history. But memoristas subvert the supremacy of the literate by turning these documents on their heads. Oral tradition organizes colonial caciques into a hierarchy that recapitulates Cumbal's section system, not the chronology of the Royal Provision. Even more subversive are contemporary historians' readings of the nineteenth-century legal papers associated with the El Zapatero dispute, in which the narrators utterly disregard the facts laid out in the documents. Instead, they emphasize details, like the bull and the hitching post, that do not appear in the written record, details they learned from their grandparents in the years before the documents were rediscovered.

In essence, contemporary storytellers and activists, who were instrumental in repossessing El Zapatero in 1975, have done their historical research backwards, creating a history and then corroborating it with paper, thus lending symbolic value and power to the written word. In other words, they confront the legal system and force it to play according to *their* rules by using the written word and legal papers to legitimize their own oral memory. Instead of molding the oral memory to correspond with the dictates of the written form, the story of El Zapatero, a narrative of loss, conceptually liberates the Cumbales from the written legal system that has imprisoned them, permitting them to take the law into their own hands through political militancy.

SEVEN

The Art of Ethnic Militancy

IN JUNE OF EVERY YEAR, the state-sponsored commemoration of the Día del Campesino or the Day of the Peasant is celebrated throughout the Colombian countryside, accompanied by the flowery discourse of local officeholders, the cacophony of small-town bands, the aroma of barbecued beef furnished by politicians in search of votes, and the distribution of seedlings to be planted on eroded mountain slopes. In highland Nariño the celebration has been renamed the Día del Indígena or Day of the Indian by cabildos anxious to be recognized as Indian. While the senator flies in from Bogotá, the municipal mayor delivers his speech in the town plaza, seedlings are exchanged for votes, and the band erupts into unmelodious song, the communities for whom the celebration is intended stage their own festivities in the casa de cabildo or in the public space of repossessed lands. Shielded from the gaze of local mestizos, cabildantes deliver their own speeches, and the public is treated to dramatic presentations and the music of rural bands. Militant art recalls the exploits of the colonial caciques, the horrors of conquest, and the achievements of the modern land-claims movement. Visual image and verbal cliché prompt the audience to reflect upon the rhetoric of the contemporary Indian movement, on the one hand, and the narratives of community historians, on the other.

Cumbales and neighboring Muellamueses use song and drama to assert an indigenous nationalism that reinforces their commitment to the construction of a distinct ethnic identity while it acknowledges their membership in the broader Colombian nation. On the one hand, militant art emphasizes cultural specificity through recourse to a history conveyed through texture, obtained through the dense combination of sound, movement, image, and story as opposed to the single-channel narrative. Texture is achieved through the choice of themes and cast of characters, the design of costumes, and the use of language. On the other hand, implicit in the artistic production of ethnic activists is a recognition that indigenous historical experience intersects with that of other Colombians. The shared nature of the past compels Indians to clarify what it means to be both Pasto and Colombian, a task that the artists accomplish through appeals to a national Indian political discourse.

Artistic Representation and History

Selective Reconstructions of the Past

Dramatic presentation and musical composition are not new to the highlands of Nariño. Theater and spectacle have been an integral part of the celebration of Christian festivals since the colonial period: Holy Week and Advent processions include reenactments of biblical scenes, biblical tableaux are prepared for Epiphany, and Spanish-language Nativity plays punctuate the Christmas season.[1]

Contemporary theater and musical presentations are, in contrast, frequently secular in nature, performed for neighbors in rural schoolhouses or for broader cross sections of the population at large cabildo meetings; some of the more politically active sectors of Panán have introduced secular, historical theater into Epiphany Carnival. Even before the advent of the land-claims movement, young people organized secular theater groups, presenting the disappearing customs of their elders without making reference to land struggles. Although these actors were acquainted with Nativity plays, it is equally likely that they were introduced to drama at school.

The composition of secular songs, in contrast, can be traced directly to a colonial-era forebear. News of the antitaxation rebellions of the turn of the nineteenth century, whose hub was in nearby Túquerres, was broadcast in the form of *coplas* or rhymes, which have been transcribed in the documentary record.[2] The songs we will be examining, like the coplas, are important for their original lyrics and not for their accompanying music, which is borrowed from popular songs.

Recognized by the cabildo as official community organizations, artistic groups are frequently short-lived. Their membership is drawn from the youth of neighboring veredas, some of whom are anxious to support the land struggle while others are just looking for a good time.

Such organizations play a central role in integrating young people and women into political life by providing a chance for those not directly involved in the all-male and highly politicized cabildo to participate in public activities. Members of theater groups usually attend most cabildo meetings and join cabildo-supervised grass-roots organizations, such as the juntas de acción comunal. They are active participants at large public encounters where their artistry is presented on stage. In other words, theater is an avenue for the incorporation of young people into cabildo affairs. It is thus no accident that, a few years down the line, some of the young male actors become cabildantes, their theater experience having groomed them for political office.

In communities in which historians are generally older men who were once active in cabildo affairs, music and drama also serve as vehicles for more youthful forms of historical interpretation. The members of Los Cumbes, a Cuaical drama group, identify themselves as memoristas on the title page of their scripts:

> HISTORY OF THE ARTISTIC GROUP LOS CUMBES, representatives of this great history that arises out of very young people, as is THE ARTISTIC GROUP LOS CUMBES, who memorized this great event. . . .[3]

Artistic performance thus creates a space in which historical knowledge can be interpreted by new sectors previously without access to historical interpretation, and shared with a broad public.[4] The past that artists dramatize is a selective construction, based in part on the scanty historical documentation that Indians have had access to and in part on the actors' and singers' personal experience. More than narrative portrayals of particular historical milestones, artistic interpretations of the past serve as mnemonics, references to other more complete stories (Cohen 1985). For example, in the song "El indio lucha por su tierra" (The Indian Fights for His Land), composer Valentín Cuaical makes but brief reference to the events that took place the first day of Cumbal's repossession of the Llano de Piedras:

Las cinco de la mañana	At five in the morning
llegamos a nuestro Llano,	we arrived at our Llano,
y todos con un farol,	everyone with a lantern,
con la herramienta en la mano.	with tools in hand.
Ya salen los enemigos	Now the enemies come out,
con palo, piedra y tronantes,	with sticks, stones, thunder,
y todos los campesinos	and all the peasants
los sacan a puro trote.	remove them at a trot.

Las once de la mañana	At eleven in the morning
ya llega mi coronel,	the colonel arrives,
y todos los campesinos	and all the peasants
quieren dialogar con él.	want to converse with him.
Nosotros los cabildantes,	We the cabildantes
también tenemos teniente,	also have our lieutenant,
porque somos una nación	because we are a nation
y somos independientes.	and we are independent.
El barrio Nueva Granada,	Barrio Nueva Granada,
los blancos nos desafían.	the whites challenge us.
Mi cuerpo se hará pedazos,	My body may be cut in pieces,
pero la tierra sí es mía.	but the land is surely mine.

Oral accounts of the struggle for the Llano de Piedras are considerably more elaborate, describing all manner of personal experience. For example, Lastenia Alpala still captivates her audience when she recounts how, at the time in her late seventies, she hid a comrade's pistol in her milk pail, thus spiriting it past government soldiers:

> A boy, whom I think might have even been a relative, said, "Señora, please carry this."
> It was a revolver, and without saying anything, I received it.
> And then [the police] grabbed him and made him put up his hands.
> And there I was with the revolver under my arm.
> Then they said, "Go ahead to jail, you such-and-such Indians."
> Then they mistreated us.
> Well, they kept on taking us, they led us.
> Then, I remembered and I said to myself, "Soon I'll fall," I said, "and then the revolver will fall." I opened the milk bucket and I put it in there, all nice, and I covered it up.
> And it was true: later on I stumbled on a brick, since it was night, and I fell face down. "Clink!" The revolver in the bucket.
> And the soldier said, "Oh!" He said—here I'd be discovered—"What is that you're carrying in that bucket?"
> And I said, "The cups I brought to drink coffee with."
> "Oh, fine," he said. (Lastenia Alpala, Vereda Quilismal)[5]

Written accounts are more rigorous in adhering to the chronology of the event. Diomedes Paguay, in his pamphlet *De como recuperamos nuestro Llano de Piedras* (On How We Repossessed Our Llano de Piedras), records all the meetings, battles, and encounters that transpired during the occupation of the Llano. Songwriter Cuaical, in contrast, highlights only the major themes that most people remember: the peaceful entry by the Indians that met with violent reprisals on the part of the local mestizos, the dialogues with government officials, and, most important, the awakening of a national consciousness in the cabildo. As he was an active and influential supporter of the Llano-era cabildo, Cuaical's telescoped history of the occupation highlights the official version of the events, including meetings with the police and reaffirmations of cabildo autonomy, as opposed to the more idiosyncratic accounts of other oral narrators.

The past is reconstructed selectively according to the needs and dictates of the present, providing people with a model of reality toward which they can strive. Among the Pastos, the contents of this model are grounded to a large extent in the distant past, offering a glimpse of what indigenous autonomy might look like once the cabildo wins its struggle. This model is centered around the historical event that has had the most traumatic effect upon native Colombians: the Spanish invasion. Its importance is evident in the signs that the veredas of Muellamués carried to the 1988 celebration of the Day of the Indian:

Vereda Santa Rosa presents the problems of Medardo Erazo.
Vereda Riveras presents a marriage with its indigenous traditions
    and customs, with our authorities and their special law that pro-
    tects us, Law 89 of 1890. Long live the Day of the Indian!
Vereda Chapud presents the trickery by the whites in the year 1560
    of Chief Bernardo.
Vereda Guan Puente Alto is present at the Day of the Indian with the
    following: the burial of Chief Nutibara and the Gaitana, arrested
    by the Spaniards.
On the Day of the Indian the vereda Cristo is present with the rejec-
    tion of the land cooperatives in the resguardos of the Southwest.
Comunidad presents the passion and death of our race; this occurred
    in the year 1536.[6]

Four of the six plays treat conquest themes, portraying Spanish authorities—for example, the local landowner, Medardo Erazo—who swindle native lords—sometimes local caciques, such as Bernardo, but also figures from Colombian national folklore, such as Nutibara and La Gaitana. One of the other two presentations is the reenactment of a traditional marriage ceremony, a theme common to Nariñense theater groups. The Muellamués rendition is particularly interesting because the vereda in question linked its depiction of traditional marriage customs with support of the cabildo, perhaps prodding the audience to remember that, in the earlier part of the century, cabildos were charged with the moral education of the community and frequently obligated courting couples to get married. But even this portrayal of recent history is intimately connected to the memory of the Spanish invasion. The banner incorporates a slogan in favor of defense of resguardo legislation, in particular, Law 89 of 1890, which is frequently confused with colonial-era titles. Even though this particular play treats a relatively recent theme, its creators have situated it within the broader framework of the conquest and colonial periods.

The selectivity of these presentations is due, in part, to the paucity of available historical documentation. Cabildos' incursions into regional archives are inspired by the need for copies of colonial-era briefs in the course of land claims. Given that these documents provide useful, albeit abbreviated, information on colonial political actors, conquest plays that draw upon them concentrate almost exclusively on naming conquest-era hereditary chiefs and colonial-period Spaniards.

It is possible to distinguish some of the other sources from which the historical interpretations of these dramas are drawn. The funeral of Nutibara, for example, opens with the preconquest burial of a hereditary chief, his body covered with gold jewelry. The image was taken from a poster advertising a museum exhibit of pre-Columbian goldwork; the poster hangs in many cabildo offices.[7]

In a fascinating analysis of a sixteenth-century *relación* describing the conquest of Querétaro, Mexico, Serge Gruzinski (1985, 40) demonstrates that its Otomí authors used costumes and dances from colonial festivals as templates for describing pre-Columbian armies. The Muellamués theatrical version of the traditional wedding similarly employs ritual as a source of historical evidence. Other dramatic portrayals of weddings I have witnessed highlight the process of negotiation between the families of the bride and groom and the accompanying exchange of cooked food. The Muellamués play depicts the wedding ceremony itself, complete with priest and mass. This is reminiscent of farcical reenactments of weddings that take place at the "Sacada de la Vieja," a secular ritual performed at the completion of house construction, in which the woodland spirit or *vieja* hidden in the beams is removed from the house. A similar reenactment of the marriage ceremony used to be held every year at Epiphany Carnival in Chiles.

History and Ethnic Typologies

Insistence upon the conquest-era roots of contemporary indigenous experience is a product of more than the paucity of historical data.

It also reflects the authors' acceptance of the ethnic typologies of the dominant society, in which Indians are relegated to the historical past (Berkhofer 1979; Dorris 1987; see Fabian 1983). Similarly, militant theater situates Indians in distant locations, especially in the tropical lowlands. In *Historia de una esclava indígena del Gran Cumbal, estando llegada a una casa de dos extranjeros de mal humor* (History of an Indian Slave from Gran Cumbal, Arrived at the House of Two Bad-Tempered Foreigners), a Los Cumbes actor states that the power of Indians originates in the jungle: "You didn't know that we, the Indians, got our learning through telepathy or from the breezes that cover the four winds of the Colombian Amazon."[8]

The practice of using geographic displacement to define Indian "otherness" also characterizes traditional Nariñense ritual and dance. The Jambo dancers of Panán, for instance, represent the people of Mayasquer on the warmer slopes of the cordillera over looking the Pacific lowlands; the word *jambo* is a common variant of *yumbo*, a term used in highland Ecuador to signify the lowland outsider (Salomon 1981; see also Poole 1990). Many of the actors in contemporary Nativity plays carry baskets made in Mayasquer, as if to equate terrestrial distance with the temporal remoteness of Christ's birth. Like the Mayasqueres, who are believed to have the ability to transform themselves into animals and to fly, the characters of contemporary political drama are portrayed as having supernatural abilities that take them beyond the realm of contemporary human society. Note, for instance, a script by Los Cumbes: "This great history confirms the intelligence of the forefather caciques, who could transform (human) aspects into animals of the jungle and other such important things."[9]

The national Indian movement has, in some respects, transported the image of the Indian into the twentieth century and up the cordillera to the highlands. For many contemporary Colombians, the distinctive costumes of the Guambianos of the department of Cauca or the Ecuadorian Otavaleños—both examples of successful modern highland communities—now convey the impression of "Indianness." These same images sometimes substitute for lowland representations in militant drama. Thus, for example, the winning entry in Panán's Epiphany Carnival depicted the caciques María Panana and Cumbe with their children, dressed in Otavaleño and Guambiano clothing.

But in the popular Colombian imagination Indians are increasingly associated with the production of ethnic art, a stereotype used over and over by Nariñense actors (see Crain 1990). Equally influential in creating this image is the fact that the only available evidence of the pre-Columbian past is found in ceramic artifacts. The Muellamués version of the conquest shows people peacefully going about their every-day lives, painting small statues of birds (plate 9). Similarly, one of Los Cumbes' plays, in which miserable sharecroppers overthrow a greedy and exploitative landlord, is entitled *Historia de nuestra artesanía indígena de nuestro Gran Cumbal* (History of Our Indian Handicrafts from Our Gran Cumbal). As will become evident later, the prime example of handicrafts in Nariño is the woolen cloth produced by local weavers which until recently was the mainstay of the rural costume (plate 10).

Rewriting History

In *How Societies Remember,* Paul Connerton (1989) suggests that in most societies ritual is the most powerful source of historical knowledge. Commemorative ceremonies in particular serve as vehicles for historical interpretation, insofar as they not only remind participants of events but *re-present* them, thereby lending an instrumentality to history by shifting its locus from the past to the metaphysical present. Once history is inscribed, not on paper but in bodily activity, that claim upon the past is strengthened (see de Certeau 1984). According to Connerton, commemorative ceremonies "do not simply imply continuity with the past but explicitly claim such continuity . . . by ritually re-enacting a narrative of events" (Connerton 1989, 45).

Cabildo ceremony effectively relives the past by voicing the same words that were used to grant land rights to the caciques in the colonial period. It is thus no accident that these ceremonies are frequently reenacted in militant theater. But re-presenting history implies more than repeating events of, or rituals signifying, the past; in Nariñense drama it also signifies the concomitant *correcting* of history.[10] Muellamués portrayals of the conquest depict early battles in which the Indians are always the victors (plate 11). Los Cumbes sets its characters in the timeless past, living in grinding servitude to large landowners, but the Indians always win in these plays, which close with slogans of the contemporary land-claims movement.[11]

But even if history is corrected by dramatic forms of establishing connections to a heroic indigenous past, the triumphs of conquest-era caciques are situated in a European historical framework. Remember, for instance, that Vereda Comunidad named its play *The Passion and Death of Our Race,* a very clear reference to the life of Christ. The roots of this Christian framework originate in the religious spectacle of the past. Traditional drama was always religious in nature, teaching universal Christian history to the native South American faithful. Holy Week processions, for example, were essentially a series of biblical tableaux in which people impersonated biblical characters, moving across the countryside in a chronologically organized pageant of Judeo-Christian tradition.[12] I observed a truncated version of the elaborate processions of the past in Panán in 1987, which included a host of *pasos* or tableaux, but only one that was locally inspired—the cabildo with its banner, trailing behind the cross of Christianity and the souls of humanity. In this procession native history is absorbed within the framework of the universal.[13]

Similarly, voices of the Indian movement have rewritten native history so that it corresponds to, legitimizes, and is legitimized by the Christian past. Manuel Quintín Lame, a turn-of-the-century Páez militant, whose published works have influenced the Indians of Nariño, included Indians in his reworking of the Nativity, much as did native Peruvian chroniclers of the colonial period:

> The cradle of Knowledge is hidden under cruel mountains, as is told in the dreams of the Indian who ascended to visit the newborn in that straw cradle, who was a guest in one of the halls of the "House of Bethlehem," he who left the philosopher's stone, etc., that Indian who brought a gift of gold to the man and King of Kings. (Lame 1971 [1939], 13)[14]

Although militant theater employs Christian metaphors, these predominantly secular plays are situated within a culturally specific vision of the past in which historical chronology is reconstituted to conform to the hierarchical organization of topographic space. The Muellamués commemoration of the Day of the Peasant, for example, is celebrated with a series of plays presented by veredas, although at the performance I witnessed they were not presented in hierarchical order. The history presented by Cumbal theater groups is frequently localized, situating historical caciques in specific veredas. Such local histories are loosely organized according to the section hierarchy, as is evident in the following Los Cumbes speech. Here the veredas are represented by their most common surnames:

> Because whites know that we were created in the forest, the most distant and forgotten plains. But we were created with our own blood and very strong, to know that we are Indians and descendants of our cacique Cumbe and our *cacica* [female cacique] María Panana. Because this ancestry will never be lost, because from there the Alpalas, the Tapies, the Quilismales, the Cuaicales, the Tarapueces, the Chinguades, etc. were reborn.[15]

Finally, the space of dramatic representation expands to encompass the territory as a whole instead of remaining confined to a stage. At a 1986 celebration, the Muellamueses portrayed the history of native carriers on the Camino de Barbacoas by walking actors and audience along the road running through the resguardo.

The Power of Images

Cacique Cumbe

The history embedded in Pasto drama and song is not revealed through narrative but through images that move people to remember the past and also to act upon it. The power of images originates in the present, in concrete activity. Pierre Nora contrasts this active and malleable past with history, by calling it memory:

> Memory, history: far from being synonyms, they are opposites. Memory is life, borne by living groups and in their names, it is in permanent flux, open to the dialectic of remembering and of forgetting, unconscious of its successive deformations, vulnerable to all of its uses and manipulations, susceptible to long periods of latency and to sudden revitalizations. History is the always problematic and incomplete reconstruction of that which is no longer. Memory is a still-active phenomenon, a living link to the eternal present; history, a representation of the past. . . . Memory is rooted in the concrete, in space, gesture, image and object. History only attaches itself to temporal continuities, to evolution and to the relations between things. (Nora 1984, xix; translation mine)

I am not speaking here of history in the chronological sense, but of the forging of a connection with the past by re-creating it in the present, a process that, as has already been noted, Connerton maintains is most powerfully expressed through ritual.

Image lies at the heart of national identity. Vague, abbreviated, and sometimes stereotyped, it supplies the foundations for a sense of nationality:

> [National] identity is essentially a discourse: its building blocks are images, terms and words that we acquire in our infancy, in school, in the newspapers. In all forms of communication, discourse about identity is configured through symbols, sentences, myths, stereotypes, vague notions, collective

images. Descriptions [of identity] are also elements in its creation. (Melo 1989, 28; translation mine)

In Cumbal and Muellamués, many such images are culled from readings of resguardo titles. Little is known about the meaning of or the historical referents associated with these symbols, because they are only scantily described, if described at all, in the documents. Nevertheless, or perhaps precisely for this reason, they move people to action. The power of such symbols was expressed to me in the following story about the repossession of the Llano de Piedras. Confronted by repression, people invoked the name of cacique Cumbe to justify their actions:

> The police would say to them, "Who tells you to repossess the land?" or "Who is it that goes first? It has to be someone."
> Then they would say, "No, no one tells us. I don't know. You don't even know the people who are going. We go to the land, but don't know who [sends us].
> "It's that the cacique lights our way. We're going to the land and everyone gets up. The cacique lights the way in dreams." (Bernardita Chirán, Vereda Cuaical)[16]

Cumbe's name is borrowed for countless music and theater groups, which frequently call themselves by some variant of "Los Cumbes," and the cacique is invoked time and again in plays and in music (plate 10). Cumbe does not appear in any colonial-era documents; the power of his image derives from the link between past and present that is established through the use of a name that so closely approximates the name of the resguardo.[17]

The invocation of the referentless image of Cumbe conforms to traditional Andean forms of representation. In the pre-Columbian Andes, the significance of visual images depended upon oral exegesis (Cummins 1988). For example, the knots and colors of the *quipu*, the Incaic mnemonic device composed of knotted strings, represented abstract categories of knowledge that had to be interpreted by the *quipucamayoc*, the person who made or translated the quipu. The quipu did not encode information in itself, but served as a mnemonic for recalling knowledge deriving from another source, in this case, from its interpreter (Ascher and Ascher 1981). Similarly, Cumbe's name serves as a stimulus for the recall of events to be remembered and interpreted by the listeners.

According to Susan Sontag, photographic images are made meaningful to the viewing public only when they are articulated within a previously constituted ideology:

> Though an event has come to mean, precisely, something worth photographing, it is still ideology (in the broadest sense) that determines what constitutes an event. There can be no evidence, photographic or otherwise, of an event until the event itself has been named and characterized. And it is never photographic evidence which can construct—more properly, identify—events; the contribution of photography always follows the naming of the event. What determines the possibility of being affected morally by photographs is the existence of a relevant political consciousness. Without a politics, photographs of the slaughter-bench of history will most likely be experienced as, simply, unreal or as a demoralizing emotional blow. (Sontag 1977, 18–19)

Similarly, Cumbe is made meaningful to the Cumbales only within the context of the ideology of their movement, whose program developed after native historians began to interpret local history.

Young memorista playwrights and songwriters recast the past in images framed by contemporary ethnic ideology. For instance, embedded within Los Cumbes' *Historia de nuestra artesanía indígena. . .*, a story of the exploitation of Indian sharecroppers and artisans, doña Dorita Cumbal cautions the community to maintain its ideology of support for the cabildo, territorial autonomy, repossession of lands, and cultural revitalization:

> But let us forget dinner, my children. Come here a moment. I will tell you a few beautiful things. You will see, my children, I will leave you these grand experiences, so that when I die, you have these great memories from your mother. First of all, you must be good Indian children, and very affectionate with everyone you meet, and defenders of your rights that your grandparents left you. Also, you must be very smart Indians in working your lands, which our cabildos have left us, and you must not sell off these rights. Because history teaches us that we should not sell our land, but continue to work it to sustain ourselves by it, and you will see that in this way you will live wonderful and contented lives. Second, I tell you to continue to weave this beautiful flannel for our clothing and that of our brothers. Also, you should continue to revive the treasure that is being lost, so that you can decorate our very important clothing.[18]

The need for the Indian movement to express its demands in general terms, applicable across groups and comprehensible within the political and cultural terminology of the dominant society (Diskin 1991; Jackson 1989; Ramos 1988), is exemplified in this somewhat wooden speech by a series of what could almost be called formulaic utterances. These utterances fall into two groups: those that allude to the historical roots of indigenous rights and those related to cultural revitalization.

The first group emphasizes historical claims to land through reference to rights inherited from previous generations, through admonitions against selling lands to outsiders, and through entreaties to work hard. All three are staples of the rhetoric, imagery, and demands of the national movement. More regionally specific are the second group of utterances, which, drawing upon commonly held beliefs of the dominant society, guard against the loss of cultural traits, particularly the typical Nariñense peasant costume.

The ideological framework so aptly conveyed by these utterances is most thoroughly experienced by the actors themselves, for whom theater constitutes a form of political education. The young memoristas develop a familiarity with cabildo ideology and with resguardo history as they prepare and learn their lines. What they ultimately create, though, are images that the audience must situate within its own framework.

Visual images are essential to historical representation as it is expressed through militant theater. On one level, they are all that the audience receives in the course of these dramatic productions, given that the untrained voices of the actors rarely project enough to be heard by the public. But on a more fundamental level, across the Andes knowlege is acquired through the act of seeing. The active quality of seeing is expressed in colonial-era Quechua prayers and in contemporary women's songs, in which divine knowledge is acquired through sight (Harrison 1988). Among the Colombian Páez, seeing is integral to political ritual and mythology related to the legitimization of land tenure (Rappaport 1985).

The Texture of the Past

What the audience sees in these dramatic presentations is a series of static images whose meaning is conveyed through *texture*. In a study of the symbolism of community among black migrants to Washington, D.C., Brett Williams describes the re-creation of rural Carolina culture in the metropolis as it is manifested in foodways and in gardening. She emphasizes that Carolina customs convey a sense of texture, of "dense, vivid, woven, detailed narratives, relationships, and experiences," which take on meaning as they are relived through expressive forms that "rely powerfully on repetition, improvisation, and the exploration of sometimes narrow situations through many emotional, sensory, interpersonal, and reflective voices" (Williams 1988, 47).

The texture of Nariñense theatrical images is manifested largely through the visual, but also the aural, channels, depicted most clearly in costume and in the names and language of characters (see also Guerrero 1991). Texture and image recall the history of everyday life rather than political history, which is frequently expressed through plots and in speeches.

In Muellamués, preconquest Indians are frequently portrayed with tropical forest attributes (Plate 13). Warriors are seminaked, wearing grass skirts, feathers, and face paint; caciques wear tunics (plate 14). Panán's cacica María Panana, appearing at the 1987 Carnival, donned a modest but makeshift tunic, similar to those worn by theatrical caciques (plate 12). Almost all pre-Columbian Indians are decked out with "gold" jewelry made from metallic paper, an attribute that costume designers learned from archaeological exhibitions. Golden headbands hold in place the long hair that these characters typically exhibit. Long hair was a prevalent symbol of Indianness in nineteenth-century watercolors of Indians (Ardila and Lleras 1985) and was also employed by Páez activist Manuel Quintín Lame in an appeal to his indigenous roots.

Costumes conveying a sense of the more recent past, and sometimes even the distant era of the caciques, are generally constructed from the clothing that old people still wear: double-weave woolen ponchos and flannel trousers for men; wool folleras and shawls for women. Everyone barefoot or is shod with *alpargates* or hemp sandals (plates 10 and 14). Such garb is by no means aboriginal in origin; it is worn by non-Indian peasants throughout the Colombian and Ecuadorian Andes. Nevertheless, it has assumed a symbolic importance in the Nariñense Indian movement, representing indigenous culture as it used to be. The display of this clothing is interpreted as a form of cultural revitalization.

Non-Indian characters sport stereotypical costumes that are almost a parody of twentieth-century mestizo dress. Priests are identified by their red capes, pith helmets, leather boots, and ties (plate 15). Spanish soldiers wear leather jackets and sunglasses, as would a modern-day landlord (plate 11).

Clearly, theatrical costume is hardly historically authentic. Conquest-era chronicler Pedro de Cieza de León (1962 [1553]) lays any doubts to rest with his description of Pasto clothing:

Their dress is [such] that the women wear a narrow mantle in the manner of a sack, with which they cover themselves from their breasts to their knees; and another small mantle on top, which falls over the long one, and all of them are made of grasses and of the bark of trees, and some are of cotton. The [male] Indians cover themselves with a mantle that is just as long, which must be three or four *varas* [approximately 3 meters], which they twist around the waist and again around the throat, and the remaining strand is placed on top of the head, and on their dishonest parts they wear small loincloths.[19]

Contemporary theatrical costume is meant to convey historical meaning through contemporary stereotype and cliché as well as by distancing the observer from the historical subject. The distancing is produced by the use of clothing that is recognized as being from the past, either because it is tropical lowland in appearance or because it corresponds to the costume of the earlier part of this century. Both of these representations are fueled, as we have seen, by commonly held stereotypes of Indians. It is thus not so much the accuracy of the costume as the associations it elicits that is at stake here (see Layne 1989). Nariñense theater has a different function from the illusory and nostalgic appeals to historical accuracy found in contemporary North American reenactments of the past (Handler 1988; Handler and Saxton 1988; Huxtable 1992; Lowenthal 1985). It is not meant to arouse a sentimental appreciation of earlier lifeways; instead, it invokes history in order to activate militant sentiments in the present.

Costume also provides the major vehicle for historical expression in processional spectacle. Biblical characters do not *do* anything; they are simply represented by virtue of their clothing (ϝ te 16). The personal reminiscences of comuneros who participated in the processions of the past, which were considerably more elaborate than the one I observed in Panán, contain descriptions that are essentially lists of costumes.[20] Raúl Fueltala, for example, always played King Saul ⁚ . the Good Friday celebration in Chiles, taking his place in a procession ranging from sixty to one hundred pasos. He remembers the texture of the procession, especially the clothes he wore and the props he carried:

So I got to be the King.
And, sure, I had to ready the horse. The horse was decorated with a cape, adorned even to his gilded hooves, with that yellow paper, the reins, the bit, his head, everything, the saddle covered with a cape that shined with stars and ornaments.

The King himself, then, rode out, that's right, and I was dressed in white with a cape and with a sword and also with a king's goblet.

I would steer my horse, with the sword and carrying the goblet and with a nice crown, everything.

And I came after the Centurions. The Centurions would go ahead, and then they shouted out to me from the list, "King Saul, your turn!"

Then, I would have to follow, and behind me, those who were next. (Raúl Fueltala, Vereda la Libertad, Panán)[21]

Texture was similarly conveyed by the backdrop of some of the more elaborate pasos. Fueltala remembers how Adam and Eve were portrayed on Good Friday in Chiles:

R.F.: Eve was a woman, and so she had to wear her undergarments and cover herself with leaves, covered with those bijao leaves, girdled like a follera, wrapped here on her body, all dressed in leaves.

And Adam, the same thing.

That's why, all of it, it all depicted, it all formed Paradise, all of it.

J.R.: What was Paradise like?

R.F.: Paradise was formed, was made with a large garden, with boughs. They hung fruit there, in short, all of that. That was Earthly Paradise, which Adam and Eve left.

And they continued on like that in the parade until they reached the church again, until the Galillean was inside, that is, Jesus of Nazareth. (Raúl Fueltala, Vereda Libertad, Panán)[22]

Don Raúl's sense of the past, as it is recorded in his narration, is not organized according to a chronological series of events. Instead it obeys a sequence of images that are arrayed over topographic space, duplicating in commemorative ceremony the close relationship between time and space that pervades the native Nariñense historical memory.

Images are also created through the use of language in these plays. The Pasto language disappeared during the nineteenth century, and the indigenous peoples of highland Nariño are all monolingual Spanish speakers. Playwrights employ various methods of re-creating the aboriginal tongue, both to convey what it meant to be an Indian in the past, and to show that many young people plan to embark on the impossible task of linguistic revival. Los Cumbes portrays the mother tongue through the use of nonsense syllables. Indigenous names, some Pasto and some from far-flung regions of Colombia, also convey a feeling of linguistic autonomy: Cruz Angela de los Cumbes, Cristián Sotavento, Sebastián Panán. Perhaps the most touching example of the role language plays in supplying texture (additionally, an example of the dramatic rewriting of history) is a Muellamués conquest play in which actors, probably return migrants from Quito, speak Quechua while a narrator declares over the loudspeaker that the community has finally recovered the lost Pasto language.

Toward a National Indian Discourse

An examination of Colombian Indian manifestos led Michel de Certeau (1986, 227) to declare that the discourse of indigenous organizations is marked by cultural and geographic specificity, not by the construction of a common ideology and language. Nevertheless, as I have mentioned on a number of occasions, the exigencies of communication with other ethnic militants and with the dominant society in part foster a common political language. In Cumbal, and I suspect in other communities, militant drama plays an important role in the creation of a national Indian discourse, conveyed through texture and image, much like the costume and language I have already described.

Cumbe and Manuel Quintín Lame

The birth of a pan-Indian discourse is especially clear in the scripts written by Miguel Angel Alpala, director of Los Cumbes. Miguel Angel is a young man from a poor family in Cuaical. Being landless, he was forced to seek work in the Putumayo, where he spent several years as a wage laborer, returning in the mid-1980s to participate in local Liberal party politics under the tutelage of the man elected governor for Quilismal in 1987. Never having finished primary school, Miguel Angel does not write with ease; nevertheless, the scripts he wrote for Los Cumbes are typed. Although I was permitted to make photocopies for my own use, the scripts were not reproduced for the actors, who only imperfectly memorized their lines, aided by the formulaic utterances they contain:

> We, the Indians, detested by that Greater "Cumbal" of the white Spaniards, *who arrived that October 12, 1492, at the lands called Guananí, which today we call Colombia.*[23]

also:

> The son of an Indian will sit on the throne of knowledge, to defend our own blood, blood that for a long time *has been hidden by our fierce vengeance.*[24]

and finally:

> *Prehistory echoes our ancestors, their homes there on that hill where the house of the divinity is buried, according to the prehistory of Bochica, who through signs or parables found truth in the sublime rays of the sun: when it shined from the east and in this way it consecrated the ceremonies of the gods that our ancestors adored.* But the adventurers who arrived on October 12, 1492 in the name of civilization, brandished knives in their hands with the intention of robbing us of our lives and of those great riches that we had inherited from our ancestors, the caciques. And today we, the Colombians, are accompanied by valor, and *united like a concert of angry eagles, we will achieve our defense,* so that we are done justice, and so that we are protected by the competent authorities of the whole nation, of all of Colombia, and for all Colombians.[25]

Each of the phrases I have highlighted is a quotation by Alpala from Manuel Quintín Lame's *Los pensamientos del indio que se educó dentro de las selvas colombianas* (The Thoughts of the Indian Who Was Educated in the Colombian Jungles), published under the title *En defensa de mi raza* (In Defense of My Race (Lame 1971 [1939]).[26] Lame was a Páez sharecropper who moved the Indians of Cauca and Tolima to demand their rights to reclaim land, to an autonomous political authority (the cabildo), and to an autonomous territory (the resguardo). His political demands, formulated in the early part of this century, still from the cornerstone of contemporary Indian mobilization. Lame's status within progressive and indigenous circles is such that his name is synonymous with indigenous resistance.[27]

Lame wrote his book in 1939, but it was not published until 1971, several years after his death. The treatise swiftly became a tool for political education in indigenous communities, including in Gran Cumbal, where several copies circulate. David Cuásquer of Panán was inspired by the book to compose a song about Lame, highlighting his struggles in Cauca and Tolima, and situating his interest in education within the context of growing ethnic consciousness in Nariño:

Guillermo León Valencia	Guillermo León Valencia
negó la educación,	denied him education,
Caudillo Quintín Lame	Leader Quintín Lame

siguió la organización.	kept organizing.
Cumbales y Pananes	Cumbales and Pananes
se unieron para luchar,	united to fight,
lo mismo los Mayasqueres,	the same with the Mayasqueres,
con Chiles van a ayudar.	who'll help with Chiles.
Los grandes terratenientes	The large landowners
guerrearon en Chaparral,	made war in Chaparral,
para ampliar las haciendas,	to extend their haciendas,
nuestra ley terminar.	to finish off our law.
Caudillo Quintín Lame	Leader Quintín Lame
al monte se fue a educar,	went to the hills to learn,
para dejar una historia,	to leave a history,
los libros para educarnos.	books to educate us.[28]

Even before its publication, *Los pensamientos* was a source of inspiration for the Indians of Ortega, Tolima. It was only after repeatedly hearing unusual metaphoric language uttered by the people of Ortega that editor Gonzalo Castillo-Cárdenas began to suspect that some kind of template existed for their clichés, resulting finally in his discovery of Lame's manuscript (Castillo-Cárdenas 1987, 1–3). Note how Lame's book operates as a model for dramatic dialogue in Cumbal:

1. *October 12, 1492:* The playwright makes repeated reference to Columbus's arrival in America, although the Spaniards would not invade the Pasto region for some four decades. The insistence upon 1492 echoes Lame, who repeatedly asserts that 1492 was a turning point in indigenous experirnce. Lame frequently opposes 1492 to 1939, the year in which his book was completed, since he perceived the 447 years between 1492 and 1939 as marking a period of Indian oppression that would end with the appearance of his treatise. The playwright calls Colombia by an alternative name, "Guananí," the aboriginal name of the Bahamian island on which Columbus made his landfall. Lame had repeatedly used the concept of "Guananí" to refer to aboriginal territorial autonomy: "And so tomorrow a communion of Indians will be born, the legitimate descendants of our Guananí land, the descendants of those hated tribes persecuted by the non-Indian" (p. 19).[28] Both Lame and playwright Miguel Angel Alpala use 1492 and the name "Guananí" as mnemonic devices: Lame, to recall the cataclysm of the Spanish invasion and the existence of a separate and autonomous indigenous experience; Alpala, to recall Lame.

2. *Reclaiming the Throne:* Lame's treatise is profoundly messianic, proclaiming his role as savior of Colombia's indigenous peoples, who would liberate Indians from the darkness of ignorance through the power of his knowledge. Then justice would be done: "That crime is

hidden, sirs; but that justice will come, when the Colombian Indian reclaims his throne, etc., etc." (p. 21).[30] Similarly, the playwright makes reference to the coming millennium, when the aboriginal throne will be reclaimed and Indian blood, long hidden, will once again be visible. Lame writes that his knowledge was acquired through nature, not through a formal education, a concept David Cuásquer takes up in his song. In the treatise, Lame likens his intelligence to the flight of birds:

> *Atallo cundulcunca,* bird or condor's nest. That condor of my mind and that eagle of my psychology, an Indian psychology that was conceived when the condor or condors passed by, like a concert of swallows that visit the seasons. Those condors sought their abodes in the high peaks, and others in the shadows of ancient oaks. They shout out in the midst of the immense solitude that accompanied me. (p. 65)[31]

The same flight of birds becomes a metaphor for knowledge and political awareness in the Los Cumbes' script where "united like a concert of angry eagles, we will achieve our defense."

3. *Prehistory:* The lengthy passage in the play that situates the source of knowledge in prehistory, in particular in archaeological remains, and identifies the sun as a mouthpiece of this knowledge, is also reminiscent of Lame's writings. *Los pensamientos* states that humanity learned its crafts—goldwork and stone carving—from the sun; it also makes reference to the Chibcha god, Bochica (p. 24). For Lame, history is encoded in the remains of this glorious past:

> Now I ask you, why has the anger of the centuries or of the ages not been able to destroy or erase up to today those legends that mark the Cemeteries of our prehistory; Cemeteries that are found, some in the bowels of the earth and others form the bed of extensive lakes of waters, and others are the deposits of the great riches of my Sovereign ancestors, who dominated multitudes. And that [in] this court of Sovereign Indians many were not the sons of woman, like a "Sinviora," founder of the temples of the sun Divinity and who also taught the Indians how they should adore the sun. (p. 76)[32]

All three themes—the cataclysm of 1492, the messianic future, and the roots of knowledge in the aboriginal past—are interpreted pragmatically, articulated in metaphoric language and in potent images that entreat indigenous theatergoers to, in Connerton's words, represent their past within their present conditions. The playwright appeals to the audience's memory of Lame's words as a stimulus for recalling the demands of the Cumbales' own movement.

It is indeed significant that native Nariñense theater draws upon a printed source for its nationalist verbal images, for the written word has served as a vehicle for communication with the dominant society since the colonial period. In effect, written language is one of the points of intersection between Colombian Indians and the national society, one of the interpretive spaces in which we can begin to comprehend how these communities are, in fact, Colombian. Colombian law, which is itself encoded in written form, requires that resguardos supply documentary evidence of their existence in order to maintain their character as autonomous political and territorial units. Writing thus forces Colombian Indians to consult the past in order to justify the present.

Nevertheless, in the past two decades, written language has also become a vehicle for communication among Indians themselves. The leadership of Nariñense resguardos reads and contributes to the national Indian newspaper, *Unidad Indígena,* and cabildos routinely produce pamphlets and leaflets in the course of their struggle. As Benedict Anderson (1983) has suggested in his analysis of nationalism, the printed word generates the sensation of an "imagined community." Among Colombian Indians the printed word fuels an awareness of a broader indigenous community that exists beyond the confines of the locality, a community even broader than the unity created by regional Indian organizations. Cumbal playwrights invoke the existence of this imagined community by drawing upon Lame's published works for the formulaic utterances they recite in their plays.

Playwrights and Memoristas

If the purpose of militant drama is to expand the space of historical interpretation so that it includes sectors heretofore excluded from the analysis of the past, it is only partially successful. Theatrical expression may serve as a vehicle for the reconstitution of a sense of community on the artistic plane. Communal activity helps to make personal reminiscences and memoristas' histories publicly meaningful. In theater, historical mnemonics permit the collectivity to relive past experience and, thus, to reappropriate it for use in the present (Shopes 1986). In this respect, militant theater represents a democratization of historical expression. This new approach to historical interpretation, furthermore, is successful inasmuch as it recasts in secular form the religious spectacle of the past that once provided people with a sense of universal history. But when we consider militant theater against the backdrop of memorista history, it is considerably less successful in its objectives. In comparison to the narratives of the memoristas, which themselves incorporate only a few historical referents, these plays display a conspicuous poverty of historical detail. The young actors seem to have neglected their homework, for they display little knowledge of the contents of pertinent documentation or the experiences recounted by memoristas.

The space of dramatic presentation might be better understood, however, as an opportunity for young people to learn *how to remember* history as opposed to *what should be recalled*. Like memoristas, militant dramatists insert historical referents into a framework describing experiences of the present or the recent past. While memoristas weave this background with threads originating in narratives of recent experience—foodways, agricultural practices, the Camino de Barbacoas, the sufferings of the men who extract ice from Mount Cumbal, cabildo ritual—actors evoke the quotidian and the recent through their portrayal of costume. The names of the caciques of the titles are thus projected against a contemporary and experiential backdrop. Likewise, quotations from Lame are selected out as familiar images and are deployed in a visual field built upon turn-of-the-century clothing.

Notwithstanding the amateurish historical analysis of the playwrights in comparison to that of the traditional historians, it is precisely by emphasizing recent experience to the detriment of historical explanation that militant actors constitute themselves as a new brand of memoristas. If their dramatic training leaves them with little in the way of historical data, it introduces them to the craft of the community historian, whom they learn to emulate. In time, some of the best of this youthful group will take up the mantle of the cabildo, acquire a greater fluidity in interpreting the past, and eventually become memoristas in their own right. How they articulate their historical knowledge in the future—whether through oral narrative, newspaper articles, political rhetoric, song, or some other medium—will become evident in future years.

Conclusion

T HE FIRST FEW WEEKS OF 1987 inaugurated a year of conflict in Cumbal. A new cabildo, just elected in December, took part in the ceremonies and celebrations accompanying its transition to power. Oaths of office were taken at the office of the mestizo municipal mayor, where the 1986 cabildo relinquished its staffs of office to the 1987 authorities. The formal ceremony was followed by festivities at the homes of the eight outgoing and eight incoming cabildantes. The first Sunday of January, the new governor opened a meeting of his new administration with fiery pro-recuperación rhetoric and refreshments served all around. His supporters anxiously awaited transfer of the archives, when each regidor would receive his vereda's inventory of documentation prepared by his predecessor and would undertake the laborious task of comparing the painfully written list with the huge stack of usufruct documents stored in the archive cupboard.

But events did not move so smoothly. The outgoing cabildo from Cuaical and the incoming one from Quilismal had been locked in an ongoing controversy during the past year. José Elipcio Chirán, governor in 1986, was reluctant to hand the reins of government over to Alonso Valenzuela. His reasons were numerous. Chirán could not stomach the way Valenzuela manipulated his connections to a Liberal party politician in order to marshall resources already earmarked for the resguardo. Furthermore, Chirán could not abide by Valenzuela's methods: when he was governor in 1981 and in 1985, the years the cabildo received the repossessed haciendas El Laurel and La Boyera, Valenzuela was accused of taking more than his fair share of land for himself and his associates. Chirán, however, was as guilty of some of these offenses as Valenzuela. As an active member of the pro-Arellano faction of the local Liberal party, he was equally at fault for introducing partisan politics into cabildo process, and while he was indeed more scrupulous than Valenzuela in the distribution of repossessed lands, Chirán was known for his wealth in an otherwise poor community.

Nevertheless, more was at stake than partisan politics and the ethics of land claims. José Elipcio Chirán is the grandson of Lastenia Alpala, great-nephew of former governor Hilarión Alpala, nephew of former president Efraín Chirán, and cousin, son-in-law, brother-in-law, or compadre of a host of other former cabildantes. His president, Salomón Cuaical, son of don Benjamín, also hails from a long line of cabildantes. In contrast, Alonso Valenzuela is the first of the "Chulde" wing of the Valenzuela family to occupy the governorship. Gilberto Valenzuela, his uncle and another "Chulde," was elected president. In bygone days, the Valenzuelas not only were locked out of positions of authority but were accused of opposition to the cabildo. The bitter dispute I observed in 1986–87 is undoubtedly rooted in the centuries-old hold on power that Chirán's family enjoyed, a hold now threatened by the new-found attractiveness of cabildo office that accompanied recuperación politics.

The rivalry swiftly came to a head when Chirán and the 1986 cabildo breached custom by refusing to turn the archives over to the new authorities. Some of Valenzuela's younger and more hot headed supporters broke into the cabildo office, prompting bitter criticism on the part of many of the older spectators. Some days later, a rumor crept from house to house in Cuaical: Valenzuela's men had stolen the cabildo archives. The scandalous allegation was never borne out, however. Within days, the intact archives were handed over to the cabildo of 1987, and the political year commenced.[1]

My anecdote condenses the dominant themes of this book: the construction of ethnic identity, the ethnography of literacy, and the use of historical methodology in anthropology, for it is through a memorista reading of the archives—by José Elipcio Chirán's family and associates—that a contemporary Cumbal ethnic identity, whose contours are determined by the cultural stereotypes and the legal precepts of the dominant Colombian society, is shaped and maintained. How, precisely, this occurs is at the center of anthropological debate, but is conspicuously absent from the work of many Andeanists, in large part because of their reliance upon the oral domain and the priority they place upon the study of isolated, traditional Andean communities.

The Construction of Ethnic Identity

The vast majority of Colombian Indians confront pervasive stereotypes of the dominant society in their efforts to defend their ethnic distinctiveness. Highland populations, many of them, like Cumbal, composed of monolingual Spanish speakers, have been integrated for centuries into regional and national markets as peasant producers or as proletarians. Since the colonial period they have actively inserted themselves in national political life as litigants, most recently as ethnic militants. Their recent successes are notable: international support for land claims; widely publicized participation in the writing of the new constitution; two voting seats in the Senate. Equal space was given in the most recent official compilation of Indian legislation to distinct legal codes newly drafted by indigenous organizations of Nariño, Cauca, and other highland regions (Colombia 1990, 798–829). Yet in the popular imagination—and, I suspect, behind closed doors in government offices—highland militants are perceived as being "less authentic" and "less Indian" as they become increasingly more adept at asserting their rights through the use of legislation and the mass media (Gros 1991; see Zúñiga Eraso 1986, n.d.). That is to say, as Colombian Indians reformulate their image of themselves in a struggle to maintain their ethnic distinctiveness in late twentieth-century Colombia, their historical role as forgers of their own destiny is denied them by the very dominant society that obliged them to follow the path of cultural invention in the first place.

Anthropologists are increasingly studying cultural invention, once viewed as inauthentic and spurious (Hobsbawm and Ranger 1983), as a dynamic and continuous process that must be interpreted in its historical and social contexts. Whether we take as our focus the creation of an official culture to satisfy the nationalistic aspirations of Euroamericans (Handler 1988), the invention by members of the dominant culture in a third world country of an image of subordinated ethnic groups (Flores Galindo 1988; Poole 1992), the interpretation of tradition by fourth-world intellectuals in advanced capitalist societies (Clifford 1988; Hanson 1989; Landsman and Ciborski 1992), or the codification of that tradition by indigenous people resisting colonialism (Bowen 1989; Keesing 1982), cultural invention takes place across cultural boundaries, within particular cultural contexts, and at precise historical junctures.

How, and on what basis, an identity or a culture is created at any particular point in time—the study of the specificity of invention—is the task of the anthropologist. Nicholas Thomas underscores the distinctive, almost iconic, nature of what he calls "cultural imagining":

> The community that is imagined is not simply conceived of in its empirical complexity; its distinctiveness is understood, rather, through particular resonant practices and characteristics. In a dialectical process, the group and the particular practices are redefined as they come to connote each other. (1992, 215)

Certain historical junctures, which Raymond Fogelson (1989) calls "epitomizing events," are of particular significance for the creators of new cultural images. These junctures are not historical occurrences that actually took place in the past; rather, they are the dramatization in imaginary events of processes that unfolded over the long haul.

In Cumbal, the clearest example of an epitomizing event is the bestowal of resguardo title by Mauricio Muñóz de Ayala, bearer of the Royal Crown, upon the colonial caciques who knelt on the plain in the company of their counterparts from neighboring communities. This image, drawn from eighteenth-century titles that repeatedly record such ceremonies in the course of the decades-long dispute that finally granted title to Cumbal's hereditary chiefs, resonates in the everyday practices of the cabildo. Bearing its staffs of office decorated with rings called crowns, which are implanted vertically in the soil, the resguardo council routinely grants usufruct rights through an almost identical ceremony. The portrait of a chiefly possession ceremony, reproduced today in oral accounts, in written narrative history, and in theater, is reinforced through readings of nineteenth-century court transcripts, in whose pages Indians are denied their rights to land through disruption of such rituals. The image is amplified in oral narratives that attribute the loss of these disputes to the presence of hitching posts, which replace implanted staffs of office, legitimizing mestizo claims to the land.

Vicente Rafael, in a reference to *Noli me tangere*, the 1886 novel by Filipino nationalist José Rizal, compares Tagalog listeners "fishing out" references from a sermon by a Spanish priest to the broader subaltern strategy of decontextualizing representations by colonial authorities:

> The laughter in this scene, as in similar passages in the novel, arises as we witness the congregation skid from word to word without connecting what they hear to the priest's actual message. Instead, they "fish out" discrete words from the stream of the sermon, arbitrarily attaching them to their imaginings. Curiously enough, the drift away from the content of the sermon only pulls them back with "redoubled attention" to Fa-

ther Damaso's speech. It appears that the natives are compelled to submit to the priest's authority despite, indeed because of, the fact that his sermon is *almost* incomprehensible. (1988, 2)

Listening-as-fishing is mirrored, suggests Rafael, in the Tagalog appreciation of writing for "the play of voices (rather than the emergence of *a* voice) to which it gave rise, thereby making of reading a process akin to guessing" (ibid., 54).

This is an apt image for comprehending how the Cumbales read colonial documents: their contents are decontextualized from their colonial legal setting and subsequently recontextualized within the more familiar surroundings of everyday life. Colonial referents are recast, moreover, within the framework of the oral narrative of the memorista, in which personal reminiscences are juxtaposed with colonial epitomizing events. This is not so much Rafael's arbitrary "reading-as-fishing" as it is Indians' calculated reframing of legal discourse in their own narrative idiom. Their thought processes can be traced, in part, through the perusal of community archives, where marginal notes highlighting pertinent terms in typescript copies of colonial titles are reproduced in first drafts of letters to government authorities, as was the case in the letter the 1950 cabildo sent to the Ministry of Mines.

The Cumbales' choice of the legal channel as primary source material for the generation of self-representations brings to mind the related question of who defines and authorizes a particular form of discourse (Feierman 1990, 31). By concentrating upon historically situated peasant intellectuals as the producers of discourse and practice, Steven Feierman succeeds in answering this question for the Shambaa area of Tanzania, without losing sight of the relations that envelop peasants within historical processes of the broader society (see Rappaport 1990b).

In Cumbal as well, local intellectuals called memoristas produce a politicized ethnic discourse. They draw upon the legal record because, in order to reclaim aboriginal lands, they must speak the dominant society's language of jurisprudence. Yet, while in the last instance we might say that the relative weight and power of the Colombian establishment decides whose discourse is to be authoritative, the effective transformation of legal language by local intellectuals redefines their relationship to the dominant society. This is patent in the broader national society's acceptance of indigenous self-representation in their law books and legislative bodies. On the local level, it is clear in the state's recognition of indigenous claims achieved through militant action, such as the occupation of haciendas.

As in Feierman's Tanzanian example, the study of the indigenous invention of culture in highland Colombia must take into account the changing contexts and the pressures brought to bear on local intellectuals. In the late nineteenth century and in the 1930s, heavy-handed government authorities persuaded certain sectors of indigenous communities to use the law as a basis for rejecting their ethnic identity and choosing the road of deindianization. Other actors, such as the cabildo of Cumbal, instead chose to embrace legal language as a means toward cementing their identity through litigation. In the 1970s, indigenous appropriation of the strategies of the broader peasant movement transformed the channels through which legal discourse was transmitted. With the advent of the Indian movement, the narratives of the memoristas fueled more radical and infinitely more successful attempts at repossessing lands.

The choice of which genre will provide a vehicle for ethnic discourse is also determined by the historical and the social position of the local intellectual. While contemporary cabildantes, building upon on close readings of law and of the titles, define their ethnicity through political rhetoric and the formulation of policy, younger people redefine the contours of their identity through dramatic presentations that draw upon the dominant society's cultural definitions of Indianness, which they have culled from the print and visual media.

The Ethnography of Literacy

An examination of the role of law in the elaboration of ethnic discourse in Cumbal presupposes that close attention will also be paid to indigenous literacy. I am not concerned here with the general implications of literacy and its constitution as a category in opposition to orality, a discussion that has little bearing on the questions at hand (Finnegan 1988; Goody 1977; Halverson 1992; Ong 1982; Street 1984). Instead, I have turned my attention toward how contending parties to a long standing dispute use the written record; in order to grasp how a subordinated ethnic group redefines the literate canons of a distant historical period and of an alien society in a contemporary legal idiom (see Appadurai 1981).

Such an orientation to the place of the written word in a community whose daily life transpires in the oral sphere demands an examination of how a series of discursive systems overlap and interpenetrate one another across a broad spectrum of genres. Cumbal's relationship to literacy involves considerably more than the transformation of speech into writing and writing into speech, although the conscious manipulation of the two channels is unquestionably a central concern of my analysis (see Stock 1990).

In contrast, an appreciation of the ethnography of writing in Cumbal must take into account a series of overlapping forms of literate communication, ranging in genre from the legal brief to the personal diary, varying in time from the eighteenth century to the present, differing in author from the colonial Spanish scribe to the contemporary ethnic militant and his or her mestizo adversary. As each example of literate exchange is read a second or third time, its contents reinterpreted in light of the contemporary concerns of the reader, it is reevaluated outside of the written channel, adding to the existing body of oral narrative or redefining people's attitudes toward material culture. And in turn, the memories inscribed in tangible things and those that the memoristas embellish with their own personal reminiscences reverberate in later readings of the same written texts as well as in the preparation of alternative literate tracts, such as contemporary history pamphlets or the scripts of plays. The resguardo titles have been read and reread on numerous occasions, by different historical actors, to the point that the memory of their contents has little in common with the information they actually record.

This process of reformulation of testimony occurs both within and across cultures participating in a legal dialogue. As Alessandro Portelli has eloquently demonstrated in his analysis of the conditions under which a written transcript was produced of the 1981 trial of presumed members of the Red Brigades charged with the 1978 murder of Italian Christian Democrat Aldo Moro, the formal legal discourse into which oral testimony is translated inexorably alters its meaning:

> The degree of interpretation is much higher than in normal transcripts, and the complexity of experience is tendentially reduced to discrete legal categories in forms that, at times, actually anticipate the verdict. (1991, 251)

The power to assign new meanings to particular oral accounts by reinterpreting them in the written legal record turns testimony into truth as, for example, when oral lists are transformed into writing by the prosecutor:

> By assimilating the list typographically to a written document it makes it easier to perceive the testimony as fact rather than words. Cognitive manipulation is achieved with no factual manipulation. (Ibid.)

And this legal truth becomes historical truth when the records supply evidence for historians bent upon reconstructing the trial (ibid., 269).[2]

The fixity of the written "truth," however, was highly debatable in the trial of the Red Brigades, where tens of thousands of pages of transcript inhibited judges, jury, and the defense from making use of their contents. The interrogation of witnesses ultimately involved the oral confirmation of an unwieldy and unreadable written record (ibid., 264–65).

Such is also the fate of the numerous legal papers that the Cumbales employ in the construction of their ethnic discourse. Much of the thousand-odd-page Royal Provision, which records colonial-era chiefly testimony, was translated from Pasto to Spanish and reformulated in eighteenth-century European legal language; it thus no longer transmits a colonial Pasto observer's image of events. The mass of papers produced in the mid-nineteenth-century dispute between the cabildo and mestizo strongman Segundo Sánchez over the hacienda El Zapatero similarly proved indigestible for twentieth-century readers, who reinterpreted its contents through the epitomizing events of the bull and hitching post. Under such circumstances, it becomes difficult to defend the fixity of written over oral communication.

More fixity accrues to the legal form in which these thousands of pages of written testimony are cast. Transported across cultures and time, modes of registering legal evidence in turn influence other genres of written and oral expression.[3] It is not accidental that the legal format, which permeates a vast range of Latin American literary genres, is also the principal vehicle for historical expression in Cumbal. In the indigenous community, where the legal document has served as the primary means of communication with the dominant society, the legal format influences both written and oral narrative. Yet, while contemporary indigenous appeals to the archive mirror the literature of the dominant society in their persistent fascination with legal writing, they are also colored by distinctly local forms of discourse. In addition to the weight carried by the personal reminiscences of memoristas, historical evidence is also processed through the filter of the six-section hierarchy, which restructures events in time in accord with the arrangement of points in space.[4] Furthermore, contemporary historical discourse in Cumbal is highly dependent upon the language of pan-Indian militancy, in which appeals to documentary history employ the terminologies of ethnographic description and of the human rights community.

Methods for an Ethnography of History

In a narrative mosaic of oral testimonies of the social and political tumult of 1968, her own personal reminiscences, and reflections upon her life today, Italian historian Luisa Passerini contemplates the essential paradox of popular memory:

> Memory narrates in the vivid tones of lived experience. But what interests me is not the vivacity of its inferences, nor its loyalty to reality. . . . Instead I am attracted by memory's claim to make a history of itself, which is much less and perhaps something more, than social history.
> The enterprise is difficult because it at once encounters a paradox. . . . To make itself into history, this subjectivity must assert itself as antihistorical. It must annul itself, distance itself, destroy. (1988, 39; translation mine)

The same paradox must be faced in the study of politically inspired history-making in Cumbal. The genres through which indigenous popular memory is expressed are antihistorical insofar as they subvert their very sources, transforming document into image, condensing chronology and converting time into space, altering actuality so that it becomes possibility, resituating the present so that it appears as the past. Contemporary readings of Deed 228 present a case in point.

A record of the ambiguous actions of mid-eighteenth-century political actors, Deed 228 is, I have argued, a legal justification of land loss, athough it officially recognizes communal indigenous possession of Gran Cumbal. In the twentieth-century cabildo letter to the Ministry of Mines, however, Deed 228 becomes a sacred text recognizing indigenous sovereignty. Its contents are altered as multiple historical referents from the texts of other time periods are assembled within the conceptual space occupied by the title. Spanish official Mauricio Muñóz de Ayala's tracing of resguardo boundaries is juxtaposed with contemporary personal reminiscences of the extraction of ice and sulphur from Mount Cumbal and with the memory of independence hero Simón Bolívar. Colonial, republican, and modern referents are, moreover, interpreted through the vehicle of the modern possession ceremony, whereby usufruct is transferred from cabildo to smallholder. In other words, plucked from—or fished out of—their original narrative context, historical referents and legal documents become icons.

If secondhand accounts so radically alter the contents of Deed 228, subsequent interpretations in other genres depart even further from the original. When the contents of Deed 228 are rendered in dramatic dialogue, for example, the title is cast in the metaphor of a jaguar's paw, with 228 claws corresponding to the notarial reference under which the title was catalogued in 1908. Although such an image has little to do with events that transpired in the distant colonial era, it is helpful for locating the document in the archives. The confrontation of Spanish and indigenous authorities exemplified by the document is rewritten in dramatic action so that the Indians win. The result is a good deal more inspirational than a conquest play would be for a land-claims movement. And Deed 228 is invoked in song through a series of highly compact images: cacique Cumbe and the Royal Crown, a gloss for the title itself as well as for staffs of office and the repossessed lands of the Llano de Piedras. Some of these image are derived only partially from the written record: the central figure of cacique Cumbe does not appear in the title, and caciques also may be modeled after museum posters or may conform to the dominant Colombian stereotypes of how Indians should look.

If the Cumbal memory is *antihistorical*, it is by no means *ahistorical*. While it rejects any loyalty to the past as documented, it is meaningful only as long as it acknowledges the power of history. It is only by tracing contemporary Indians' relationship to their forebears that the cabildo can justify its struggle for land; in keeping with Colombian law, this is only possible through the collection of historical documentation. The paradox of memory presents a challenge for description and analysis: how do we present the antihistorical character of memory without portraying it as ahistorical? I close this book with some reflections on this issue.

In this book I have tried to move between the Cumbal construction of the past and the documentary record as a means of identifying both the historical circumstances in which memoristas have practiced their craft and the extent to which they are loyal to the written evidence they cite. This has meant a thorough investigation into the holdings of community archives as well as the examination of documentary repositories in Colombia and in Ecuador, where I was fortunate to find the very briefs upon which memoristas have depended for their data. It was thus possible to compare written texts with oral reminiscences in a variety of circumstances.

Written sources, nonetheless, cannot be digested as monoliths. The long life of each document, the multiple readings it has been given over the centuries and the countless uses to which it has been put, the continuous reinterpretation of written evidence against the backdrop of the oral memory, are all testimony to the multilayered, pliable, and ambiguous nature of the documentary record.

I have presented Cumbal's history as it arises in the course of the analysis instead of grounding the entire study in a historical framework. This has allowed me to place Cumbal popular memory, and not my own reworking of documentary sources, at center stage. Similarly,

I have chosen to organize the book by genre, inserting historical references at those points at which they are pertinent.[5] Thus, for example, citations from colonial-era chiefly genealogies, nineteenth-century observations on the antiquity of the six-section system, and contemporary personal reminiscences of Chiles' Good Friday procession complement rather than detract from Cumbal modes of presenting the past. Image, texture, and temporal juxtaposition are neither obscured nor rendered ahistorical by their subordination to chronology.

Cumbal memoristas move within a wide spectrum of interpretive genres. Although oral narrative contains a wealth of significant historical information in itself, I have harnessed it to examine other forms of representing the past. Some of these, such as song and theater, are a common feature of ethnography. Others, such as the encoding of historical referents in topographic space or costume, have been studied widely by anthropologists. Yet others, for instance, the preparation of legal briefs and political pamphlets, are treated more infrequently in the literature (see de Certeau 1986). It is my contention that all of these genres—and not only those of narrative or ritual—must be explored simultaneously as intertexts that constantly impinge upon one another (see Comaroff and Comaroff 1992, ch. 6).

What is needed, then, is an ethnography of history in which orality is not privileged over written communication (Boyarin 1989, 1992; see Clifford 1988; Tyler 1986, 1987), even among those who are not generally characterized as participants in the world of literary production. Indeed the Cumbales or any other Latin American indigenous group can only be construed as completely oral if we disregard their historical relationship to the nation-state to which they belong.

Yet how we combine written and oral sources is not quite so simple. In the words of John and Jean Comaroff (1992, 34), we must "construct our own archive," consisting of both the orthodox evidence approved by "guardians of memory" and sources closer to the everyday lives of people. The archive should include more than those forms of historical or anthropological evidence traditionally employed by the two disciplines.[6] Moreover, it must transcend the barriers imposed by the guardians of memory in the subaltern community as well as in the dominant society.

An effective ethnography of history, however, must be much more than that. It cannot just reconstruct an anthropologically informed historical narrative using a combination of orthodox and unorthodox sources produced by both the powerful and the powerless. As Greg Dening writes, histories must be treated as "collapsed time," the continuous reinterpretation over time of many texts (1988, 11). Our job is to excavate the manifold meanings attached to these multiple and multiform texts, to create what Dening fittingly compares to a "memory palace" (ibid., 100), in which the complex process of making history, as opposed to its final product, is our goal.

Notes

Introduction

1. My use of the word "community" is actually a gloss for the Colombian legal term *parcialidad indígena*, or indigenous community.

2. Little is known about the Pasto language. A vocabulary or grammar of Pasto has not yet turned up in the documentary record. Pre-Columbian Pasto sociopolitical and economic organization has been studied by a number of scholars, including Landázuri (1990), Rappaport (1988), Salomon (1986), Uribe (1977–78, 1985–86), and Uribe and Cabrera (1988). The fate of the Pasto under Spanish domination has been studied by Calero (1987, 1991) and by Moreno Ruíz (1970).

3. Andeanists are currently criticizing such static and simplistic notions of Andean culture. See, for example, Urton (1990) on the colonial construction of the Inca origin myth; Flores Galindo (1988) on historically sensitive alternatives to monolithic conceptions of what is Andean; Poole (1992) on modernist redefinitions of Andean culture through photography; Nash (1979) and Seligmann (1989), whose ethnographies of miners and market women take us to the margins of the indigenous world, blurring cultural boundaries. Colombianists Dover, Seibold, and McDowell (1992), Findji and Rojas (1985), Langebaek (1992), McDowell (1989), and Rappaport (1990b), and Ecuadorianists Guerrero (1991), Harrison (1989), Ramón Valarezo (1987), Salomon (1986), and Weismantel (1988), among many others, have opened new northern vistas for Andean research.

4. Notaría Primera de Pasto [NP/P], 1908 [1758], "Expediente sobre los linderos del Resguardo del Gran Cumbal," Escritura 228 de 1908.

5. El 12 de octubre de de 1981 entramos a Boyera. Si el 12 de octubre vino el invasor, el 12 de octubre de 1981 el Gran Cumbal se puso frente a esta invasión. El 1 de julio de 1987 entramos en batalla, como lo hizo el 20 de julio

Simón Bolívar en la Batalla de Boyacá. Pudimos todos los colombianos decir que estábamos fuera de los españoles. Pero ese 20 de julio de 1987, le vamos a decir a Colombia que volveremos a decirles a los terratenientes, frente a la agresión de los terratenientes, el Gran Cumbal responde, "¡Fuera los terratenientes!"

The words of oral narrators are distinguished from other quotations by ragged right-hand margins and by brief paragraphs that many times begin with discourse markers such as "entonces" (translated as "then"). I am not attempting to capture the intricacies of ethnopoetics in the way that Basso (1985) or Tedlock (1983) have suggested; such a detailed rendering of orality in writing is not relevant to the arguments I am making in this book. Instead, I have chosen a compromise solution, adapted from Salomon and Urioste's translation of the Huarochirí manuscript (Salomon and Urioste 1991, 34–35) and based upon my own memory of the speech patterns of the narrators.

6. There is, of course, more to this metaphor than meets the eye. If Alonso Valenzuela was anxious to disassociate himself from Arellano's political faction, he did not plan a break with the Liberal Party. At the time, he was the local leader of a different political group associated with another of Nariño's Liberal senators.

7. In a study of the recovery of traditional agricultural technologies by indigenous organizations in the Ecuadorian Andes, Bebbington (1992) argues that agricultural innovation serves as a form of cultural maintenance insofar as it provides an alternative to out-migration.

8. Nor is datura, called *guanto* in Cumbal, valued for its hallucinogenic properties. Datura pods used to be sown with potato seed to ensure, through sympathetic magic, a harvest as abundant as the fruit of the guanto tree. My interlocutors assured me that this practice, which they now regard as questionable, bears no relation to the use of guanto as a fumigant.

9. For a discussion of the tradition of walking community boundaries, see Radcliffe (1990). I have no evidence that this ritual was performed by Cumbales in the past, except in those instances in which land was in dispute and the colonial authorities required an *inspección* to determine the boundaries of plots.

10. *M.T.:* Porque de ver la belleza que estaban los agujeros, valía la pena tomar el agua de ahí. Tomaron agua los demás compañeros. (*J.R.:* Entonces, ¿eso no era algo que los mayores les habían dicho, sino que Ustedes mismos decidieron hacerlo?) *M.T.:* Nosotros mismos decidimos hacerlo así, eso es.

See also Archivo del Comité de Solidaridad con las Luchas Indígenas, Pasto [ACSLI/P], 1982, "Informe del Primer Recorrido en Reconocimiento de los Linderos del Gran Cumbal," 3–5.

11. *M.T.:* Llevamos la escritura allí, la llevábamos, y mirando la escritura, de acuerdo a la escritura, íbamos viendo el punto, y mirábamos la escritura y vimos el punto donde era. Por lo menos, de ahí al otro día fuimos al Cerro de Doña Juana, que dice—hoy le han puesto otro nombre, que Doña Luisa—pero en todo caso, en la escritura así cita al cerro. Y tuvimos la oportunidad, casi lo íbamos haciendo eso con hechos. (*J.R.:* ¿Cómo con hechos?) *M.T.:* Con hechos. Que llegamos al punto, no mirábamos de acá no más, sino llegábamos, tu-

vimos la oportunidad de llegar al propio Cerro de Doña Juana. De allí se mira hacia otro lindero que se llamaba el Cerro del Rollo, y el Cerro del Rollo se miraba lejísimo. Estaba buen tiempo, se miraba por la mañana—a eso de las nueve de la mañana, no más, y después se tapa, eso tiene, tiene eso allá en las montañas que se tapa de niebla y no se mira nada. De allí pudimos, fuimos por los linderos: no fuimos por el camino de Miraflores, sino una cuchilla abajo por donde limita la Escritura 228.

12. See, for example, Assembly delegates Orlando Fals Borda and Lorenzo Muelas Hurtado's "Informe-ponencia sobre los pueblos indígenas y grupos étnicos," *Gaceta Constitucional*, 8 April 1992, 2–8.

13. See AICO (1992), among the pamphlets and position papers of the Colombian Indian movement listed in the bibliography, for a summary of the political platform of these senators.

14. Manuel Quintín Lame's influence in Cumbal is considered in further detail in chapter 7.

15. Chapter 1 documents this process in Nariño.

16. CRIC produces its own pamphlet series, which provides insight into the history of the organization (CRIC 1973, 1974), and its own newspaper, once called *Unidad Indígena* and now renamed *Unidad Alvaro Ulcué. Unidad Indígena* has become the periodical of the national Indian movement. See also a history of CRIC by its leadership (CRIC 1981; Morales 1979).

17. The reaction of the cabildo of Cumbal to the domination of the land struggle by indigenous ANUC activists in 1977 and 1978 is documented in an unpublished manuscript by Diomedes Paguay, *De como recuperamos nuestro Llano de Piedras*.

18. AISO's position regarding CRIC is documented in a number of pamphlets (Gobernadores Indígenas en Marcha 1980, 1981, 1985; AISO 1985). The history of AISO is documented by Findji (1992).

19. The southern portion of highland Nariño has not suffered the extreme violence that has characterized the rest of Colombia during the past decade. Most of the violent episodes I have heard of—and the number is considerable, although it does not approach that of other Colombian regions—have not been politically motivated. Nevertheless, conflicts arising from the land struggle have spawned a number of violent interludes, including severe beatings of indigenous militants by police, soldiers, and representatives of landlords, as well as a smaller number of deaths. The murder of Ramiro Muñóz was clearly politically motivated; however, his assassins have never been discovered.

20. Resguardos are granted territorial and political autonomy under articles 329 and 330 (Colombia 1991; 101–2), leaving the Indian movement with the complex task of developing guidelines for culturally distinct modes of delimiting territory and governing themselves.

Chapter One

1. En el principio la gente española en España, en Europa, por allá, fundaron las guerras y por allá vivía la gente estrecha; allá ya no tenían tierra a donde trabajar. Entonces, Cristóbal Colón dijo y pensó, y entre compañeros se

fueron a navegar, y dijeron que se había tierras. Entonces, ellos navegaron seis meses. Entonces, los otros compañeros le iban a matar a Cristóbal Colón, pero ¿a dónde es que lo van a matar, que no hay nada de tierra? Entonces, como ya habían ido cerca, vió a lo lejos, vió una luz aclarar y le aclaró la luz, y entonces vieron que se había tierra. Entonces, bajando en la orilla del mar, bajaron los [sic] tres hojas de papel de la Ley 89 de 1890, y entonces vió y dijeron que se había tierra. Entonces, en Colombia no existía gente blanca. En Colombia era pura gente india.

2. On the nineteenth-century liquidation of resguardos, see Friede (1972). Bergquist (1986) has written extensively on governmental transformations of the 1880s and their influence on economic policy. See Bonilla (1979), Jimeno and Triana (1985), and Triana (1980) on shifts in Colombian Indian policy during the same period.

3. Notaría Primera de Pasto [NP/P], 1908 [1758], "Expediente sobre los linderos del Resguardo del Gran Cumbal," Escritura 228 de 1908. A longer but less complete version of Deed 228, the *Real Provisión* or Royal Provision, also serves as a source of history in Cumbal: Notaría Primera de Ipiales [NP/I], 1906 [1712–58], "Expediente sobre los linderos del Resguardo del Gran Cumbal," Escritura 997 de 1906. Both of these eighteenth-century documents were registered with the municipal authorities at the beginning of the twentieth century. See chapters 3 and 5 for contemporary reinterpretations of the colonial titles.

4. Daniel Pécault (1987) suggests that violence, restricted democracy, and the absence of state power at the regional level are essential characteristics of the Colombian political system. The mid-nineteenth-century loss of El Zapatero exemplifies the absence of the state at the local level: municipal authorities ignored Supreme Court decisions and usurped the hacienda from the cabildo by force. The significance of the loss of El Zapatero and native narrators' use of conflicting bodies of national law interpret the history of this struggle are analyzed in chapter 6.

5. For instance, while other Pasto chiefs controlled the activities of long-distance traders called *mindaláes,* who paid their tribute in merchandise as opposed to foodstuffs, no such individuals are listed for Ancuya (Archivo General de Indias, Sevilla [AGI/S], 1558, "Traslado del libro de tassaciones . . . "; AGI/S, 1570–71, "Tassacion de los tributos de los naturales de las ciudades de San Joan de Pasto . . ."). For an analysis of the multiethnic character of Ancuya in the early colonial period, see Salomon (1986).

6. En atención al artículo tercero de la Ley 89 de 1890, por el se ve que se puede formar cabildo en donde se haya establecido parcialidad de indíjenas más como en él espresamente dice que eso se cumplirá siempre que estuviera establecida; más como en este lugar no ha existido ni existe hasta la presente tal parcialidad que usted se refiere en su nota, por consiguiente no pueden practicar ninguna instalación por no ser reconocidos por ninguna autoridad de este Distrito i por lo mismo, este funcionario no puede atender a su exitación que me hace por ser ilegal la posesión en que pretende (Archivo Central del Cauca, Popayán [ACC/P], 1895, "Expedientes relativos al resguardo de Ancuya" n.p.; the following citations in this section are taken from this document).

7. En atención en no haber antes existido parcialidad de indíjenas en este Distrito por no haber constancia en esta oficina, los que se presentaron con el carácter de indíjenas de Ancuya comprobarán el hecho de serlo para ser atendidos conforme a la ley.

8. Respecto a los individuos hoy presentados a este despacho con el carácter de indíjenas de Ancuya, el señor secretario sentará una diligencia en que se individualice cada uno para que designe el lugar en donde ha existido i desde qué fecha tiene conocimiento que ha dejado de haber parcialidad en este Distrito.

9. 10.000 indios vivimos en estas dos provincias, desde Ipiales, Túquerres i Ancuya, que somos perseguidos i inquietados i engastados por los enviciosos de nuestros terrenos de resguardos, que a pretexto de compras i ventas se han llevado la mayor parte de nuestros terrenos de resguardos que el Rey de España nos dejó amparados.

10. Pero todos somos descendientes de nuestros antiguos tributarios de quienes tenemos nuestros títulos que aseguran nuestros terrenos.

11. Similarly, the Pasto resguardos of Túquerres and San Juan and the Quillacinga resguardo of Males were threatened with extinction when their titles could not be located. The archive of the cabildo of Túquerres, in which the resguardo title was preserved, was robbed on three occasions between 1920 and 1935, forcing the cabildo to seek documentation of its existence in distant archives (Archivo de la División de Asuntos Indígenas, Bogotá [ADAI/B], 1939–52, "Expedientes relativos al Resguardo Indígena de Túquerres"). San Juan, created in 1881 when it split from Ipiales, had documentation only of those land disputes registered in the notary of Ipiales in 1906; these were not judged to be admissible for maintaining resguardo status (ADAI/B, 1940–60, "Expedientes relativos al Resguardo de Indígenas de San Juan, Nariño"). The title to Males had been duly deposited in government offices in Pasto in 1935, but it was lost in 1938 when the building in which it was stored was burned during a strike. In 1948, the Ministry of Agriculture declared the title lost, not having found it in the notary offices of Pasto. A marginal note in the documentation of the liquidation of the resguardo indicates, however, that the title lay unlocated in both Ipiales and in the ministry's own archives (ADAI/B, 1937–50, "Expedientes relativos a la extinción del Resguardo Indígenas de Males, Nariño").

12. For the colonial history of the Quillacingas, see Moreno Ruíz (1970) and Calero (1987, 1991). A general economic history of the area in the colonial period is provided by Guerrero (n.d.).

13. On the economic conditions that heralded the liquidation of the resguardos, see Zúñiga (n.d.). The interpretation that follows of the destruction of Quillacinga resguardos is fleshed out in more detail in Rappaport (1990a).

14. On the persuasiveness of government arguments in favor of private property, see the proceedings of the liquidation of Males (ADAI/B, 1937–50). Similar pressures continue to operate in Cumbal, where some of the comuneros of Cuetial (Vereda Nazate) preserve deeds of private property as collateral for obtaining bank loans. On the influence of deindianized Indians over their indigenous neighbors, see documentation from Consacá (ADAI/B, 1939–

50, "Expedientes relativos a la división del Resguardo Indígena de Consacá, Nariño"). Documents from the División de Asuntos Indígenas generally do not include clear page numbers.

15. ADAI/B, 1939–50.

16. Sus miembros gozan de un nivel cultural semejante al del resto de la población campesina del país (ADAI/B, 1948–50, "Expedientes relativos a la división del Resguardo de Chachagüí, Nariño").

17. Linguistic change was thought by some to be key to the creation of a broad layer of mestizos in Indian areas, a goal proposed as a solution to the chronic labor shortage in the Colombian countryside (Uribe Uribe 1907). For the official study of Males, see ADAI/B (1937–50).

18. El número de habitantes de ésta Parcialidad, es de ciento sesenta y ocho personas, gente ésta que toda se halla completamente civilizada, puesto que todos son blancos y medianamente educados (ADAI/B, 1939–50).

19. La Ley 89 de 1890 fue expedida para indígenas incivilizados, casi salvajes, que apenas habían sido reducidos a la vida civilizada, cuando se los consideraba incapaces de administrar por si mismos sus bienes, y cuando los primeros indígenas de una tribu estaban en número reducido, y todo ha cambiado con los sistemas modernos de educación y sus facilidades, un indígena es un verdadero hombre suficientemente educado, capaz de administrar sus bienes por si mismo (ADAI/B, 1937–50).

20. Y por esta razón, no es justo seguir viviendo la vida insipiente de aborigen, aunque esto sólo se entiende ahora por tradición al origen de los pueblos de la América meridional (ADAI/B, 1939–50).

21. Pero, desgraciadamente ahora con el cambio de gobierno, las autoridades de este lugar como Alcalde y Personero Municipal que patrocinan al Cabildo de indígenas a cuya administración dependimos, nos están haciendo una cruda campaña de persecución en nuestras actividades económicas paralizandonos en el trabajo y privandonos de que sea productores de los mencionados viveres, así: tratan de despojarnos de las parcelas a pretexto de que no somos indígenas según la bastarda ambición de los despojadores que se están apoderando de las parcelas que quitan a otros indígenas agricultores, de modo abusivo y arvitrario con todo el fruto del trabajo (ibid.).

22. An interesting example is Deborah Poole's analysis of cattle rustlers in the Peruvian province of Chumbivilcas, where what distinguishes Quechua peasants from local power-holders is not so much culture or ethnic identity (the two groups are culturally and linguistically similar) but the power that inheres to each sector (Poole 1988).

23. All of these people, as well as the townspeople of Cumbal, can be referred to as mestizos, implying a cultural identification with the dominant Colombian society, not membership in a racial group.

24. El, como se había ido al cuartel, y él casi el lenguaje, el propio, ya lo ha perdido. El no declaraba bonito, sino es que decía Juan Bautista Cuaicual, no decía Cuaical.

25. Cuando llegó el papá al cuartel, que entonces ya preguntó por Juan Bautista Cuaicual, que entonces ya el portero ya le comunicó que "Acá lo busca un

hombre, que dizque es de Cumbal, y que vaya Usted." Entonces decían elay—
claro, ¿sería cierto o no?—que entonces que él salió de esta manera, así se fijó
para allá a la puerta y el viejecito que estaba así parado, así dizque vió para
allá, dizque le dijo y, "¿A quién ves hijito? Yo soy tu papá, Juan Ramón Cuaical." "¡Ah! Cuaical, ¿no?" Que dizque dijo, "Vine a ver, a ver si ya nos vamos."
"A ver, pues," es que dijo, ahí se hizo ya el cerrado, "Lo que diga pues, mi
comandante," es que dijo, "Lo que diga, a ver, pues, ya me da el paz y salvo
pues, nos iremos", que ha dicho, pero. Y entonces, "Tú, viejecito, ¿serás mi
papá? Entonces, yo habrá necesidad de hincarme."

26. Que dentraba adentro a la cocina y como así tenemos los cuyes, que
andaban por ahí, por la sala, dizque decía, "Y ese animalito que anda por ahí,
debajo del rincón, diciendo 'Lui, lui,' ¿qué animalito es?" "Esos son los cuyes,
hijito," dizque decía la mamá. Ahora que, "¿Que no te acordás? Esos son los
cuyes." Y la mamá dizque le decía, "Ese es de cojerlo, de pelarlo." "¡Hum!" es
que decía, "A ver, pues, ¡hum! A ver, cójalo uno, a ver, pues, pélalo."

27. In *Being Indian in Hueyapan,* Judith Friedlander (1975) observes that
much of what Indians perceive as marking them as indigenous is actually of
Spanish colonial origin.

Chapter Two

1. In other formerly Pasto communities, such as Muellamués and Panán,
the cabildo is composed of a governor, his alternate (*suplente*), one or several
mayors (*alcaldes*) and constables (*alguaciles*), and a treasurer (*fiscal*). I suspect
that Cumbal's cabildo is organized differently because it is a composite community, created out of the union of a series of colonial-era chiefdoms, a historical process I will outline in the following pages. Narrators tell of the existence
of a parallel *cabildo de obras* or cabildo of good works, organized along the lines
of neighboring councils, which supervised the comuneros' moral standing,
requiring them to attend mass and to marry their lovers, among other things.

2. Muellamués, immediately to the north of Cumbal, is organized into upper and lower moieties, each with a distinct section hierarchy (see Gómez del
Corral 1985).

3. The series of four parcialidades originally began with Cuaical, moving
on to Quilismal, Guan, and Tasmag, while today the rotation commences with
Guan, followed by Tasmag. Remnants of the original section order are still
observable in the terrain: immediately south of Guan is a small piece of land
that still belongs to Quilismal. This suggests that colonial-era Cuaical occupied
the territory that today is Guan, since Cuaical preceded Quilismal in the colonial hierarchy. I have no explanation for this transformation in the section hierarchy, and can only guess that as non-Indians acquired medium-sized plots in
the valley, indigenous families were forced to migrate to higher altitudes, thus
inverting the order.

4. Colonial-period tribute censuses, which provide us with an image of the
organization of these chiefdoms, are found in the Archivo Central del Cauca,
Popayán (ACC/P, 1722–1810, "Numeraciones de la Provincia de los Pastos").

The 1940 document for Ipiales is from the Archivo de la División de Asuntos Indígenas in Bogotá (ADAI/B, 1940–43, "Expedientes relativos al Resguardo Indígena de Ipiales"). Although no direct evidence of the presence of pre-Columbian section hierarchies in the Pasto area exists, we can speculate as to such existence on the basis of ceramic iconography. Tuza bowls, made by the pre-Columbian Pasto, frequently depict a series of individuals, houses, or animals arrayed in a circle around a central motif; sometimes the center takes the form of an eight-pointed star. Both the surrounding representations and the central star might be interpreted as signifying the decentralized but hierarchical unity of the cacicazgo. Tuza iconography is reproduced and analyzed by Francisco (1969) and by Uribe (1977–78); its possible relationship to territorial hierarchies is interpreted by Rappaport (1988).

5. ACC/P, 1722–1810. Colombian and Ecuadorian archives contain countless documents providing information on land loss among the Pastos. The longer version of Cumbal's title, called the *Real Provisión* or Royal Provision, is an excellent source for the study of the relationship among land loss, forced migration, and the constitution of the modern section system (Notaría Primera de Ipiales [NP/I], 1906 [1712–58], "Expediente sobre los linderos del resguardo del Gran Cumbal").

6. Los que inscribimos vesinos de la parcialidad "Tasmag," ante Usted atentamente desimos: que es evidente que todos los terrenos comunales de este distrito forman un sólo cuerpo, i este terreno va distribuyendose a todo individuo que no tenga en donde mantenerse; pero hay que advertir, Señor Alcalde, que toda esta porción de terreno está dividida en pequeñas secciones, con la denominación de "parcialidades," i cada una de ellas está demarcada con sus respetivos linderos, i representada por un Rejidor, i este para su dominio doméstico i para observar sus costumbres antiguas, necesita conocer los linderos de cada parcialidad (NP/I, 1892 [1873], "Balerio Cuaycal, regidor de la parcialidad de Tasmag . . . ," f. 465r).

7. Llegado las doce del día pues, ya compadecía toda la comunidad, ya sus veredas y demás. Entonces, era allí en el convento: allá iba el alcalde con el secretario, allá formaba el acta para el nombramiento del cabildo. Entonces, allá se seguía, ya los regidores, ya los que pone la comunidad, por fulano, por fulano. Entonces, ya seguían ya por Guan, por fulano de tal, iban pasando ahí por delante del cura, del alcalde, ya diciendo, "Otro por fulano de tal." Y en eso, él que ya salía con mayor número de votos, ese ya quedaba fijo. Y así hasta la hora de llegar a gobernador. Cuando ya llegaba al gobernador, decían fulano de tal, entonces gritaba toda la comunidad.

Don Benjamín is describing cabildo elections before the advent of the land struggle, at which time the office of governor became contested ground and the winner was decided by ballot instead of by voice vote. The outgoing cabildo has always named a slate of candidates, to be opposed by a second slate of independent candidates called the "community" slate, as don Benjamín recounts.

8. Sí, pero, todos van guacho, guacho, por supuesto en minga, pues. Entonces unos ya los dejan. Entonces a lo que, si ya acaban por allá, ya el canto,

entonces ya los peones se sabían salir. Decían, "Me voy a descansar." Decian, "Yo ya acabé. Tiene que traerme el patrón, entonces la volteada para yo regresar," decían, "a sacar a los más quedados."

9. Urton (1984) documents the same form of territorial division of communal work in a Peruvian Quechua community, focusing on the agricultural labor of individual families as well as on mingas called to sweep the town plaza. He notes that the determination of work spaces at mingas is highly contextual, shifting from one occasion to another and determined through the use of sight lines.

10. Lists of governors for the late seventeenth and early eighteenth centuries are found in ACC/P, 1671–1747, "Cartas cuentas de la Provincia de los Pastos." Information regarding chiefly succession and parcialidad membership is recorded in the Real Provisión (NP/I, 1906 [1712–58]). See also analysis by Rappaport (1988). Rotational systems are also documented for the colonial Maya (Farriss 1987) and the Nahua (Lockhart 1985).

11. Those who oppose land claims come from a variety of backgrounds. Some are wealthy peasants who fear the cabildo will distribute their lands to the land-poor. Others are landless laborers attached to haciendas or employed by the municipal authorities. Here, as in many cases, the most dispossessed are the most conservative. But, for the most part, I discovered that those labeled *contrarios* were nothing of the sort. Most had simply opted out of participation in the land-claims movement for various reasons: because they had enough land and little time to dedicate to communal activity; because they were in dispute with the current cabildo for any one of a variety of reasons unrelated to land claims; or simply because they were poor, old, or infirm, and did not have the money needed to sign up as participants in land-claims actions. Even those who support the cabildo's strategy are frequently silent when it comes to criticizing the communal authorities. Although women have virtually no voice in the contemporary cabildo, in the colonial period there were some *cacicas* or female caciques in Pasto communities. Nevertheless, it is unclear whether these women wielded political power or were simply cited in the documentation as members of noble families. The best-known cacica of the oral tradition is María Panana of Panán.

12. Archivo del Cabildo Indígena del Gran Cumbal, Nariño [ACIGC/N], 1919–25, "Libro copiador de actas de devociones de la iglesia . . . ," and 1961, "Libros copiadores de devociones. . . . " Cabildo sponsorship of feasts ended in the 1950s, when an adequate number of sponsors could no longer be found. A pro-Indian director of the local Division of Indigenous Affairs also played a central role in halting feast sponsorship, condemning the practice for occasionally leading comuneros to sell their lands to offset the large expenditures that festival sponsorship occasioned. Festival sponsorship in the Aymara community of Jesús de Machaca follows a rotative order (Albó 1972).

13. ACIGC/N, 1919–25.

14. NP/I, 1906 [1712–58].

15. Panán's mythical *cacica* or female cacique was María Panana, who does not appear in the documentary record. Juan Chiles, cacique of Chiles, is cited

in colonial legal papers, but he is also a mythical figure (Mamián 1992, 29). On the mythologizing of historical caciques among the Páez of Cauca, see Rappaport (1985, 1990b).

16. *Diario Oficial,* 5 July 1869.

17. These decrees are also listed in Deed 228, the resguardo title, and are itemized in chapter 5.

18. This is also a common feature of such Chibchan languages as Guambiano and Páez (Jon Landaburu, personal communication).

19. El Rey le confirmó [la Real Provisión] el 25 de enero de 1758, pero *más adelante* había otros títulos . . . por los años de 1746 y de 1630.

20. Cumbal concepts of time are really not so extraordinary once we admit that our own notion of temporal process is itself a cultural construct. Moreover, it is the product of a particular historical period. The notion of human agency in history is relatively recent in European thought. Linear notions of time represented in horizontal space, with humans at the pivot of temporal process, only became important during the Renaissance. In earlier centuries, the cosmos was arranged in a vertical hierarchy and humanity was not perceived as standing at the center of time (Bakhtin 1984, 363–64).

21. Bueno, eso sería por veredas, trayendo pues, el ingeniero. Repartió primeramente, se hizo los lotes por veredas y se hizo caminos, entradas, salidas, ¿no? Para que haiga por donde andar. Y cada vereda se hizo un acta en primer lugar, un acta que cada regidor maneje un acta con los afiliados de cada vereda, ¿no? Y pues, sí se hizo ya el reparto ya, a metros, a lo que les alcanzó. Después ya repartió el cabildo lo que les alcance a cada persona, a metros.

22. The Llano de Piedras was expropriated from the non-Indian townspeople, who were not remunerated for their loss as they had never legally purchased the land. Hacienda owners, in contrast, frequently hold title to their farms, which were illegally usurped from the resguardo so long ago that an adequate paper trail of deeds and contracts could be created. The return of haciendas to the cabildo is administered by INCORA, which purchases the lands from hacendados at well below market rates; title is then transferred to the indigenous community, which does not pay the government anything for the reclaimed territory. Such a policy is relatively recent in Colombia, following on the heels of the agrarian reform of the 1960s. In the 1930s, only a decade after the Llano de Piedras was usurped by the mestizos, the cabildo of Cumbal attempted to reclaim it by holding nocturnal ceremonies granting comuneros usufruct rights in the valley. These rights were short-lived, however, since mestizos always reoccupied the Llano at daybreak. This unsuccessful attempt at reconstituting the resguardo in the Llano de Piedras followed an approach similar to that of recent recuperaciónes in that land distribution was coordinated at the vereda level. Government officials do not always understand the need to divide reclaimed lands into veredas. In fact, when I requested a copy of the map of the Llano de Piedras from the official cartographic agency, I was told that not only was there no existing map dividing the Llano into veredas,

but that it was an impossibility, since two veredas could not carry the same name in a single municipality.

23. NP/I, 1892, "El Cabildo de Cumbal pide la protocolización . . . ," and 1892 [1883], "Protocolización de los títulos. . . ."

24. That this has long been the case is apparent in a series of nineteenth-century deeds illustrating that at that time, the first sections of both Muel-lamués and Cumbal were called Guan (NP/I, 1889b, "Venta del terreno Guan en el distrito de Guachucal . . . ," and 1898, "Escritura de venta de acción y derecho que tiene en los terrenos comunales pertenecientes a la parcialidad de Guan en el distrito de Cumbal . . ."). Mirror images are also a common motif in Tuza iconography, suggesting that contemporary structures of topon-ymy quite possibly have pre-Columbian roots (see Rappaport 1988).

Chapter Three

1. Entonces este señor Braulio Quilismal, entonces era muy tomador. Y por allá por Piedra Ancha [Mallama] y por esos lugares ya pues, habiendo ya la carretera ya del tráfico para Barbacoas, que entonces por allí ponían siempre mucho guarapo, y él por ahí pues, claro, se tomaba sus guarapos, se emborra-chaba, y con esa carga llegaba a Barbacoas cuando ya estaba terminando el mercado. Entonces, claro de vender, vendía. Pero ya vendía perdiendo el pre-cio. Entonces, venía a dar cuenta al patrón. Entonces el patrón le iba anotando no más—don Ramón Revelo—la pérdida que iba sufriendo. Entonces, en tanto viaje y así, don Braulio Quilismal, contaban que se fue alcanzado ya en dinero. Entonces cuando ya no tuvo de donde pagar ese dinero, entonces como aquí tuvo el potrero, que entonces lo entregó esto a don Ramón Revelo y a Dolo-res Revelo.

2. Así contaba en la escritura. Sí, yo la conocí la escritura de esos tiempos. Eso habían vivido por allí, lo habían tenido. Yo la leí la escritura y, hasta el documento de Braulio Quilismal, que le habían dado el cabildo. Había sido hecho por un Valerio Quilismal, había sido secretario en el 1860, y el presidente había sido don Manuel María Alpala en ese tiempo en 1860. Yo, por ahí los habían tenido los papeles. Yo los leí y la escritura también.

3. Esta es una historia muy bonita, de que deja, pues, en qué acordar. Y esto es pues, un ejemplo para los demás, los jovenes que vienen, pues, enseguida, y para que se den cuenta lo que precisamente los mayores han luchado en la recuperación, y ya con pensamiento claro, con ideas, pues, nuevas.

4. On the importance of collecting the history of such mundane topics as price changes, so popular with many narrators, see Salomon (forthcoming). The inclusion of these sorts of subjects in historical discourse is a cultural artifact. We need only look at the relatively recent acceptance of social history in Europe and North America to conclude that the history of everyday life was for a long time undervalued as a topic of historical interpretation in Western academic circles. The canons of academic history also influence the scope of historical interpretation in other social milieux. Passerini (1987, 41) observes,

for example, that the politically committed leftist men in her sample of working-class autobiographies from Turin generally opted for canceling out their individual private lives from their accounts; Cumbal narrators, in contrast, weave their private lives into their histories of the cabildo.

5. Pues, la diferencia de la historia y un cuento, pues, bueno: que un cuento se lo inventa, pues. Casi muchas veces es mentira, ¿no? Yo creo que, claro que alguno que piense le voy a decir un cuento pues, se saca de la cabeza, pues, se la hace una mentira al otro para que se ría un rato, o estar contento con el otro. Pero esta historia es una cosa de que es cierta, y lo que ha pasado con nuestros mayores, y lo que se ha hecho en la recuperación, porque estamos de presentes.

6. Quechua grammar accounts for the difference between information witnessed by the speaker and heresay by the use of suffixes. As occurs in the following quotation from Cumbal, Central Peruvian highland Quechua testimonial modes are intimately connected to topography, which provides a direct evidential connection between past event and present experience (Howard-Malverde 1990).

7. Porque yo pues, también iba para allá, pero yo no vía nada. Decían "La Moledora, la Moledora," pero ¿dónde está la Moledora? Los que ibamos para allá, que por allá es una piedra que está en el monte. Pero yo quiero verla, pues. Nadie, "Hacerse acá, camine, acá está. Yo le amuestro, aquí está." Porque uno hay que ver y creer. Porque de otra manera, mientras no vea, pues, eso es como un cuento.

8. Los mayores conversan una cosa que ha sido verdaderamente cierto, porque si fuera cuento, los cuentos han contado de otro modo y muy prontos se olvidan, pues. Y todo lo que se cree, como cuento no se puede olvidar, entonces se lo considera que es historia. Sí pues. Porque viven contando, viven contando, y uno se pregunta, "¿Y ésto no será cuento?" Entonces dicen, "Esto es una historia que me conversó tal mayor," dicen, y vuelta si el otro mayor vive, dice, "Usted lo conversó tal esto," dice, "Si ese mayor me contó así, que antes fué así."

9. In Andoke, a language spoken in the Colombian tropical lowlands, the social position and knowledge of the speaker determines the genre in which an utterance is classed (Jon Landaburu, personal communication). Genre is similarly important in distinguishing between mythic and other accounts in Quechua (Allen n.d.b; Howard-Malverde 1990) and in Aymara (Arnold and Yapita 1991).

10. In *First-Time*, Richard Price (1983) provides the reader with photographs and brief biographical sketches of the Saramaka historians whose accounts he compiles. This attention to specific individuals contributes to our appreciation of Saramaka intellectuals as creative individuals instead of as anonymous informants (see also R. Price 1990; S. Price 1990).

11. Van a caminar. "Cuando en ese tiempo," decía mi abuelo, "de Tulcán para arriba, de esas estancias, esos páramos, había unos chaparros, ¿no? Y entonces de unos caminos muy estrechos." Entonces claro, ya iban con conocimiento de que los caminos eran así, pero bien, como a pie iban, "Pues, como-

quiera hemos de llegar de Tulcán para arriba," decía, "Ya nos fuimos," decía, "preguntando por donde podemos llegar más breve a Quito." Entonces es que decía, "Por eso," sabía decir mi papá señor, entonces decía el, "yo diré que la gente puenda es," decía, "una gente sana y de caridad."

12. I was never able to record an interview with Hilarión Alpala because he refused to talk with me. However, Helí Valenzuela, whom don Hilarión trusted, was fortunate to be able to tape an interview with him.

13. Bueno, los mayores pues, pongámoslo que haigan tenido—porque mucho más allá, pues, los mayores sí han sabido historia: ahí también, el finado Fernando Taimal, pues, ha sido un historiador buenazo, el finado José Domingo Paguay también, de los mayores de antes. Pero esas historias sería que los hijos las acabaron, o ¿cómo tan harían para vez que nosotros no tener más prelación de nada, pues? Y los que las han conservado, las tienen y saben. Nosotros, como no hemos llegado a tener esas historias, no. . . Sabe lo mismo que dicen la Ley 89, no sé la Ley 89 pues. Ahí en que unos entramos a la mesa del cabildo, a unos nos prestan y a otros no nos prestan. Apenas el gobernador, el presidente, estaba a manos de ellos, y para que uno no se dé cuenta ni salga más adelante, no le prestan. Entonces, uno puede tener más experiencia, pasando—claro, como dicen algunos—dicen, "Pasó Usted por la mesa, sabe la ley." Pero ¿qué vamos a saber de leyes ni historia? Porque no ha llegado a nuestras manos, ni siquiera lo hemos repasado, así tuviéramos memoria para que nos quede.

14. Many people believe that the Cuaical/Quilismal monopoly on historical knowledge has been shattered only recently, with a loosening of the hold these two veredas have on political power in the resguardo. This loosening was brought about in part by the democratization of the land struggle and by the increased influence of the clientelism of Colombian party politics on cabildo political process. It is interesting to note that when I asked people who they thought would comprise the coming generation of historians, I was consistently given the name of three-time governor Alonso Valenzuela from Tasmag. He however was the least interested in history of anyone I met in Cumbal.

15. De repente en una cueva así que estuvo, vió un barro adentro, así hondo, y la rama como choza, es que lo vió sentado un sapo, una rana, una rana sentada ahí. Entonces, ella es que dijo "Y ahora, ese sapo, acá se ha venido a estar. Acá ha venido a estar ese sapo." Lo vía. Entre más lo vía, porque la rana tiene unas puntas negras y unas amarillas, eso, sí. Entonces, las amarillas, es que los vía amarillando, disque lo vía. Vuelta se fijaba más, vuelta en otro rato ya recogía la leña. Lo miraba vuelta, vuelta lo vía más es que brillaba. Entonces de repente es que se fijó bien. "Y ahora," es que dijo, "esas pintas, ¡qué amarillas! Y ahora, ¿por qué será el modo que ha sido ese sapo?" Entonces, es que lo vió con corona. Entonces, ella lo que disque pensó es, "¡Ah!" Es que dijo, "Razón yo he oído decir que los moscos y los animales tienen su rey: los sapos han sabido tener también su rey," disque ha dicho.

16. "Una vez, no me acuerdo con quien, nos fuimos," decía, "a divisar. Un día que no había una nube en el cielo." Y se pusieron a divisar. "Por eso no está lejos," decía mi hermano, "el Pacífico, pues se veía." Pero él decía que vió

así. Después ya había sabido cuando, decía, "nosotros divisamos una porción de cerros pequeños, no más, y todos nevados la punta. Y ahora, ¿dónde será ese poco de cerros? Yo siempre he leído," disque dijo, porque sabía leer, "Pero como no me han contado ni he visto en las historias y en la geografía yo he leído, ¿dónde será ese poco de cerros tan tupidos, como pueblo, así cordillera entera? Pero voy a preguntar." Amigos, los padres en ese tiempo. Disque preguntó a un padre Benjamín Arteaga, se llamaba, yendo a dejar la primicia que se acostumbraba. Disque le dice mi hermano, "Padre, dígnese decirme una pregunta que le voy a hacer. Diga ¿qué lugar es que ha habido un poco de cerros pero tupidísimo?" "Y ¿de dónde vistes?" "De aquí, del cerro de Cumbal, en un día despejado." Ya disque le contó como fué, "Y vimos una isla con cerros todos nevados. Eso es lo que me llama la atención. ¿Dónde es ese lugar?" Y el padre dijo, "Tonto, esos no son cerros: eso es el mar, eso es el Pacífico."

17. Cuando yo todavía estaba en la escuela, yo ya era ya muchacho, ya de unos 14, casi 15 años, fue el último año que estuve en la escuela; yo tuve siete años de escuela, me dió mi padre. Entonces, mi padre tenía un amigo allá en Carlosama, llamaba Manuel Cuaical. Y entonces él había sido cabildante, gobernador. Y entonces, él había ganado un pleito y era como ser, abogadillo. Y entonces, él, como era muy amigo de mi papá; mi papá hasta le sabía alquilar una yunta de bueyes para que vaya a trabajar a Carlosama. Y entonces, viendo que yo así leía, estudiaba, entonces le dice a mi papá, "¿Y por qué no le compra una ley? Yo le vendo," dijo, "una ley. Yo tengo," dijo, "del cabildo," le dijo. "Yo tengo," dijo, "la Constitución Colombiana." Entonces, yo hasta la Constitución estudié. La Constitución hasta la copié. Esa, la Constitución Política de Colombia era, había sido dada en 1886, la primera Constitución y entonces fue reformada en 1910. Entonces, la del '86 hasta yo la copié la Constitución, porque no era mucho largo. Era pequeña no más la Constitución, o sea la madre de las leyes. ¡Elay! Entonces, ese hombre le vendió un cuadernillo de la Ley 89 indígena a mi papá, y entonces, yo estudié esa. Yo por eso, desde ese tiempo sabía la Ley 89, las facultades del cabildo y las tierras, y que ese era la protectora de la raza indígena. De esos modos yo aprendí, supe la Ley 89, y supe lo que era respetar la gente indígena, como dice, para el repartimiento de las tierras.

18. Y venían otros militares. Y también venían para caridades de víveres y ropa y plata de las demás poblaciones que no se habían destruido. Pero todo venía para los blancos.

Don Fernando calls the local townspeople "whites," once again, a reference to cultural identification and not race. Younger Cumbales, however, employ an ironic racial slur when they insist the townspeople are really "mestizo," pointing to their bronze skin color.

19. A.C.: Por eso, mi papacito sabía tener esos papeles que quedan. (J.R.: ¿Papeles de qué?) A.C.: Diciendo las demarcaciones que han sido los primeros títulos de este Cuetial. Sabían ver, o los prestaba que los estudie otras personas que podrían.

20. De como recuperamos nuestro Llano de Piedras (Of How We Repossessed

Our Llano de Piedras) is an undated typescript that has not been circulated in the community.

21. On the influence of reading in nineteenth-century working-class England, see Vincent (1981). Vincent's study of working-class autobiographies led me to ask memoristas for the names of the books they had read or owned. Like other memoristas, don Benjamín's *historia patria* is colored by the "great men" theory of history and the chronological orientation of such books as Henao and Arrubla.

22. El archivo pues, también hacen inventario. Era el regidor de cada vereda que tenía que hacer un inventario de los documentos que han existido, los documentos antiguos, los documentos fenecidos que ya no tienen ya valor; esos eran un volumen aparte. Pero ahí constaba tantos documentos fenecidos, ahora sí, tantos documentos que están girando en la actualidad, elay. Eso iban ahí, leyendo, año por año, que en qué año, cuáles documentos, de quiénes, y de quiénes fulanos: iban nombrando el nombre del individuo, el nombre del terreno, de la vereda, e iban ahí pasando el número de documentos en, allí en unos libros que hay hasta ahora, elay. Eso. Y entonces, cada regidor, por medio de un inventario, el inventario o sea volumen de piezas, ese lo entrega el presidente con el secretario, al presidente del cabildo nuevo y al secretario del cabildo nuevo. También ese es el volúmen que dicen de piezas, ahí son tanta cuestión de sumarios, de pleitos, de resoluciones, de circulares, de así del gobierno, de uno cualesquiera asuntos civiles. Ese es un volúmen grande: ahí van algunos documentos así de los tiempos pasados, como la Escritura 228.

23. Archivo del Cabildo Indígena del Gran Cumbal, Nariño [ACIGC/N], 1935, "Inventario de las piezas y más diligencias . . . del mismo año 1935." See also ACIGC/N, 1940, "Inventario de las piezas y más diligencias . . . del año de 1940."

24. Note that Deed 228 was retrieved in the 1970s and therefore does not appear in don Benjamín's inventory. A good example of the incorporation of earlier documentation into court transcripts is the body of evidence presented by the caciques of Tuza in their dispute with the hereditary chiefs of Puntal (today Bolívar, Ecuador) over maize lands: Archivo Nacional del Ecuador, Quito [ANE/Q], 1792, "Titulos y ynstrumentos de los yndios y casiques. . . . "

25. Lord (1964) and Yates (1966) have examined the way formulaic utterances and striking images serve as props for the oral memory. Although I found their work useful in formulating my ideas, I employ these concepts in an entirely different manner. First, there is Cumbal's distinct relationship with the written historical record. The majority of men under age forty are at least marginally literate and use writing as a source of information. Even though literacy was limited in the past, there were always some individuals who could decipher the written word and interpret it for their compatriots. There are indications that indigenous scribes were operating autonomously in Pasto communities as early as the mid-seventeenth century (Archivo Histórico del Banco Central del Ecuador, Ibarra [AHBC/I], 1654, "Protocolos y testamentos a cargo de Juan Francisco Guapastal . . . "). Second, contemporary narrators

do not use clichés and images as props for memorizing their tales but as brief reminders of historical referents. While memoristas may formulate these images in detail, other comuneros may leave them left in their raw and iconic state. More appropriate to the Cumbal example than Lord and Yates is Walter Benjamin's notion of historical images as practical memories summoned to confront threatening circumstances (Benjamin 1969). Taussig (1987) suggests that such images are employed metaphorically rather than literally in the course of resistance to domination, which he studies in a lowland setting not far from Pasto.

26. Mary Weismantel (1988, 144–45) suggests that the plant commonly called *nabus* is a wild food gathered in time of hunger and should not be translated as turnips. Since turnips were included in sixteenth-century tribute lists (Archivo General de Indias, Sevilla [AGI/S], 1558, "Traslado del libro de tassaciones . . . "), I am hesitant to identify the food that the Cumbales call nabos with Weismantel's *nabus*.

27. Clichés and archetypes also provide models for structuring the historical memory in other regions. Passerini (1987, 20–24) examines similar recurrent images among female working-class narrators from Turin, who recall their experiences under Fascism.

28. Archivo Central del Cauca, Popayán [ACC/P], 1722–1810, "Numeraciones de la Provincia de los Pastos," signatura 3041 (1722).

29. Esta hacienda la compraron los señores Miguel Tarapués, Bernardo Tarapués, y Manuel Tarapués, los dos hermanos y el otro particular, pero todos fueron Tarapueses. Los dos hermanos fueron Miguel y Bernardo, el otro fue Tarapués, pero particular, como le estoy contando, que somos particulares, pero Tarapués. Por ejemplo, como le dije yo, yo soy Tarapués con todos los Ursulos, como le han dicho, Tarapués Ursulo, porque de Bernardo Tarapués hubo una hija que ha llamado Ursulina, y de esa descendencia venimos hasta aquí: por eso a nosotros nos dicen Tarapueses Ursulos, porque nuestra madre bisabuela ha llamado Ursulina, hija de Bernardo. Y de Miguel son los otros Tarapueses; los Eugenios son de Manuel [*sic*]. De esa descendencia había un cuaderno grande que habían hecho como árboles. Que habían hecho tres árboles de los tres Tarapueses, y estos iban descendiendo, ¿no?, del uno, del otro, y del otro, la descendencia, iban los hijos, los nietos y las generaciones. . . . Yo dependo del primer árbol, que es don Bernardo y de él es doña Ursulina, y de Miguel son los Eugenios, de Manuel son los Alcántares, pero son tres Tarapués.

30. Don Nicolas Garcia Paspuel Tusa casique principal de los pueblos de Tusa, Puntal, y Angel, jurisdiccion de la Villa de San Miguel de Ybarra, hijo legitimo y heredero de don Thomas Garcia Paspuel Tusa casique principal que fue de dichos pueblos y nieto legitimo de don Sebastian Garcia Paspuel Tusa y viznieto legitimo de don Xptobal Garcia Paspuel Tusa y de doña Francisca Tusa, casiquez principales que fueron de dichos pueblos, ya difuntos (ANE/Q, 1771, "Autos de proclama de don Matheo Garcia Paspuel Tusa . . . ," f. 2r).

Chapter Four

1. The importance of considering the entire range of historical knowledge, including that contained in such non-narrative genres as short sayings or names, is emphasized in the work of Cohen (1980, 1989) in Uganda and Price (1983) in Suriname. Michel de Certeau (1984) underscores the dangers of abstracting history from everyday life, claiming that such abstraction removes knowledge from its context of interaction and manipulation, and places it instead within a new and isolating scientific framework, which, ultimately, robs it of all meaning. Blount's examination of the social context of genealogy-making (Blount 1975) presents a good example of de Certeau's assertion.

2. Y en birtud del decreto de esta otra parte y titulo de cazique con que rrequerio al dicho justicia mayor don Ambrosio de Prado y Sayalpud cazique de la parcialidad de Cumbal, cojio por la mano al dicho don Ambrosio de Prado y lo sento en una silleta pequeña de madera en prezencia de los yndios e yndias de la dicha parsialidad de Cumbal y a los yndios mas principales de dicha parcialidad les quito las mantas y las echo en el suelo y se las mando lebantar y le huuieron cada uno una reberencia y los abraso a estos todos que hizo en señal de posesion y verdadera posesion la cual se la dio real agtual corporal del quazi sin contradizion de persona alguna y zin perjuicio de otro terzero que mejor derecho tenga (Archivo Nacional del Ecuador, Quito [ANE/Q], 1694, "Materia seguida por don Ambrosio de Prado y Sayalpud . . . , " f. 4v).

Chiefly testaments from earlier periods include keros and other artifacts of chiefly rule, such as strombus shells and *qompi* or fine fabrics (Archivo Histórico del Banco Central del Ecuador, Ibarra [AHBC/I], 1592, "Testamento de don Cristóbal Cuatin . . . , " f. 1v; AHBC/I, 1605, "Testamento de doña Catalina Tuza . . . , " ff. 2r–v.; ANE/Q, 1735, "Thomas Rodriguez de Herrera, con fray Jose Pintado . . . , " ff. 87r–v, which includes the 1624 will of doña Luisa Actasen of Túquerres). Cardale de Schrimpff (1977–78) details the importance of cloth as an indicator of authority among the Pastos, as does Murra (1975) for the southern Andes.

3. The first mention I have found of caciques carrying staffs of office is in the late colonial period (Archivo Histórico del Banco Central del Ecuador, Quito [AHBC/Q], 1748, "Autos seguidos por doña Estefania Pastas . . ." f. 262v, and ANE/Q, 1764, "Autos de don Marthin Cumbal Aza . . . ," ff. 1v–2v).

4. *B.C.:* El bastón que se conserva donde el señor Benjamín Cuaical tiene más de 200 años. Fue el primer dueño Juan Agustín Cuaical. Siendo joven bailó de danzante 12 años consecutivos. Enseguida pasó a poder de Fidel Cuaical. Después de Fidel Cuaical, pasó el bastón a poder de Valentín Cuaical, que fué mi padre. Después lo conservo yo hasta la actualidad, Benjamín Cuaical, y con este bastón, acabó Juan Agustín Cuaical un año en Túquerres de gobernador. (*J.R.:* Y esta vara también salvó la vida de don Agustín . . .) *B.C.:* Sí señora. Esta le salvó la vida. Cuando lo iban a fusilar en tiempos de la Revolución—pero eso ya no sé en cuál año fue, el tiempo de la Revolución, como que fue en

tiempo de la guerra de Tomás Cipriano de Mosquera. No, en la de Mosquera no fué. Ahí yo no le doy ese dato, porque yo no sé en qué Revolución sería, como en ese tiempo había tanta revolución, que se revolucionaban por ganar el poder. Pero se supo que en ese tiempo en algunas de esas guerras, lo iban a fusilar a don Agustín Cuaical. El todavía, como dije ya que él fué ya abuelo, ya abuelo que más que sea, que lo sacaron ya para fusilarlo. Y entonces, cuando ya han estado para fusilarlo, entonces apareció un comandante ya de la Fuerza Armada. Entonces es que gritó: "¡Alto ahí!" es que había dicho, "Ese indio acabó gobernador en Túquerres, déjenlo." Así, ¡elay! Entonces, acabado con ese bordón, gobernador en Túquerres.

5. Unlike other indigenous communities, whose members participated as soldiers in Republican-era civil wars (see Findji and Rojas 1985; Rappaport 1990b), the Pastos were passive observers and frequently victims of the opposing armies. Older narrators still have vivid memories of army raids that took place during the last of these wars, the War of the Thousand Days at the turn of the century. These memories are sometimes linked to the history of reclaimed haciendas where atrocities took place.

6. Hermanos indígenas: yo salí un día muy por la mañana a conseguir fortuna para mi casa. Pero cierto día, me encumbré a esas grandes riberas del Gran Cumbal y, por los malos entendimientos, me pusieron cautiverio. En primer lugar, les quiero contar lo siguiente: Que entre sueños pedía auxilio. Cuando yo encontré el auxilio, me tropecé con un cordón amarrado de un frailejón, y fui a caer junto a un cajón. Cuando yo estaba muy cerca, estaba un tigre ladrón, sentado en ese cajón. Y al verme yo asustado, quise salir corriendo y este gran ladrón me quiso alcanzar del garrón. Y de verme tan asustado que yo no tuve qué decirle, que me vuelva esas cosas que nuestras son. Entonces, me dijo: indio, tus cosas, tuyas son. La cogí en la mano y me puse a verlas: encontré las cosas y maravillas más bellas. Cuando de pronto, al estar viendo éso, escuché una voz que decía: cuenta las doscientas veintiocho garras del tigre, porque de allí saldrá la Real Escritura 228 de 1906. Porque de allí tendrás tu salvación para todas tus funciones, que es la Ley 89.

The Royal Deed is used here as an alternate name for Deed 228. It is dated 1908 (the playwright inadvertently said 1906) because, in that year, the original title was registered by the Colombian authorities.

7. In the neighboring Sibundoy Valley, to the northeast of Cumbal, Inganos associate jaguars with thievery (McDowell 1989, 52–53). Perhaps the playwright, who spent several years as a wage laborer in the lowlands of the Putumayo, was aware of the importance of the feline symbol if not of what it signified.

8. El disco titula el "Cacique Cumbe." El cacique Cumbe quiere decir que él fue el viejo de aquí, él que luchó y manejaba aquí este territorio o esta parcialidad del Gran Cumbal, como hay Real Provisión o la Escritura 228. El disco reza, por lo menos: "¡El cacique Cumbe tendrá que venir! Porque es de San Pedro, de nuestro Cumbal." Anteriormente habían llamado San Pedro aquí al municipio de Cumbal. Entonces pues, dice el disco "Porque es de San Pedro, de nuestro Cumbal, donde dejó escrito la Corona Real." O sea que la Corona

Real es la Escritura 228, que esa fue expedida en la Real Audiencia en los Virreinados de Fernando VI en Quito.

9. *G.V.*: De lo que existe dentro de las comunidades indígenas, por lo menos en los bastones, hay coronas. O sea que es la corona sagrada donde el virreinado desde allá. Y sacándose la corona y besó, y le mandaba Mauricio Muñóz de Ayala, para que en vista de la Real Corona o de la Real Audiencia de Quito, así mismo lo hiciera y cumpliera el deber a él mandado como autoridad o como Alcalde Mayor de los Pastos, o sea que nosotros pertenecemos al Cacique de los Pastos. (*J.R.*: ¿Cuál es la corona del bastón?) *G.V.*: Hay una corona, un anillo, digamos que parece. Nosotros decimos anillo, no es anillo, sino es significando ya las cosas: es corona. (*M.J.T.*: Que son picaditos como corona.) *G.V.*: Si. Entonces esa es la corona. O sea que significa la Corona Real del Fernando VI. Entonces yo significo de que no es anillo, sino es una corona, y eso da más credibilidad a nosotros como indígenas de aquí del Gran Cumbal, de que está escrito, como dice la Real Provisión o la Real Corona. Entonces es que nuestros abuelos, nuestros caciques, ellos también creían en eso, y por eso es el bastón. Pusieron la corona, y existe.

10. Yten declaro que a las faldas de dicha loma por arriba tengo otra quadra de tierras que compre de Ana Ytaman que linda por vna parte y otra con dos sanjas viejas por un lado la quebrada de Quesaca y por arriba con tierras de mi hermano don Juan . . . (ANE/Q, 1746, "Autos en favor de Miguel Garcia Paspuel Tuza . . . , " f. 8r). This 1709 will of don Mathias Quatimpas, a cacique from Tuza, is contained in a later land-claims document.

Gradas are reused as boundaries in the Carlosama cacique don Sebastián Calisto's will, which is undated (ANE/Q, 1747, "Autos de don Visente Garcia Yaputa . . . "); this will also contains references to *named* zanjas. See also Caillavet (1989) on uses of pre-Columbian zanjas. Angel María Piarpuezán of Nazate told me that four types of boundary markers are used in Cumbal. Of the two he says are of ancient origin, zanjas delimit flat lands and gradas divide parcels on mountain slopes. Of more modern origin are *tapias*, pressed-earth walls found only in the lower reaches of the resguardo, and the less popular barbed wire fences.

11. Por la cabesera divida con tierras de Mateo Taramuel, sanja por medio a topar haciendo semicirculo con tierras de Julio Guadir por el un costado haciendo esquina en tierras del espresado Guadir sigue deslindando para abajo con tierras de Agustin Poso, hasta encontrar con un mojón de piedra sembrada i una mata de guamuco questá al labio de la sanja que se divide con dicho Poso por el pie cogiendo de dicha piedra ó guamuco en esto mojones por medio, deslinda con terrenos de Crisanto Acpala á topar a otra piedra sembrada i mata de "chilco" que se halla alabio de la sanja i entrada de Balentin Cuaycal, y por el ultimo costado, sigue lindando por arriba con la misma entrada i sanja, hasta dar al primer lindero que al principio se dijo (Archivo Personal de Salomón Cuaical, Cumbal [APSC/C], 1872, "Documento de adjudicación del terreno Chendé").

12. The complex stratigraphy of customary and national law in an African context is analyzed by Moore (1986, 1989). For a Peruvian example of the rela-

tionship between oral/communal and written/state means of delimiting territory, see Radcliffe (1990).

13. I learned of this zanja from Moisés Tapie, who directed me to speak with Segundo Colimba, his neighbor, who had worked on its construction. Here is an interesting case of non-Indians employing aboriginal boundary markers to stake their own claims to a tract of land. Throughout Nariño, haciendas are marked by zanjas, but only infrequently are supported by written documentation. I would venture to guess that zanja construction by hacendados represents a European appropriation of an indigenous model of history to cover up for the lack of European evidence substantiating the legality of their landholdings. Hacendados use zanjas differently from Indians: landlords construct zanjas to delimit private property while Indians dig them to mark use rights to communal lands. In a sense, then, zanjas delimiting communal lands are considerably more permeable than those isolating private property. The hacendado's misuse of zanjas is corrected by the cabildo when it reaffirms usufruct rights to repossessed lands through cabildo ceremony. A suggestive account of conflicting appropriations of history by Indians and mestizo landlords is provided by Seligmann (1987) for highland Peru. Seligmann's work indicates that we cannot study indigenous notions of history in isolation but must analyze them within regional and national frameworks. For further discussion of the intersection of mestizo and indigenous forms of making and reading history, see chapter 6.

14. Connerton (1989) suggests that commemorative ceremony constitutes the major vehicle for historical remembering in most societies. His ideas are discussed further in chapter 7 in relation to theatrical presentations of history in Cumbal and Muellamués.

15. Administrando justicia en nombre de la República de Colombia y por autoridad de la ley, os doy posesión real, formal, y material de este terreno para que lo labore, lo usufructue durante el tiempo de su vida y después quedará a su legítima descendencia, por lo cual el cabildo les ordenamos que revuelquen por el suelo, arranquen yerbas, las esparzan por el aire en señal de verdadera posesión que el cabildo en méritos de justicia les da.

16. Y vino [Mauricio Muñóz de Ayala, Alcalde Mayor de los Pastos] a una inspección de quince días en ese año mismo de 1758, el cual recorrieron los linderos con Juan Tapie, así la familia Tapie los de aquí nativos. Y dentro de los quince días dió la posesión que dice y significa que hasta ahora nuestro cabildo o mi persona como presidente que me ha tocado declarar abierto el acto para dar las posesiones a los indígenas como usufructuarios de sus tierras o de sus parcelas. Es que dijo Mauricio Muñóz de Ayala: En nombre de la República de Colombia y por autoridad de la ley os doy posesión real, formal y material a los indios e indias, chinas y chinos de aquí de la parcialidad del Gran Cumbal.

17. It is only recently that Andeanists have turned from the study of the persistence of pre-Columbian cultural forms to an examination of the dynamics of the emergence of contemporary Andean culture within the historical context of invasion, domination, and resistance (see Stern 1987; Dover, Seibold,

and McDowell 1992). From this new perspective, it becomes pointless to distinguish between "aboriginal" and "European" traits; instead, the dynamics of the creation and re-creation of an Andean identity must be the focus of interpretation.

Chapter Five

1. Andeanist inclinations toward the interpretation of historical documents have resulted in a number of insightful analyses of the writings of colonial-era indigenous authors (Adorno 1982, 1986; González Echevarría 1990; Harrison 1988; MacCormack 1991; Salomon 1982; Salomon and Urioste 1991). In these studies, documents are not reserved as sources of ethnographic information but are analyzed as texts with their own internal coherence. A few studies have considered documentary literacy among contemporary indigenous groups (Radcliffe 1990; Rappaport 1987, 1990b; Rivera 1986a, 1986b; Urton 1990). Anthropologists are beginning to examine everyday literacy, such as the reading and preparation of simple maps (Orlove 1991b) or the writing of letters (Skar; n.d.). Similarly, in lowland South America, the study of literacy is in its infancy (Gow 1990).

2. This did not stop even people who hated to read from requesting and slowly studying my publications.

3. Con la solemnidad nesesaria [Don Simon Mainbas, cacique de Tuza y Puntal] manifiesta vnos ynstrumentos antiquados pertenecientes a vnas tierras que posee para que de ellas se cirba Vuestra Merced de mandar que el presente escribano le de vn tanto de todo lo que se hallare legible porque con las hinjurias del tiempo se ban consumiendo por lo que se nesesita su refacsion. (Archivo National de Ecuador, Quito [ANE/Q], 1757, "Cuaderno de los instrumentos de la escritura de venta, otorgada por don Pedro Guatinango a don Andres Gualsago y testamento de don Francisco Paspuel Guachan . . . ," f. 3r). See also the testament of Andrés Yazam (ANE/Q, 1772, "Autos de don Juan Rosero . . . ," f. 3r).

4. This clause, common to colonial-era titles, refers to the ethnic isolation that the Crown imposed upon resguardo Indians.

5. REFERENCIA: Parcialidad de Cumbal por sus yacimientos de azufre cuya explotación-extracción y beneficio del mineral data desde la REAL AUDIENCIA DE SAN FRANCISCO DE QUITO 9 de junio: 1758 52 años antes del grito de INDEPENDENCIA del 20 de JULIO: 1810.

—Los derechos adquiridos con observancia de las leyes del rey de ESPAÑA fueron declarados por la PRIMERA CONSTITUCION de la REPUBLICA que serían reconocidos, protegidos y de ninguna manera vulnerados por las nuevas AUTORIDADES.

—Y por una y otra vez el Capitán de Infantería Española, y Alcalde de JUSTICIA MAYOR DE LOS PASTOS, Don MAURICIO Muñoz de Ayala en comisión de la REAL AUDIENCIA DE SAN FRANCISCO DE QUITO refrendó la posesión, la hizo buena, y otro tanto hizo bueno el dominio a los cuatro caciques TAPIES del globo de tierras en cuyo centro vino a destacarse como una pirámide el volcán de nom-

bre EL CUMBAL. DURANTE ocho días el Capitán de Infantería tuvo que identifi-
car uno por uno de los linderos naturales con los que quedó circunscrito el
globo de las tierras concedidas a las indiadas en la cabeza de sus caciques.
HECHO lo cual pacientemente de la linderación a que fueron llamados los demás pueblos, el Capitán de Infantería Española se puso de rodilla en la pampa,
y luego ciñándose la corona de oro de su rey, su señor natural, en alta voz hizo
entrega de la tierra en su tenencia, en su posesión, en su mismo dominio a los
caciques, representantes genuínos de sus pueblos de CUMBAL. Y a la vez quedaba el descrito globo de tierras limpio de negros, de españoles y de todo
advenedizo. ENTONCES como hoy sigue lo accesorio a lo principal: era la tierra
de importancia máxima, sin igual, ya que élla le daba a la indiada de comer
aunque con su trabajo, y a sus ganados los pastos de cada día les proporcio-
naba espontáneamente y en abundancia.
—ASI es como se adquirió la tenencia, posesión y propiedad, frente a todas
las gentes con ayuda del Rey, su REAL AUDIENCIA DE SAN FRANCISCO de QUITO
sus Capitanes de Infantería y sus Alcaldes Mayores de Justicia.
—CON gran seso la ley 35 de 1943 convino en que la NACION por medio de sus
ténicos [sic] habría los trabajos de EXPLORACION. Lo racional, lo primero es
buscar, dar con los yacimientos que nada rinden, que nadie se los beneficia,
que nadie les saca ni ha sacado provecho. (Art. 2o. de la memorada ley 35). DE
suerte que en el artículo 2o. se previno que había que explorar, buscar lo que
aun ni vez alguna ha sido laboreado, beneficiado—rendido provecho merced
al trabajo. NUESTROS mayores, desde tiempos inmemoriales, en que no se sabe
de fijo cual fue el primer día, han explotado, sacado, para tener con que vivir
así la nieve, en bloques, como el azufre. SE han cargado a sus espaldas, por
esas laderas abajo del Cumbal, bloques de nieve y cantidades de azufre. Abajo
en el punto del LIADERO es donde ya echan la carga en sus bestias para irse a
los mercados de Colombia y el Ecuador. NO hay ni como negarlo que ello es
una gracia, una dádiva del REY. Y que hoy la REPUBLICA vaya pretender arreba-
tarnos con la fuerza, lo que primero es trabajo aun con peligro de la vida por
esas pendientes, donde se quedó el cuero de muchos de nosotros, y lo que es
después, todavía a costa de esfuerzos, comerciar en pueblos de Colombia y el
Ecuador.
—EN la Notaría Nro. 1o de Pasto, a 9 de junio de 1908 han sido protocolizados
los títulos de que hacemos mérito, y valen para nosotros como la tabla de
SALVACION. SOMOS de la raza que necesita a gritos un nuevo redemtor, a la
grandeza de SIMON BOLIVAR.
—EN la estafeta de Cumbal jamás nos entregan la correspondencia. Ojalá que
la dirijan a Pasto, donde tenemos una persona a quien hemos facultado para
que la retire a las OFICINAS DE LA AVIANCA o del Correo Nacional.
    El once (11) de mayo remitimos nuestro primer memorial, en defensa de lo
que tenemos para trabajar y por consiguiente para vivir.
    A los otros les quedan yacimientos inexplorados, y por lo tanto inexplo-
tados, beneficiados nunca, de ellos nadie se ha ingeniado su negocio ni como
pueda ni con mucha técnica.
    Por qué es que ha de ser siempre mas sabrosa la manzana del cercado

ajeno??? (Archivo del Cabildo Indígena del Gran Cumbal, Nariño [ACIGC/ N], 1950, "Borradores de cartas del Cabildo al Ministerio de Minas, sobre los yacimientos de azufre del Cerro de Cumbal," ff. 5–6)

6. Aviso a ustedes recibo de su memorial del 2 de junio en curso, para el señor Ministro de Minas y Petróleos.

En atención a que se trata de una comunidad de Indígenas que, acaso no conozcan las leyes y decretos sobre concesiones mineras, debo decirles que si ustedes estiman que con la concesión solicitada se menoscaban legítimos derechos de la parcialidad de Indígenas de cuyo Cabildo son ustedes miembros, deben presentar ante el Gobernador del Departamento su memorial de oposición a la celebración del referido contrato, junto con los documentos que comprueben sus derechos. El Gobernador remitirá la documentación a este Ministerio y aquí se estudiará esa oposición y, si se encontrare formalmente presentada, se ordenará pasar para su decisión al Tribunal Superior de Pasto.

Mientras no se formule la oposición legalmente, nada puede hacer este Despacho en relación con su memorial referido.

Soy de usted atento y seguro servidor (ibid., f. 9).

I am indebted to Diana Digges for bringing the government's letter to my attention and for sharing her interpretation of the material in an article that further explores the two letters (Digges and Rappaport 1993).

7. Agustín Colimba of Cuaspud was frequently mentioned to me as a knowledgeable memorista. By the time I arrived in Cumbal, however, he was old and quite ill; he died during my stay, and I was never able to meet him.

8. En el cabildo ahora tiene tanta copia. Hay fotocopias; la propia está en el cabildo, la propia Real Provisión. Yo la conozco, la ví, la busqué: esa existe en la Notaría Primera del Circuito de Pasto, allá está la Real Provisión. Yo la vide. Lo único, que no pude leer. Ahí estaban los nombres de los caciques. Hasta tenía unos sellos. Esto está en papel pergamino, está la Real Provisión en Pasto. Y entonces, cuando se ofrece así las querellas, de los pleitos o así, el cabildo solicita por aparte. Solicitan allá y entonces, pero para copiar es muy trabajoso. Eso copian los escribientes, copian a la hora del sol, con lente: entonces, ha sabido parecer, entonces parece clarito. Porque a nosotros nos hicieron ver, en esas horas que estábamos allá en la consulta a que nos haga conocer la Real Provisión, la madre de las otras. Entonces, el secretario, estaba haciendo sol y nos sacó por allá a un patio, a una plazuela. Entonces dijo, "Vengan a ver, a ver si pueden leer." Entonces nosotros sí leímos. Ahí decía "De Mallorca, el Rey que ha sido de España, de Cursia [sic], de Corsica." Nosotros podíamos leer también allá en el sol.

9. Yo me fui a conversar con fulano de tal, que se llamaba Fernando Cuesta, y él tiene una escritura que ha sabido hacer los caciques la letra alrevesada.

10. Analogous mestizo reactions to the possession ceremony are recorded in the nineteenth-century documentary record (see chapter 6).

11. On the nature of colonial documentation, see González Echevarría (1990), Phelan (1967), and Vidal (1985). M. T. Clanchy (1979) describes a similar mix of literacy and ritual practice for medieval England. A good example of

the orality of colonial-era Spanish written expression is the encoding in documents of the public proclamation that accompanied legal processes. If a decision was announced thirty times in public, it was written out thirty times in the document arising out of the case (see Rappaport n.d.). In fact, early colonial literacy had a very different meaning than our own notion of writing does. In the sixteenth century language was perceived as having been composed of "absolutely certain and transparent sign[s] for things, because it resembled them" (Foucault 1970, 35). Writing, then, was an image of the truth lodged in things (ibid., 36–41).

12. ACIGC/N, 1908, "Escritura 228 de 1908"; future citations of this document will appear in the text.

13. In eighteenth-century Mexico, Nahuatl-speaking scribes mimicked the layered nature of the legal brief; they fabricated their own titles, adopting the layered form that characterized the original documents to which they did not have access (Gruzinski 1988; Lockhart 1982). But although the indigenous authors were able to mimic the layered effect of the legal record, it is not clear that they fully understood why so many documents had been juxtaposed. Eisenstein (1966) argues that it is only in the past few centuries, once print literacy became firmly embedded in European society, that historians began to distinguish between myth and history, and to organize chronological accounts of the past. In her view, then, the very form of these legal manuscripts would affect the way they are employed as historical evidence.

14. Y entonces hicieron un quejatorio. Se vinieron las parcialidades que eran de Muellamués, de Cumbal, de Carlosama, Guachucal, Panán, Mayasquer, Chiles y se echaron el quejatorio a la Audiencia Real de Quito. Y la Audiencia Real de Quito entonces les dijo el informe. Principalmente fue el quejatorio a las Antillas, a Turman [sic], a Conde, y entonces al Rey Corona. Ordenó, dice, que pase una comisión de la Audiencia Real de Quito, hacerle respetar esas tierras.

15. Don Felipe por la gracia de Dios, Rey de Castilla, de Leon, de Aragon, de las dos Sicilias, de Jerusalem, de Navarra, de Granada, de Toledo, de Valencia, de Galicia, de Mallorca, de Sevilla, de Sardeña, de Cordoba, de Murcia, de Jaen, de los Algares y Algeria, de Gibraltar, de las de Canarias, de las Indias Orientales y Occidentales y las de Tierra Firme del Mar Oceano, Archiduque de la Siria, Duque de Borgoña, Conde de Napoles, de Flandes, Tirol, de Barcelona, Señor de Viscaya y de Molina, etc., etc. (ACIGC/N, 1906, "Real Cédula o Provisión," f. 8).

16. Entonces a donde el Capitán les cogió las manos a ellos, y los sometió a la posesión, a los cuatro caciques, al llegar, a Sebastián Tarapués, Hilario Nazate, Gabriel Nazate, Bernardo Tarapués, y los sometió a esa posesión en nombre de la República de Colombia, por la autoridad de la ley, rueden. Entonces rodaron, después pajearon pajas, terrones, en verdadera posesión. Terminó ese auto y les advirtió a los que estaban oyendo de los otros, les dijo que cuidado vayan a engañar a los indígenas en contra, que el que se someta a eso, con una multa de cien patacones.

17. ACIGC/N, 1950, f. 3v.

18. El azufre tocaba llevar pues un canasto, largo y bien acomodado. Ya que está lleno el canasto, la cabeza, la frente, una manta que llamamos. Entonces, de allí llevábamos a la espalda con un buen bordón para afirmarnos, para no caernos. Y eso bajábamos al Liadero, donde entran las recuas de las yeguas. Y ahí echábamos la bestia y a entregar al pueblo.

19. Las primeras se cargaba es un bulto. Después, se mermó las cargas, que a las primeras que yo iba eran cargas pesadas de cuatro arrobas, un bulto. O sea apenas con un bulto, cada persona. Después mermaban las cargas. Acostumbrábamos a cargar carga entera, pero las cargas no pesaban, cuando eso ya, cuando más pesarían es cinco, seis arrobas.

20. La nieve se la saca con hacha haciéndole acequiecitas, cuadrándolo, por cuatro lados, oiga. Entonces, ya que están bien hondas las acequias en la nieve en el cerro, enconces se le da dos hachazos duros de cada lado. Entonces, se hace la acequia por la mitad y eche guasca con un cabestro y vamos halando y arrastrando, oiga. Hasta que llega al plano y cargarlo a la espalda. Y en el plano eso sigue adelante, oiga. Eso toca irlo teniendo de atrás, y antes tiene fuerza, y a veces se escapa de ganarle, oiga. Hasta llegar a una parte que llamamos el Liadero. Ahí teníamos paja cortada y frailejón y unas lías de cabuya para con eso envolverlo y enseguida la paja, después el frailejón, y ahí empacarlo bien bonito. Y de ahí sí, cargar las bestias y entregarse a Tulcán, Ipiales, a Túquerres. Mandar para Sandoná, Cumbitara, Tumaco, a todas partes.

21. The other most frequently repeated mnemonic for recalling the history of sulphur exploitation is the "Calzadero," the point at which the elders, unaccustomed to wearing shoes, were forced to put on homemade footwear to protect themselves from the sharp stones of the mountain. As chapter 7 will argue, contemporary playwrights cast their historical knowledge in a framework comprised largely of descriptions of clothing; this is equally true for narratives of the ascent of Mount Cumbal.

22. Se escribió con la idea de aportar a la medicina, la historia, la educación, la cultura. Pues para mí, todo, todo nos hace falta, todos los que estamos, buscar de todo, no sólo para el grupo no más entender, sino que de todas las cosas sepamos todos, y hagamos una cartilla de todas las cosas, una cartilla o un cuaderno grande.

23. Así compañeros, conoscamos quiénes son positivos y quiénes enemigos. Empecemos a caminar bien nuestro camino, más seguro día a día. Y si algo nos desviamos, pisemos despacio, pero seguros de ir, hasta que podamos dar la salida del camino, para ejemplo e historia del futuro de nuestros hijos, que dirán, "Así fueron mis padres, un día, en ese tiempo que lucharon." Porque es un derecho que nos han quitado, que fué de muchos años y de siglos.

24. Don Delfín was probably also influenced by the writings of Manuel Quintín Lame (Lame 1971 [1939]), a Páez militant whose treatise has played a central role in the framing of the demands of the Colombian Indian movement. The impact of Lame's writings on Nariñense history will be discussed in chapter 7.

25. En estos años entramos la comunidad, desmontando una parte de montaña. Los contrarios, de la loma Mengambis, nos hacían hartos tiros al monte.

Al otro día se adelantan en la misma loma, a no dejar entrar a trabajar. Con quince armas de alcance, disparaban juego seguido, y la gente indígena los arredondiábamos. Al segundo día hicimos un rancho grande para seguir trabajando y no salir más, y fue una comisión a la casa del terrateniente a decirle que ya desocupe la finca. A ruego se les dió plazo de tres días. En esos días cogieron un papal con la gente de Chiles. No encontramos al terrateniente, sino al mayordomo, diciéndole que esta tierra es de los indígenas, y enseguida zanjamos.

26. The Quechua used in the title of the magazine is an example of the profusion of Quechua loanwords in Nariñense Spanish. *Chasqui* is traditionally used in Nariño to describe the indigenous messengers that municipal officials used to carry communications to their counterparts in other localities. Only one issue of the *Chasqui* has appeared. All citations from the *Chasqui Cumbe* will appear in the text.

27. Helí was finally elected as regidor from Nazate and chosen to be cabildo president in 1990. Today he is the alternate indigenous senator in Bogotá, under the provisions of the new constitution, which created two special Senate seats for Indians.

28. Muchos tiempos han pasado en el olvido las buenas costumbres de nuestros mayores, las leyes, las experiencias de luchas, la cultura, la medicina tradicional, las creencias y las buenas formas de vida; de igual manera a los sufrimientos sometidos, a la dominación, a la discriminación racial y a la humillación económica y social.

Por tal razón es conveniente dar a conocer a la Gran Familia Cumbe sus experiencias ocultas, custodiadas en sus archivos, lo cual ha sido la base fundamental para la reivindicación de los derechos y seguir su proceso histórico como pueblos autónomos con el mayor derecho a vivir y desarrollarse como humanos en nuestra madre tierra heredada de nuestro GRAN CACIQUE CUMBE.

29. El territorio Cumbe se delimitó con mojones de referencia, como son las neolíticas piedras con agujeros o huecos, los ríos, quebradas, cerros, volcanes, lagunas y las montañas. Esta delimitación fue realizada quizá muchos siglos antes de llegar los colonizadores españoles. Los límites fueron unos acuerdos y a veces luchas entre los cacicazgos vecinos; para así conformar un territorio libre y soberano, para trabajar en él en forma COMUNITARIA en beneficio de todos los habitantes que conforman el cacicazgo.

30. El escudo, en su estructura, está conformado como base fundamental por el sol de los pastos, sostenido por dos micos Machines. Su parte superior está cubierta por dos ramilletes que representan la vegetación autóctona. En el sol se encuentran entrelazadas las herramientas y armas indígenas, además de las varas o bastón de autoridad y justicia. En el centro del sol hay una figurilla antropomorfa tal como nuestros antepasados la representaban. Su lema "CUMBE VIVE EN LOS RENACIENTES."

El Sol de los Pastos significa según nuestros antepasados "El Dios supremo," el dios que alumbra la vida y da la luz del bien a quien le rendía culto y lo adoraban con gran alegría y júbilo. Hasta hoy sigue siendo el centro de la vida para todos. Sin El el mundo se cubriría en un manto muerto.

Dentro del sol están incrustadas las armas y herramientas; varas de mando con las que los indígenas antepasados lucharon por sobrevivir, hacer producir la tierra y organizarse como un pueblo soberano, en un territorio libre, con un pensamiento propio.

Los monos Machines fueron considerados como un símbolo de fecundidad y progenitores del género viviente, fueron los dioses del TOTEN al cual le rendían sus cultos en sitios sagrados.

Los ramilletes significan la fertilidad de la tierra unida a la mano del hombre, relacionando al hombre con la naturaleza mediante el cultivo autóctono como es la papa y las plantas silvestres que sirvieron de base principal en la medicina tradicional, como en el arte e industria.

Su lema "CUMBE VIVE EN LOS RENACIENTES," tratamos de identificarnos los actuales indígenas con el pensamiento heredado de nuestros mayores. Tratamos de revivir y fortalecer todo ese conglomerado de experiencias sociales que a través del tiempo, las leyes y gobiernos se han ido esfumando en el mar del olvido e ignorancia creando así una crisis de la autonomía y llevando al indio a desconocer su raza, su pasado y sus sistemas vitales de existencia, para marginarlo en un mundo capitalista y una sociedad de consumo donde el hombre ya no es un eslabón de la comunidad sino un número perdido y desorientado.

The Cumbe crest is analyzed and compared to the contemporary heraldry of other communities in Rappaport (1992).

Chapter Six

1. The Supreme Court decision was published in the *Diario Oficial* (Bogotá), 5 July 1869. See also judicial records related to the case, Archivo del Juzgado Primero Civil del Circuito, Ipiales [AJPCC/I], 1876a, "Apelación que el Ministerio Público i Segundo Sánchez han interpuesto contra la sentencia que pronunció el Juez del Circuito de Obando en Ipiales a 20 de setiembre de 1875"; 1876b, "Copia perteneciente a los indígenas del Distrito de Cumbal, sobre la restitución del terreno 'Zapatero' y 'Tolas', por centencia difinitiva de la Corte Suprema Federal"; and 1877, "Juicio promovido por el señor Segundo Sánchez contra los indígenas del Distrito de Cumbal por los terrenos 'Zapatero' y 'Tolas.'"

2. Archival holdings documenting late colonial rebellions, to take a fascinating example, are unlikely to become sources of historical evidence because they are not useful for most legal suits pursued by the community. See, for example, Archivo Nacional del Ecuador, Quito [ANE/Q], 1803, "Expedientes relativos a los autos criminales contra Antonio Tandaso."

3. Ese hombre tenía códigos legales. Y él fue el que mandaba, gobernaba y luchaba.

4. Novelist Penelope Lively (1987, 31) argues in *Moon Tiger* that such details function to lend veracity to historical narratives:

There was a spaniel on board the *Mayflower*. This little dog, once, was chased by wolves not far from the plantation and ran to crouch between its master's legs "for succour". Smart dog—it knew that muskets are sharper than teeth. What I find remarkable about this animal is that I should know of its existence at all, that its unimportant passage through time should be recorded. It becomes one of those vital inessentials that convince one that history is true.

5. Ahora si, un viejo de los que éramos de la junta que estábamos, se levanta madrugado y se va esa mañana que ya era para meter el ganado como a mañana y se va como hoy día, se levanta y se va sin avisarles, diciendo que se va a avisar al dueño que lo venga a llevar el ternero, el torete. ¡Oh no! Llegado allá es que dijo, "Don Segundo, buenos días." "Buenos días hijo, vení." "Yo venía a decir que lo vaya a traer el toretico que se había quedado allá. Nosotros lo íbamos a meter en nuestro ganado. Se le ha quedado." "Se le ha quedado," es que dijo, pero digale, al fin pues: "Si ese no es quedado," es que le dijo: "Ese lo dejé yo. Por eso yo no salgo de la posesión. Si ese está en posesión por eso es que yo lo dejé ahí y cuidado, eso sí. Por eso yo ya voy a ir con mi ganado."

6. The cabildo has a copy of the 1976 Circuit Court sentence that finally and definitively returned El Zapatero to the community (Archivo del Cabildo Indígena del Gran Cumbal, Nariño [ACIGC/N], 1976, "Copia de la sentencia dictada . . . "). The community ultimately won its suit, but only after paying Mrs. de los Ríos, then owner of El Zapatero, a large sum of money; later reposessions were paid for by the Colombian government, and the lands passed free of charge to the cabildo. El Zapatero was divided into plots in 1976 and distributed to those residents of Cuaical who had contributed to its purchase.

7. Por eso decía mi abuelo, "Pero hijitos, yo ya no voy a durar. Ya estoy viejo. Ya me he de acabar de hoy para mañana, pero quizá mi descendencia, pero lo que les hago saber que el Zapatero, reclamen. Pregunten, juzguen en esos papeles. Esas sentencias no pierden," decía. "Esas están tranquilas en las oficinas. Averigüen," decía, "Y entonces verá lo que quizá alguno de mi descendencia quizá saldrá medio aparente," decía. Y mi hermano hizo el empeño, cierto, y sacó El Zapatero, mi hermano Hilarión.

8. In the early 1970s, El Zapatero seemed to be a smaller and thus more manageable target than the other haciendas that the Cumbales had lost during the colonial period. Moreover, those individuals most keen to adopt militant tactics were from nearby, were temporarily occupying leadership positions within the cabildo, and thus could use the hacienda as a test case for future, more extensive land repossessions.

9. Acá era siendo la cofradía de los padres. Acá en Las Tolas. Por eso era que tenían nombrado el Paridero. Asi están en los documentos. Porque ahí era solamente cofradía de ganado de los padres, dizque era. Hasta acá era. Todo esto es, todo esto había sido. Y siendo regidor en ese tiempo que había ganado, entonces esto lo dividió el regidor de esta vereda de Tasmag. Había sido un Chirán. Yo no se como llamaba ese Chirán, pero familia de todos esos Chiranes es. Eso me hace que era. Decían que ha sido el Alvaro, Alvaro Chirán. Ese lo dividió, toda la parte esa de Las Tolas, de Tasmag. Y la parte de El Zapatero, ese no lo dividió, ¡elay! Ese, á diciendo que el regidor de allá dijo que dentren no más allá, y "mas allá lo hemos de dividir. Como ahora ya está nuestro,

ahora ya está ganado. Al rato que queremos, ya hemos de. . . . " Cuando eso, ya sino él que estaba viviendo, y por el toro que dejo, y el bramadero.

10. Pasto-area documentation illustrates that, as in Peru, cofradías served as buffer zones for protecting lands and for raising the revenues that allowed caciques to retain their lands rather than sell them to pay spiraling tribute costs (ANE/Q, 1758, "Autos de don Bernardo Quatin . . . ," and 1774, "Expediente de don Lorenso Garcia Yaputa . . . "). But cofradías were also used for personal gain. The eighteenth-century caciques of Tuza (today San Gabriel, Ecuador) created cofradías in the warm maize-growing lands of Puntal (today Bolívar), later claiming them as their own property, much to the chagrin of Puntal's own hereditary chiefs (ANE/Q, 1791, "Expediente de los casiques y comun de yndios del pueblo del Puntal . . . "). Cofradías were also primary entry points for non-Indians anxious to acquire indigenous lands. There are numerous cases in the documentary record of usurpation of cofradía lands established on communal territories (ANE/Q, 1753, "Don Francisco Prado, con los indios . . . ," and 1797, "Recurso de doña Eugenia y doña Martina Cuatin . . . ").

11. Colonial cofradía contracts are reproduced in the legal proceedings (AJPCC/I, 1877, ff. 32v–33r) and oral testimony to their existence is likewise entered into the written record (ibid., ff. 84v–86v, 115v–118v). The proceedings also contain a copy of the proclamation officially expropriating the two farms (ibid., ff. 28v–29r) and Sánchez's deeds acquired when he purchased El Zapatero (ibid., ff. 26v–27r, 30r–v).

12. *Diario Oficial,* 5 July 1869.

13. Señor Presidente, la cuestión que tenéis que resolver es de alta importancia. Los ciudadanos quienes quieren saber si vos patrocinéis a vuestro Jefe Municipal Segundo Sánchez hasta el extremo de que haya burlado vuestras órdenes y las de la Corte Federal . . . en un país regido por una Constitución que garantiza la propiedad (Archivo Central del Cauca, Popayán [ACC/P], 1870, "Solicitud de Joaquín Miranda . . . ," f. 15r; future citations of this document will appear in the text).

14. El señor Alcalde procedió a darle la posesión. En este estado se presentó el señor Segundo Sánchez oponiéndose a la posesión del indicado finca "Zapatero," manifestando que era dueño de él i que estaba en posesión, i que además tenía la posesión precaria por sentencia pronunciada por el señor Juez del Circuito en su calidad Nacional, acompañando a su narración copia auténtica de la enunciada sentencia en dos fojas útiles, las mismas que se mandó agregar a estas diligencias, por lo que el señor Alcalde suspendió el acto posesorio. . . .

15. El Alcalde de Cumbal manifestó que nada importa que el Presidente del Estado lo multara, porque ni pagará la multa, ni cumplirá la sentencia. El Jefe Municipal Sánchez manifestó también que primero tomaríamos [los indígenas] posesión en los infiernos antes que en Zapatero.

16. El coadyuvante Segundo Sánchez, se dice rematador de dichos terrenos, aunque tal remate no se hizo en efecto y que él no pagó a la Nación su precio; y que abusando de la sencillez y pusilanimidad de los indios, se ha hecho dueño y poseedor de ellas (AJPCC/I, 1876a, n.p).

17. AJPCC/I, 1876b, future citations of this document will appear in the text.

18. . . . que al mismo tiempo se lansen todos los semovientes ajenos que se pasten en el para evitar en lo susecivo estas contravercias.

19. AJPCC/I, 1877, ." ff. 32v–33r; future citations of this document will appear in the text.

20. See also Notaría Primera de Ipiales [NP/I], 1886–87, "Remate de un terreno denominado 'El Zapatero' . . . ."

21. I have, for example, heard people refer to the document in the course of political oratory, but only as a kind of an oral footnote to their speeches.

22. Me preguntó a mí, el señor Alcalde, de qué, pues, qué hablara. Yo le dije en primer lugar de que eso había un título, la escritura número 228, que eso es dado por la colonia española al resguardo de los indígenas de Cumbal, y que éramos propietarios dueños. Y lo cual dijo el señor Alcalde, "Y eso, ¿quién te dijo?" Eso dijo que, "Los papeles viejos que ustedes tienen, ya es un cuento viejo que no vale ahora. Son las leyes del gobierno que eso [el Llano], pues, es ejido, de esa cantidad de tierra, ejido del municipio."

23. In early twentieth-century Bolivia, communities reconstructed colonial modes of social organization to resist the state, basing their legal claims on colonial documents. On at least one occasion, such papers were deemed "subversive" by the authorities, who disputed their legality (Rivera Cusicanqui 1986b).

24. Archivo del Cabildo Indígena de Mayasquer, Nariño [ACIM/N] 1922, "Documentos tocantes a los acontecimientos ocurridos en Santa Inés y Mayasquer en 1922." Darío and Lucinda Nazate of Tiúquer were eyewitnesses to the dispute and provided me with a detailed account of how it transpired.

25. Despues dijo él, "¡Caray! Para dejar en una olleta, no alcanza la plata. Me voy mejor a desollar el toro." Lo fué, lo mató el toro. Fué, lo que desollando, desde la boca le fue quitando la, volteando el cuero y entonces, elay, lo fue sacando. Solamente le dejó las patas desde los nudos no más. Las patas, y los nudos para abajo, con los cascos, eso sí. Lo más, lo fue sacando entero. Lo fue sacando. Le fue sacando la carne, todo lo que fue la carne, y quedó la piel. Ahora sí, la infló con cualquier cosa y le hizo secar. Ya que estuvo el toro intactico la cabeza si como que no le quitó. Los cachos es que le dejó. Ahora sí. Los cachos los hizo dorar de oro y los ojos también es que le puso unas pupilas tambien amarillas. Y los cascos también, es que le forró de oro. Y lo puso parado, ahora sí, como ya le llenó un poco de plata. Ya estaba ahí. Y le iba llenando, y el toro estaba parado ahí, y por las mañanas se levantaba y lo vía.

26. Ha sido noche de luna, noche de la menguante, [cuando Victor Tarapúes] ha estado pasando por ahí. Y ya que ha estado ya pasando ahí en el huerto de esa casa que ha sido del viejo Urbano, entonces dizque vió brillar en esa huerta, con el reflejo de la luna que da la menguante, decía. Pero eso decía mi primo, que le han conversado a él, pero no que el ha visto. Entonces que vió brillar. Entonces es que dijo "¿Qué es eso que brilla aca?" Como una vara, ya se fue acercando y más brillaba, mas brillaba. Y cuando ya estuvo

cerca y que se fijó más, había sido una culebra, dizque. Cuando ya fue cerca dizque pegó el brinco y se largó la culebra. De alli se fue, se perdió, para la zanja del, como derecho adonde "El Zapatero." Eso sí, y ya se perdió de vista, y "Yo ya no pase más, me dió miedo," es que decía. Había sido culebra que reverdeaba allá, ya es que amarilla. "Y cuando ya voy cerca, pegó el brinco y lo había quemado y se fué y se perdió."

27. "Bien entonces yo, que venía ahí", decía, "donde eran las piedras que había sido el fogón de esa casa vieja, que había sido de ese dueño." Decía ya, "Desde arriba ya lo ví de uno que bullía allí, que bullía. ¿Qué será? ¿Qué será que bulla allá? Entonces, cuando ya vine cerca," decía," ya lo distinguí que con el brillo de la luna, lo distinguí, que era gato. Eso es. Hay unos gatos colorados. Eso es. Con el brillo de la luna," decía, "ya lo ví que fue gato." Pero decía, "Ahí se ve que ese no fué gato limpio. Cuando ya bueno lo ví, que era gato. Cuando ya ví de cerca," decía, "ví un tremendo gato. Un gato, sí, pero fue deforme. Y cuando ya vine cerca, se echó el brinco y se fué," dijo, "y se cayó para la misma zanja de Chilcas, era esa zanja, yendo por el derecho de 'El Zapatero,' para adonde habia sido el encerrado de la huerta de esa casa."

28. Reichel-Dolmatoff (1972, 96) offers an interesting twist on the metaphor of the feline as the body politic in his description of the ritual that followed the killing of a puma among the Páez of Tierradentro: "The dead animal was carried triumphantly to the village where, in one of the houses, its body was laid out on a sort of altar crowned by an elaborate arch of branches beneath which the beast was put in a lifelike crouching position and surrounded by candles. The room and altar were adorned with flowers and red cloth, and the people danced around it, playing their musical instruments. At last the carcass was butchered, and each participant in the celebration was given a small morsel to eat but not before being warned that the meat should be prepared without the addition of salt."

29. Hernando Cuesta of Chiles told my collaborator, Angélica Mamián, that Mayasqueres routinely turned themselves into felines to steal poultry from their neighbors. In the Sibundoy Valley, felines are also associated with thievery: "If you dream a tiger, cattle thieves will appear / Dreaming that you are catching the tiger, you will surprise the cattle thief" (McDowell 1989, 52–53). Remember, also, the "thieving jaguar" in the dramatic dialogue quoted in chapter 4. Interestingly, though, snakes play a very different role: Darío Juaspuezán of Chiles told Angélica Mamián that he once encountered a large snake in a plantain grove and was instructed to not be afraid because the serpent was the grove's *cuidadora* or caretaker.

30. Among the Izoceños of Bolivia, the bull represents the hacendado. At Carnival, a man dressed as a bull fights the *enmascarados* or masked ones, who represent the ancestral spirits (Silvia Hirsch, personal communication).

31. The judicial and notarial archives of Ipiales are full of documentation of this procedure and of the sale of communal lands to non-Indians, with the approval of the cabildo, in times of extreme necessity. See, for example, NP/I, 1877, "Escritura de venta de un pedazo de la hacienda Cuetial . . . "; 1889a, "Rosa Chugal solicita licencia para enagenar acciones y derechos . . . "; 1889b,

"Venta del terreno Guan . . ."; 1898, "Escritura de venta de acción . . . "; 1903, "Documento de propiedad de Rosa Chirán . . . "; and Notaría Segunda de Ipiales [NS/I], 1919, "Escritura de venta del terreno Cualchío. . . ."

32. Esa zanja pues, ahí sí no le doy el dato desde cuándo existiría. Esa zanja ha de haber existido desde el tiempo que fueron los ricos, desde el tiempo de Mosquera, porque eso contaban los antepasados, que esa zanja la hicieron ellos, antiguamente, tratando de dividirse el Mundo Nuevo. Los primeros ricos que han entrado allá, los blancos. Esa no es hecha los indios, esa zanja, no. Esa es hecha los blancos, tratandose de dividirse. Por eso las zanjas.

33. El Frailejonal, llamaba ahí. Llamaba y llama todavía. Ahí era el punto de donde iba a ser la posesión. Entonces, tocaba irla a pasar la cuchilla del cerro. Tocaba pasarlo. Y ahí es una parte fría, carajo. Y de ahí para abajo tocaba ya de bajada. Cuando la señora volteó acá, el cabildo ya estuvo abajo en el Frailejonal, recibiendo la posesión. Ahí ella también se cayó del caballo y rodaba en el suelo, pensaba lejos, lejos del punto de la posesión. Pero por eso no le valió y desde ahí hasta ahora, esa lucha tuvieron, tuvo el cabildo de Chiles.

34. It is unclear whether Graciana was a mestiza or an Indian. But since she was contrary to the aims of the cabildo, she was looked upon as a supporter of mestizo politics.

35. I am indebted to Catherine Allen, Deborah Caro, and Enrique Mayer for alerting me to this and the following argument.

Chapter Seven

1. Theatrical presentations of the Reyes Magos, using Spanish scripts, were widespread in the Andes and can still be found in some regions (see, for example, Beyersdorff 1988). Until recently, such plays were performed in Cumbal by Eloy Quilismal and his brothers; other similar plays were presented in Muellamués as Moisés Tapie and Eduardo Peregüeza of Nazate informed me. In the early colonial period, sons of caciques trained at special schools in Quito were inculcated with Christian doctrine through participation in dramatic presentations. See Moreno Proaño (1979) cited in Hartmann and Oberem (1981).

2. See, for example, Archivo Nacional del Ecuador [ANE/Q], 1800, "Expedientes relativos a la muerte de Clavijo."

3. HISTORIA DEL GRUPO ARTISTICO LOS CUMBES, representantes de esta gran historia que surge de una gente muy joven como es EL GRUPO ARTISTICO LOS CUMBES, quienes memorizaron este gran evento. . . . All of my Los Cumbes quotes are taken from typed scripts, copies of which were kindly given to me by Miguel Angel Alpala.

4. The alternative venues for historical interpretation provided by theater also afford the powerless with a protected space within which criticisms of the powerful are permissable. Kris Hardin alerted me to this alternative explanation when she described to me similar theatrical presentations in Sierra Leone.

5. Un muchacho que yo se me hacía que era hasta familia dijo, "Señora, deme abrazando ésto." Había sido un revólver, y yo sin decir nada lo recibí. Y

entonces lo agarraron y lo hicieron alzar las manos. Entonces yo con el revólver en el sobaco. Entonces ya dijeron, "Sigan a la cárcel indios tales y cuales." Ya nos trataron mal. Bueno, ya nos siguieron trayendo, nos arriaron. Entonces, yo me acuerdo y dije yo, "Por más acá me caiga," dije, "y entonces el revólver cae pues." Destapé la cantina y bonitico lo puse parado, lo tapé. Y era cierto que más acá tropiezo en un adobe, como era de noche, y me caí boca abajo. "¡Chilín!" El revólver dentro de la cantina. Entonces el soldado dijo, "¡Oh!" Dijo—ya se cayó—, "Qué es que lleva en esa cantina?" Entonces dije, "Las tasas que traje para tomar el café." "Ah, bueno," dijo.

6. La vereda Santa Rosa presenta los problemas de Medardo Erazo. Vereda Riveras presenta los novios con sus tradiciones y costumbres indígenas, con nuestra autoridad y su ley especial que nos protege, Ley 89 de 1890. ¡Viva el día del indígena! La vereda Chapud presenta el engaño de los blancos en el año 1560 al cacique Bernardo. La vereda Guan Puente Alto se hace presente en el Día del Indígena con lo siguiente: sepultura del cacique Nutibara y la Gaitana por arresto de los españoles. En el Día del Indígena la vereda Cristo presente con el rechazo de las cooperativas de tierras en los resguardos del Sur Occidente. Comunidad presenta pasión y muerte de nuestra raza; esto sucedió en el año de 1536.

7. Pre-Columbian burials have been discovered throughout Pasto territory. Nevertheless, it is only when memory is jogged by something as legitimate as a museum poster that obvious historical referents are incorporated into public displays. Similarly, it was only after the appearance of *Glory*, a film about an all-black Civil War regiment, that the Massachusetts 54th Volunteer Infantry Regiment was incorporated into reenactments of the Civil War (*Washington Post*, 20 May 1990). Nutibara, the famous cacique from what is today Antioquia, is a name undoubtedly culled from school textbooks, television, or even possibly tourism.

8. Tu no sabías que nosotros los indios, tenemos nuestro estudio por medio de la telepatía o de las brizas que cubren los cuatro vientos de la Amazonía colombiana.

9. Esta gran historia constata sobre las inteligencias de los caciques antepasados, quienes podían transformar figuras a animales de las selvas y demás cosas tan importantes.

10. Bolivian cinematographic reenactments of recent events using indigenous actors recast history as what "should have happened" (Sanjinés and Grupo Ukamau 1979), which is not precisely the same as altering the events of the past. Based on working-class autobiographies from Italy, Portelli (1991, 108–10) suggests that this emphasis on possibility, as opposed to reality, is a form of protest.

11. These militant dramas are very different from the conquest plays described by Wachtel (1971), insofar as the latter was a theater of the vanquished while the former reverses history so that the Indians are the victors.

12. The tradition of Andean Christs found in the Peruvian and Bolivian Andes (see Allen 1988; Gow 1980; Nash 1979; Sallnow 1987) do not exist in southern Nariño, whose indigenous population is considerably more cultur-

ally integrated into the dominant mestizo society. Piedad Moreno and Raúl Fueltala of Panán shared with me their reinterpretations of biblical stories situating Christ in Andean landscapes. Their Christ was forced to drink bitter quinua-water instead of vinegar; he hid from the Romans in a field of the Andean lupine called *chocho* (*tarhui* in Peru), which made noise when he moved and betrayed his presence. Howard-Malverde (1981, 194–215) reports similar stories in southern Ecuador. But stories in which the Christ figure or any other saint is transformed to take on Andean messianic traits, are not told in Nariño (see also Bernal Villa 1953 and Rappaport 1980–81 on the Colombian Páez).

13. The order of pasos at the 1987 Good Friday procession in Panán were: Cruz Alta (a large cross); Turbantes (the souls of Purgatory); the Cabildo; Adam and Eve; the Sacrifice of Isaac; Joseph and His Brothers; Sampson; the Last Supper; the Prudent Virgins; Jesus, Friend of the Children; Jesus of Nazareth; the Doctors of the Law; the Holy Sepulchre; Honor Guard; Saint John and the Slaves (a statue of Saint John carried by his religious brotherhood); Our Lady of Sorrows and Her Brotherhood (an image of the Virgin carried by her brotherhood). All of the pasos were represented by comuneros. In similar processions that used to take place in Cumbal, mestizos prepared the tableaux and Indians were relegated to two pasos, the cabildo banner and the army of Turbantes; these mestizo presentations were, according to descriptions I elicited, essentially identical to the tableaux in Panán.

14. Pues la Cuna de la Sabiduría está debajo de crueles montañas escondidas, según lo dijo los sueños del indígena que subió a visitar al recién nacido que estaba en dicha Cuna de paja, que estaba hospedado en uno de los corredores de "La Casa de Belén," aquél que dejó la Piedra de la filosofía, etc., ese indígena que le llevó un regalo de oro como a hombre y Rey de los reyes.

The influence of Lame's writings, published under the title *En defensa de mi raza* (Lame 1971 [1939]), will be analyzed below with regard to their inclusion in theatrical dialogue. See Castillo-Cárdenas (1987) for an interpretation of Lame's reconciling of universal Christian history with the aboriginal past. Colonial-era Quechua author Felipe Guaman Poma de Ayala, in *El primer nueva corónica y buen gobierno* (Guaman Poma de Ayala 1980 [1615]), also cast indigenous history within a universal Christian framework; see Adorno (1986).

15. Porque el blanco sabe que somos creados tras los bosques, los páramos más lejanos y más abandonados. Pero nos hemos creado con sangre propia y muy fuerte a saber que somos indios y descendientes de nuestro cacique Cumbe y de nuestra cacica María Panana. Porque esa descendencia nunca se perderá, porque de allí renacieron los Alpalas, los Tapies, los Quilismales, los Cuaicales, los Tarapueces, los Chinguades, etc.

The speech more or less follows the section order: Alpala is a surname common in Tasmag, Tapie and Quilismal in Quilismal, Cuaical in Cuaical, Tarapués in Nazate, and Chinguad in Cuaspud. The inversion of the positions of Cuaical and Quilismal undoubtedly reflects some confusion on the part of the playwright. Those who live in Cuaical or Quilismal, the two sections that share a common territory, are frequently unaware of the vereda affiliation of their

neighbors. The playwright probably grouped all of the Cuaical-Quilismal surnames together, without distinguishing them by vereda.

16. La policía les decía, "A Ustedes, ¿quién les dice vamos a recuperar?" o
"¿Cuál es el que empieza? Uno ha de ser." Entonces que decían, "No, a nosotros nadie nos avisa. No sé. Ni se conoce a la gente que baja. Vamos a la
tierra, pero no se sabe quien. Es que a nosotros nos relumbra el cacique. Vamos
a la tierra y todo el mundo se levanta. Relumbra en el sueño el cacique."

17. The name might be a transformation of the chiefly surname Cumbal,
which appears in Deed 228 and other colonial documents. On the role of "con-
tentless" symbols in evoking meaning as opposed to carrying it, see Keesing's
(1982) overview on the construction of *kastom*, a culturally based nationalist
ideology in Melanesia.

18. Pero olvidemos de la comida, hijitos míos. Vengan un momento para
acá. Les voy a contar unas tantas cosas muy bonitas. Verán, hijitos míos, les
voy a dejar estas grandiosas experiencias, que cuando me muera, tengan que
ver por estos grandes recuerdos de tu mamita. En primer lugar, Ustedes tendrán que ser unos buenos muchachos indígenas, y muy cariñosos con todos
los que se les presenten, y defensores de sus propios derechos que sus
abuelitos les dejaron. Por otro lado, tendrán que ser unos indígenas muy
aparentes en trabajar sus tierras, que nos han dejado nuestros cabildos, y no
ser unos vendedores de estos derechos. Porque la historia nos enseña que no
hay que vender nuestra tierra, sino seguirla trabajando para mantenernos de
ella, y verán lo que así vivirán una vida muy deliciosa y contenta. En segundo
lugar les digo que sigan trabajando estos bayetones tan lindos para los trajes
de nosotros y de otros hermanos. Por otra parte seguir recuperando nuestro
tesoro que esta perdiendose para así poder decorar nuestros vestidos tan importantes.

19. Su traje es que andan las mujeres vestidas con una manta angosta a
manera de costal, en que se cubren de los pechos hasta la rodilla; y otra manta
pequeña encima, que viene a caer sobre la larga, y todas las más son hechas
de hierbas y de cortezas de árboles, y algunas de algodón. Los indios se cubren
con una manta asimismo larga, que terná tres o cuatro varas, con la cual se
dan una vuelta por la cintura y otra por la garganta, y echan el ramal que sobra
por encima de la cabeza, y en las partes deshonestas traen maures pequeños.

20. Christian (1981, 220) describes similar processions of living images in
sixteenth-century Spain. Clendinnen (1990), in a consideration of the problems
historians confront in distinguishing between "Indian" and "Catholic" religi-
osity in post-conquest Mexico, discusses these enactments in Aztec communities. An interesting example of the conflation of mythic/historical figures and
costume can be found in Guaman Poma de Ayala's (1980 [1615]) illustrations
of Inca royalty, who are described almost exclusively in terms of their costume.

21. Así, yo me tocó de ser el Rey. Entonces, claro, yo era a componer el
caballo. El caballo era bien compuesto con capa, bien adornado desde los
cascos forrados, con papel de ese amarillo, riendas, freno, la frente, todo, el
galápago tapado con capa, brillando eso de estrellas, adornos. En eso iba pues,
en Rey propio, pues eso sí, y yo iba vestido blanco con capa y con la espada

y con un copón también de rey. Iba manejando mi caballo y con la espada y cogido el copón y con buena corona, todo. A mí me tocó atrás de los Centuriones. Los Centuriones iban adelante, cuando ya me gritaban por lista, "El Rey Saúl, ¡siga!" Entonces, ahí tenía que seguir, y atrás de mi vuelta, los que les iba a tocar.

22. *R.F.:* Eva era una mujer, entonces ella tenía que ponerse su interior y taparse con hojas, tapadas de hojas de esa de bijao, fajado como una follera, fajado por acá por el cuerpo, todo, vestidos de hoja. Y Adán, lo mismo. Por eso, todo eso, todo figuraban, todo formaban, pues, el Paraíso, todo. (*J.R.:* ¿Cómo era el Paraíso?) *R.F.:* El Paraíso lo formaban, lo hacían un huerto grande, con ramas. Ahí colgaban frutas, en fin, todo eso. Así era el Paraíso terrenal, de donde salía Adán y Eva. Y seguían yendo así por el desfile hasta llegar a la iglesia vuelta, hasta meterlo adentro al Galileo, o sea, a Jesús Nazareno.

23. Nosotros, los indígenas, mas aborrecidos de este gran "Cumbal" de los blancos españoles *que llegaron este día 12 de octubre de 1492 hasta las tierras llamadas Guananí, que hoy las llamamos Colombia.*

24. *El hijo de un indígena se sentará en el trono de sabiduría,* para defender nuestra propia sangre, sangre que por largo *tiempo se ha estado ocultando por este vengativo feroz de nosotros.*

25. *La prehistoria repercute lo de nuestros antepasados, sus asientos allá en esa colina donde está sepultada la casa de la divinidad, según la prehistoria de Bochica, quien por medio de signos o parábolas donde se constataba en los sublimes rayos del sol: cuando se presentaba por el oriente y así se consagraba las ceremonias de los dioses que adoraban nuestros antepasados. Pero los aventureros que llegaron el 12 de octubre de 1492 en nombre de la civilización* hicieron blandir la cuchilla de la mano y la intención para quitarnos la vida de nosotros y esas grandes riquezas que nosotros teníamos heredado de nuestros caciques antepasados. Y de hoy en día nosotros, los Colombianos, estamos acompañados del valor, y *unidos como un concierto de águilas encolerizadas lograremos la defensa de nosotros* para que se nos haga justicia, y seamos amparados por las autoridades competentes de toda la nación, de toda Colombia, y para todos los colombianos.

26. Subsequent references to *Los pensamientos* will appear in the text.

27. A guerrilla organization was even named after Lame. See Castillo-Cárdenas (1971; 1987), Castrillón Arboleda (1973), and Rappaport (1990b) for more on Lame's biography and writings.

28. The song makes multiple references to Lame's writings. In his treatise, Lame repeatedly refers to his archrival, Popayán poet and politician, Guillermo León Valencia. His most often used example of struggle is his successful efforts at creating a resguardo in Chaparral, Tolima. As is evident from the title of the book, Lame claimed to have acquired his learning from the forest.

29. Así nacerá mañana un concierto de indígenas de esos descendientes legítimamente de nuestra tierra Guananí, descendientes de esas tribus odiadas, perseguidas del hombre no indígena.

30. Ese crimen está oculto, señores; pero esa justicia llegará, en que el indio colombiano recuperará su trono, etc., etc.

31. *Atallo cundulcunca*, pájaro o nido de los cóndores. Este cóndor de mi pensamiento y esa águila de mi psicología indígena la que se engendró cuando pasó ese cóndor o cóndores como un concierto de golondrinas parleras que visitan las estaciones del tiempo, dichos cóndores unos buscaron su morada en los altos peñascos, y otros debajo de las sombras de viejos robles, los que dan el grito hoy en medio de la inmensa soledad que me acompañó.

32. Ahora yo les pregunto, por qué la cólera de los siglos o de las edades no han podido destruír o borrar hasta hoy esas leyendas que marcan los Cementerios de nuestra prehistoria; Cementerios que se encuentran unos en el vientre de la tierra y otros forman el redil de extensas lagunas de agua, y otros son depósitos de las grandes riquezas de mis antepasados Soberanos, quienes dominaban muchedumbres y que esta corte de Soberanos indígenas varios no fueron hijos de mujer, como un "Sinviora" fundador de los templos de la Divinidad del sol y que también enseño a los indígenas cómo debían adorar al sol.

Conclusion

1. The rivalry did not cease, however. Under the sponsorship of Liberal politician Arellano, Chirán and his supporters established a landholding cooperative independent of the cabildo, through which they purchased a hacienda. Their action drew harsh criticism from cabildos throughout the region, all of whom perceived this move as a repudiation of the institution of the cabildo and not simply as a strike against Alonso Valenzuela. The cooperative did not mend fences with the cabildo until 1989, when the then-governor found himself at odds with Valenzuela, prompting an alliance between cabildo and cooperative.

2. Similarly, Greg Dening (1988, 27) writes: "Labelling an inscription as a primary source gives it a character of authenticity and immediacy. It supports the conviction that the inscriptions are the Past itself."

3. Roberto González Echevarría (1990) effectively illustrates this point in his study of the appropriation of the format governing the Spanish legal petition by indigenous and mestizo authors at various points in the history of Latin America. For instance, the *Comentarios Reales* of the colonial chronicler Garcilaso Inca de la Vega is, according to González Echevarría, essentially a literary adaptation of a letter of appeal to the Crown made by the indigenous author to legitimize his descent from his Spanish father (ibid., ch. 2). The archive even worms its way into contemporary Latin American fiction, including Gabriel García Márquez's *One Hundred Years of Solitude*, a novel that ultimately turns out to be a chronicle of the history of Macondo that is written even as it is being read (ibid., ch. 4).

4. See Johannes Fabian's 1990 translation and analysis of a Swahili history from Zaire, in which forms of oral representation influence written language. Fabian's commentary focuses, for the most part, on the transposition of lexical features in the written record.

5. A good example of this approach is David Lan's *Guns and Rain* (1985), a study of how spirit mediums were harnessed by guerrillas during Zimbabwe's

struggle for independence. Instead of organizing his analysis chronologically according to his own interpretation of the past, Lan situates his historical narrative in a culturally-specific framework that incorporates myth and personal reminiscences.

6. Indigenous writers from North and South America provide hints as to some of these sources, including contemporary political broadsides and local newsletters, the contents of family albums, even tattered school textbooks, commercial music recordings, and old identity cards. See Mamani Quispe (1988), Momaday (1977), Rivera Cusicanqui (1986b), Vizenor (1984).

Glossary

amparo Royal grant of protection. In southern Nariño, understood to denote royal decrees bestowing land rights upon indigenous communities.

cabildante Cabildo member, whether elected, as are the governor and the regidores, or appointed, as are the teniente and the secretary.

cabildo Annually elected council administering resguardo affairs. The cabildo of Cumbal includes seven elected members, the governor and six regidores, and two appointed members, the teniente and the secretary. All but the secretary carry staffs of office.

cacique Pre-Columbian or colonial-era hereditary chief.

cacicazgo Pre-Columbian or colonial-era hereditary chiefdom.

Camino de Barbacoas Colonial-era and nineteenth-century footpath and later bridlepath linking highland Nariño with the riverine port of Barbacoas on the Pacific coast. Indians from Cumbal, Guachucal, Colimba, and other Pasto communities worked as carriers on this trade route, conveying merchandise, and even people, on their backs.

casa de cabildo Cabildo office.

cofradía Religious fraternal organization, frequently leasing lands. During the nineteenth century, cofradía lands were repossessed by the national government and placed on public auction.

comunero Resguardo member. Resguardo membership is generally determined by descent and maintained through residence, although it is possible to acquire comunero status through application to the cabildo.

contrario Individual opposed to cabildo's recuperación strategy.

deed Legal document validating rights to private property (*escritura* in Spanish).

Deed 228 Cumbal's 1758 resguardo title, providing the outer boundaries of Cumbal, Panán, Chiles, and Mayasquer.

document Legal document validating usufruct rights to land (*documento* in Spanish).

junta de acción comunal A locally based public works committee recognized and supervised by the cabildo.

Law 89 of 1890 Central piece of Colombian Indian legislation defining the nature of resguardos. The 1991 constitution nullifies Law 89, which is to be replaced by as-yet-unwritten legislation.

memorista Native historian, usually a former cabildo member or a close relative of cabildantes.

minga Andean communal work party.

páramo Marshy plain at the top of the cordillera in the northern Andes.

parcialidad Colonial-era subunit of a cacicazgo. Also, term used in the nineteenth century to refer to sections or veredas.

recuperación Political process of repossession of usurped lands by occupation, cultural and economic revitalization. The most important repossessed haciendas in Cumbal are La Boyera (1985), El Laurel (1981), the Llano de Piedras (1975), and El Zapatero (1975).

recuperador A follower of the cabildo strategy of land repossession. The opposite of *contrario*.

regidor Alderman elected by the adult members of a vereda to represent them at the cabildo. The regidor's functions include acting as an intermediary between the cabildo and the vereda, solving minor disputes, and distributing repossessed lands to vereda members.

resguardo Indigenous territorial unit comprising communal and inalienable lands administered by elected councils and legitimized by colonial titles.

Royal Provision/Real Provisión Mid-eighteenth-century record of a dispute between hacendados and the caciques of Cumbal and Nazate. Used by twentieth-century cabildos as a source of historical information and as evidence of community boundaries.

teniente Cabildo officer whose obligations include maintaining order at cabildo meetings, sending messages from the governor, and completing other non-decision-making tasks assigned by the governor. The teniente is appointed by the governor and belongs to the same vereda.

terrateniente Large landowner, frequently employing sharecroppers. Terratenientes in Nariño generally own cattle ranches ranging from 50 to 300 hectares in size.

vereda Rural neighborhood. In Cumbal, the six veredas are represented by regidores and are arranged in a territorial hierarchy. Veredas are alternately called sections in the text. The six veredas of Cumbal, in hierarchical order, are Guan, Tasmag, Cuaical, Quilismal, Nazate, and Cuaspud.

List of Narrators

Cumbal (vereda in parenthesis)

Alpala, Hilarión (Quilismal)**
Alpala, Lastenia (Quilismal)
Alpala, Miguel Angel (Cuaical)
Alpala, Nestor (Nazate)
Aza, Rosa Elena (Tasmag)
Chalparizán, Alvina (Nazate)
Chirán, Alejandro (Cuaical)
Chirán, Bernardita (Cuaical)
Chirán, Efraín (Cuaical)
Chirán, José Elipcio (Cuaical)
Colimba, Agustín (Cuaspud)
Colimba, Pastor (Nazate)*
Colimba, Segundo (Nazate)
Cuaical, Benjamín (Cuaical)
Cuaical, Mercedes (Tasmag)
Cuaical, Salomon (Cuaical)
Cuaical, Valentín (Cuaical)
Grupo Artístico "Los Cumbes"
  (Cuaical)

Imbago, Alonso (Nazate)
Mimalchí, Fernando (Tasmag)
Mimalchí, José Abrahán
  (Tasmag)
Paguay, Diomedes (Guan)
Paguay, Julio (Tasmag)
Peregüeza, Eduardo (Nazate)
Piarpuezán, Angel María
  (Nazate)
Puerres, Mesías (Cuaspud)**
Quilismal, Eloy (Quilismal)
Taimal, Miguel (Guan)
Tapie, Moisés (Nazate)
Tarapués, Efrén (Nazate)
Tarapués, Manuel Jesús (Nazate)
Tarapués, María Isabel (Nazate)
Tarapués, Nestor (Nazate)*
Valenzuela, Alonso (Tasmag)
Valenzuela, Gilberto (Cuaical)
Valenzuela, Helí (Nazate)
Valenzuela, Oligario (Quilismal)

*interview by Luz Angélica Mamián
  Guzmán
**interview by Helí Valenzuela Mites

Panán (vereda in parenthesis)

Canacuán, José Delfín (El Placer)
Cuásquer, David (Panán Centro)
Cuásquer, Nazario (Panán
  Centro)
Fueltala, Manuel (La Libertad)
Fueltala, Raúl (La Libertad)
Moreno, Piedad (La Libertad)
Nazate, Segundo (Panán Centro)

Chiles (no vereda affiliations)

Cuesta, Hernando*
Juaspuezán, Darío*
Malte, Rosario*
Salazar, Francisco*

Mayasquer (Vereda Tiúquer)

Chinguad, Lastenia
Nazate, Darío
Nazate, Lucinda
Quilismal, Alfredo
Quilismal, Jorge
Quilismal, Roberto
Tarapués, Alonso

Bibliography

Archival References

Archivo Central del Cauca, Popayán (ACC/P)

1671–1747. "Cartas cuentas de la Provincia de los Pastos," *Archivo Colonial*, signatura 1193 (1671); sig. 3017 (1721); sig. 3074 (1722); sig. 3112 (1723–26); sig. 3250 (1724); sig. 3171 (1726); sig. 3218 (1732); sig. 3518 (1732); sig. 3799 (1736–39); sig. 3880 (1742); sig. 4137 (1743–47).

1722–1810. "Numeraciones de la Provincia de los Pastos," *Archivo Colonial*, signaturas 3031, 3039–41, 3046–47 (1722); sig. 3451 (1727–30); sig. 3215 (1732); sig. 5035 (1767–68); sig. 6056 (1788); sig. 7470 (1810).

1870. "Solicitud de Joaquín Miranda como apoderado de los indíjenas de Cumbal," *Archivo de la Antigua Gobernación del Cauca ("Archivo Muerto")*, paquete 108, legajo 32.

1895. "Expedientes relativos al resguardo de Ancuya," *Archivo de la Antigua Gobernación del Cauca ("Archivo Muerto")*, paquete 221, legajo 51.

Archivo del Cabildo Indígena del Gran Cumbal, Nariño (ACIGC/N)

1906. "Real Cédula o Provisión," *Asuntos Varios* (*see* Notaría Primera de Ipiales [1906 (1712–58)]).

1908. "Escritura 228 de 1908," *Asuntos Varios* (*see* Notaría Primera de Pasto [1908 (1758)]).

1911. "Amparo 131 de 1922," *Asuntos Varios* (*see* Notaría Primera de Ipiales [1892 (1883)]).

1919–25. "Libro copiador de actas de devociones de la iglesia habierto el 19 de abril del año de 1919," *Asuntos Varios*.

1935. "Inventario de las piezas y más diligencias pertenecientes al mismo archivo del cabildo del mismo año 1935," *Asuntos Varios*.

1940. "Inventario de las piezas y más diligencias pertenecientes al mismo archivo del cabildo del año de 1940," *Asuntos Varios*.

1950. "Borradores de cartas del Cabildo al Ministerio de Minas, sobre los yacimientos de azufre del Cerro de Cumbal," *Asuntos Varios*.

1961. "Libros copiadores de devociones abierto por el cabildo del año de 1928," *Asuntos Varios*.

1976. "Copia de la sentencia dictada por el Juzgado Civil del Circuito de Ipiales, de fecha 5 de abril de 1976, al proceso ordinario, sobre reivindicación del terreno de resguardo denominado 'Zapatero', adelantado por el Resguardo de Indígenas de la Parcialidad de Cumbal, en contra de la señora Luz América de los Ríos Herrera," *Asuntos Varios*.

Archivo del Cabildo Indígena de Mayasquer, Nariño (ACIM/N)

1922. "Documentos tocantes a los acontecimientos ocurridos en Santa Inés y Mayasquer en 1922."

Archivo del Comité de Solidaridad con las Luchas Indígenas, Pasto (ACSLI/P)

1982. "Informe del Primer Recorrido en Reconocimiento de los Linderos del Gran Cumbal."

Archivo de la División de Asuntos Indígenas, Bogotá (ADAI/B)

1937–50. "Expedientes relativos a la extincion del Resguardo Indígena de Males, Nariño."

1939–50. "Expedientes relativos a la división del Resguardo Indígena de Consacá, Nariño."

1939–52. "Expedientes relativos al Resguardo Indígena de Túquerres."

1940–43. "Expedientes relativos al Resguardo Indígena de Ipiales."

1940–60. "Expedientes relativos al Resguardo de Indígenas de San Juan, Nariño."

1948–50. "Expedientes relativos a la división del Resguardo de Chachagüí, Nariño."

Archivo General de Indias, Sevilla (AGI/S)

1558. "Traslado del libro de tassaciones quel muy magnifico señor licenciado Tomas Lopez hizo en la gobernacion e provincia de Popayan," *Audiencia de Quito*, 60:1.

1570–71. "Tassacion de los tributos de los naturales de las ciudades de San Joan de Pasto y Almaguer de la governacion de Popayan hecha por el señor licenciado Garcia de Valverde," *Audiencia de Quito*, 60:2.

Archivo Histórico del Banco Central del Ecuador, Ibarra (AHBC/I)

1592. "Testamento de don Cristobal Cuatin, principal del pueblo de Tuza," 1339/244/1/M.
1605. "Testamento de doña Catalina Tuza, principal del pueblo de Tuza," 1335/295/1/M.
1654. "Protocolos y testamentos a cargo de Juan Francisco Guapastal, escribano nombrado de Tulcan," 1140/39/6/M.

Archivo Histórico del Banco Central del Ecuador, Quito (AHBC/Q)

1748. "Autos seguidos por doña Estefania Pastas pretendiendo el cacicazgo del pueblo de Pastas en la provincia de los Pastos para su hijo don Gregorio Garcia Putag contra don Tomas Sapuis Aça," 19/2, ff. 125–265.

Archivo del Juzgado Primero Civil del Circuito, Ipiales (AJPCC/I)

1876a. "Apelación que el Ministerio Público i Segundo Sánchez han interpuesto contra la sentencia que pronunció el Juez del Circuito de Obando en Ipiales a 20 de setiembre de 1875."
1876b. "Copia perteneciente a los indígenas del Distrito de Cumbal, sobre la restitución del terreno 'Zapatero' y 'Tolas', por centencia difinitiva de la Corte Suprema Federal."
1877. "Juicio promovido por el señor Segundo Sánchez contra los indígenas del Distrito de Cumbal por los terrenos 'Zapatero' y 'Tolas.'"

Archivo Nacional del Ecuador, Quito (ANE/Q)

1694. "Materia seguida por don Ambrosio de Prado y Sayalpud, sobre el cacicazgo de Cumbal," Fondo Popayan, caja 13.
1735. "Thomas Rodriguez de Herrera, con fray Jose Pintado, sobre las tierras de Yanguel," Fondo Popayán, caja 55.
1746. "Autos en favor de Miguel Garcia Paspuel Tuza por unas tierras que heredo de su abuela," Fondo Indígenas, caja 63.
1747. "Autos de don Visente Garcia Yaputa, gobernador, y el comun de yndios del pueblo de Carlosama, con don Mariano Paredes, sobre las tierras nombradas Yapudquer y San Sevastian, en los Pastos," Fondo Popayán, caja 75.
1753. "Don Francisco Prado, con los indios, sobre el Salado de Pasto," Fondo Popayán, caja 86.
1757. "Cuaderno de los instrumentos de la escritura de venta, otorgada por don Pedro Guatinango a don Andres Gualsago y testamento de don Francisco Paspuel Guachan en la causa que siguen don Hernando de Cuatinpas y don Pedro Garcia, principales del pueblo de Tusa, con don Antonio Luna, sobre tierras," Fondo Indígenas, caja 77.
1758. "Autos de don Bernardo Quatin y demas casiques de los pueblos de la jurisdiccion de Pasto, sobre el amparo de mas tierras de comunidad," Fondo Popayán, caja 99.

1764. "Autos de don Marthin Cumbal Aza, sobre el cacicazgo de Cumbal," *Fondo Popayan*, caja 111.

1771. "Autos de proclama de don Matheo Garcia Paspuel Tusa para el cacicazgo de los pueblos de El Angel, Puntal y Tusa, en la jurisdiccion de la Villa de Ibarra," *Fondo Cacicazgos*, caja 35, vol. 62.

1772. "Autos de don Juan Rosero, vecino de la Provincia de los Pastos, con los indios de Tulcan, sobre unas tierras," *Fondo Indígenas*, caja 97.

1774. "Expediente de don Lorenso Garcia Yaputa, casique, y el comun de yndios de Carlosama, sobre tierras," *Fondo Popayán*, caja 139.

1791. "Expediente de los casiques y comun de yndios del pueblo del Puntal, con los casiques del pueblo de Tusa, sobre tierras," *Fondo Cacicazgos*, caja 3 (Carchi).

1792. "Titulos y ynstrumentos de los yndios y casiques del pueblo de Tusa sobre la propiedad de vnas tierras," *Fondo Cacicazgos*, caja 3 (Carchi).

1797. "Recurso de doña Eugenia y doña Martina Cuatin, contra don Francisco Rodriguez Clavijo, por despojo de tierras y maltrato," *Fondo Popayán*, caja 232.

1800. "Expedientes relativos a la muerte de Clavijo," *Fondo Popayán*, caja 246.

1803. "Expedientes relativos a los autos criminales contra Antonio Tandaso," *Fondo Rebeliones*, caja 6.

Archivo Personal de Salomón Cuaical, Cumbal (APSC/C)

1872. "Documento de adjudicación del terreno Chendé."

Notaría Primera de Ipiales (NP/I)

1877. "Escritura de venta de un pedazo de la hacienda Cuetial, vendido por Agustin Erazo y esposa a Manuel Salvador Chalparizan, por 47 pesos."

1886–87. "Remate de un terreno denominado 'El Zapatero' en el distrito de Cumbal, al señor Sánchez."

1889a. "Rosa Chugal solicita licencia para enagenar acciones y derechos en el sitio denominado Piedra Tabla, correspondiente a los antiguos terrenos de reversión de las comunidades indígenas de Carlosama, teniendo pruebas de su suma pobreza," t. 1.

1889b. "Venta del terreno Guan en el distrito de Guachucal, por Rafael Serafín Cuaspud, a Juan Ramón Moreno," t. 1, f. 49, Escritura 324.

1892a [1873]. "Balerio Cuaycal, regidor de la parcialidad de Tasmag, pide se efectuen diligencias de deslinde entre las parcialidades de Tasmag y Cuaycal," ff. 463–80.

1892b. "El Cabildo de Cumbal pide la protocolización de los títulos de propiedad de los terrenos Llano de Piedras y Consuelo, Guan, Cuaical, Quilismal, Tasmag, Nasate y Cuaspud, que son parcialidades pertenecientes al distrito de Cumbal," t. 2, f. 397.

1892c [1883]. "Protocolización de los títulos que poseen los indígenas de Cumbal en los terrenos denominados Llano de Piedras, Consuelo y Cuaspud,"

f. 424, Escritura 131 (copy consulted is a 1911 transcription, "Amparo 131 de 1922," in ACIGC/C, *Asuntos Varios*).

1898. "Escritura de venta de acción y derecho que tiene en los terrenos comunales pertenecientes a la parcialidad de Guan en el distrito de Cumbal, por Manuel Colimba Ortega, a Mesías Cháves," t. 2, f. 1011.

1903. "Documento depropiedad de Rosa Chiran, del punto llamado Duguespud, en la parialidad de Guan, adquirida por compra brecha a Sofonias Mites," t. 1, f. 115.

1906 [1712–58]. "Expediente sobre los linderos del resguardo del Gran Cumbal," Escritura 997 de 1906 (copy consulted is a 1944 transcription of the 1906 registry of title, "Real Cédula o Provisión," in ACIGC/C, *Asuntos Varios*).

Notaría Primera de Pasto (NP/P)

1908 [1758]. "Expediente sobre los linderos del Resguardo del Gran Cumbal," Escritura 228 de 1908 (transcription consulted is located in ACIGC/C, *Asuntos Varios*).

Notaría Segunda de Ipiales (NS/I)

1919. "Escritura de venta del terreno Cualchío, en Cuetial, de José A. Aza a José Tarapués," t. 1, ff. 1–158.

Newspapers and Periodicals

Chasqui Cumbe, Cumbal
Diario Oficial, Bogotá
Gaceta Constitucional, Bogotá
Unidad Indígena, Bogotá
Washington Post, Washington, D.C.

Pamphlets, Political Documents, and Position Papers

Autoridades Indígenas de Colombia (AICO). 1992. "Elementos para la construcción de una política indigenista del estado colombiano," presentation of the Movimiento de Autoridades Indígenas to the Comisión de Política Indigenista, 14 August 1992, Bogotá.

Autoridades Indígenas del Sur Occidente (AISO). 1985. *Por qué hoy nosotros luchamos distinto.*

Consejo Regional Indígena del Cauca (CRIC). 1973. *Nuestras luchas de ayer y de hoy.* Popayán: Cartilla del CRIC, no. 1.

———. 1974. *Como nos organizamos.* Popayán: Cartilla del CRIC, no. 2.

———. 1981. *Diez años de lucha: historia y documentos.* Bogotá: CINEP, Serie Controversia, 91–92.

Gobernadores Indígenas en Marcha. 1980. *CRIC 1980: comunidades en lucha y Comité Ejecutivo.* Cali: Mimeo.

———. 1981. *Cómo recuperamos nuestro camino de lucha.* Cali: Mimeo.

———. 1985. *Nuestra idea y los problemas de hoy.* Cali: Mimeo.

BIBLIOGRAPHY

Published References

Adorno, Rolena, ed. 1982. *From Oral to Written Expression: Native Andean Chronicles of the Early Colonial Period.* Syracuse, N.Y.: Foreign and Comparative Studies, Latin American Series, no. 4.

———. 1986. *Guaman Poma: Writing and Resistance in Colonial Peru.* Austin: University of Texas Press.

Albó, Javier. 1972. "Dinámica en la estructura intercomunitaria de Jesús de Machaca." *América Indígena* [Mexico] 32:773–816.

Allen, Catherine J. 1988. *The Hold Life Has: Coca and Cultural Identity in an Andean Community.* Washington, D.C.: Smithsonian Institution Press.

———. n.d.a. "The Incas Have Gone Inside: Pattern and Persistence in Quechua Iconography," manuscript.

———. n.d.b. "Time, Place and Narrative in an Andean Community," manuscript.

Anderson, Benedict. 1983. *Imagined Communities: Reflections on the Origin and Spread of Nationalism.* London: Verso.

Appadurai, Arjun. 1981. "The Past as a Scarce Resource" *Man* (n.s.) 16:201–19.

Ardila, Jaime, and Camilo Lleras, eds. 1985. *Batalla contra el olvido: acuarelas colombianas, 1850.* Bogotá: Ardila & Lleras.

Arguedas, José María. 1985. *Los ríos profundos.* Bogotá: Oveja Negra.

Arnold, Denise, and Juan de Dios Yapita. 1991. "Oral Images of the Structures of Folktales in Highland Bolivia." Paper presented at "Textuality of Amerindian Cultures: Production, Reception, Strategies" conference, Institute of Latin American Studies, University of London, May 1991.

Ascher, Marcia, and Robert Ascher. 1981. *Code of the Quipu: A Study in Media, Mathematics, and Culture.* Ann Arbor: University of Michigan Press.

Bakhtin, M. M. 1981. *The Dialogic Imagination.* Trans. Caryl Emerson and Michael Holquist. Ed. Holquist. Austin: University of Texas Press.

———. 1984. *Rabelais and His World.* Trans Helene Iswolsky. Bloomington: Indiana University Press.

Barre, Marie-Chantal. 1983. *Ideologías indigenistas y movimientos indios.* Mexico: Siglo XXI.

Barthel, Thomas S. 1986 [1959]. "Agua y primavera entre los atacameños," *Allpanchis Phuturinqa* [Cuzco] 18(28):147–84.

Basso, Ellen. 1985. *A Musical View of the Universe: Kalapalo Myth and Ritual Performance.* Philadelphia: University of Pennsylvania Press.

Bebbington, Tony. 1992. *Searching for an 'Indigenous' Agricultural Development: Indian Organizations and NGOs in the Central Andes of Ecuador.* Centre of Latin American Studies, University of Cambridge, Working Papers 45.

Behar, Ruth. 1986. *Santa María del Monte: The Presence of the Past in a Spanish Village.* Princeton, N. J.: Princeton University Press.

Benjamin, Walter. 1969. *Illuminations.* Trans. Harry Zohn. Ed. Hannah Arendt. New York: Schocken.

226

Bergquist, Charles W. 1986. *Coffee and Conflict in Colombia, 1886–1910*. Durham, N. C.: Duke University Press.

Berkhofer, Robert E., Jr. 1979. *The White-Man's Indian: Images of the American Indian from Columbus to the Present*. New York: Vintage.

Bernal Villa, Segundo. 1953. "Aspectos de la cultura páez: mitología y cuentos de la parcialidad de Calderas, Tierradentro." *Revista Colombiana de Antropología* [Bogotá] 1(1):279–309.

Beyersdorff, Margot. 1988. *La adoración de los reyes magos: vigencia del teatro religioso español en el Perú andino*. Cusco: Centro de Estudios Rurales Andinos Bartolomé de las Casas.

Bloch, Marc. 1953. *The Historian's Craft*. New York: Vintage.

Blount, Ben G. 1975. "Agreeing to Agree on Genealogy." In *Sociocultural Dimensions of Language Use*, ed. M. Sanches and B. G. Blount. New York: Academic Press.

Bonfíl Batalla, Guillermo. 1987. *México profundo: una civilización negada*. México: Secretaría de Educación Pública.

Bonilla, Victor Daniel. 1979. "¿Qué política buscan los indígenas?" In *Indianidad y descolonización en América Latina: documentos de la Segunda Reunión de Barbados*. Mexico: Nueva Imagen.

Bowen, John R. 1989. "Narrative Form and Political Incorporation: Changing Uses of History in Aceh, Indonesia." *Comparative Studies in Society and History* 31(4):671–93.

Boyarin, Jonathan. 1989. "Voices around the Text: the Ethnography of Reading at Mesivta Tifereth Jerusalem." *Cultural Anthropology* 4(4):399–421.

———. 1992. *Storm from Paradise: The Politics of Jewish Memory*. Minneapolis: University of Minnesota Press.

Caillavet, Chantal. 1989. "Las técnicas agrarias autóctonas y la remodelación colonial del paisaje en los Andes septentrionales (siglo XVI)." In *Ciencia, vida y espacio en Iberoamérica*, vol. 3, ed. J. L. Peset, Madrid: Consejo Superior de Investigaciones Científicas, Estudios Sobre la Ciencia, no. 10.

Calero, Luis. 1987. "Pasto, 1535–1700: The Social and Economic Decline of Indian Communities in the Southern Colombian Andes." Ph.D. diss. University of California, Berkeley.

———. 1991. *Pastos, Quillacingas y Abades, 1535–1700*. Bogotá: Biblioteca Banco Popular.

Cardale de Schrimpff, Marianne. 1977–78. "Textiles arqueológicos de Nariño." *Revista Colombiana de Antropología* [Bogotá] 21:245–82.

Castillo-Cárdenas, Gonzalo. 1971. "Manuel Quintín Lame: luchador e intelectual indígena del siglo XX." Introduction to Manuel Quintín Lame, *En defensa de mi raza*, Bogotá: Comité de Defensa del Indio.

———. 1987. *Liberation Theology from Below: The Life and Thought of Manuel Quintín Lame*. Maryknoll, N.Y.: Orbis.

Castrillón Arboleda, Diego. 1973. *El indio Quintín Lame*. Bogotá: Tercer Mundo.

Celestino, Olinda. 1982. "Cofradía: continuidad y transformación de la sociedad andina." *Allpanchis Phuturinqa* [Cuzco] 17(20):147–66.

————, and Albert Meyers. 1981. *Las cofradías en el Perú: región central*. Frankfurt: Vervuert.

Christian, W. A. 1981. *Apparitions in Late Medieval and Renaissance Spain*. Princeton, N. J.: Princeton University Press.

Cieza de León, Pedro de. 1962 [1553]. *La crónica del Perú*. Madrid: Espasa-Calpe.

Clanchy, M. T. 1979. *From Memory to Written Record: England, 1066–1307*. Cambridge: Harvard University Press.

Clendinnen, Inga. 1990. "Ways to the Sacred: Reconstructing 'Religion' in Sixteenth Century Mexico." *History and Anthropology* 5:105–41.

Clifford, James. 1988. *The Predicament of Culture: Twentieth-Century Ethnography, Literature, and Art*. Cambridge: Harvard University Press.

————, and George E. Marcus, eds. 1986. *Writing Culture: The Poetics and Politics of Ethnography*. Berkeley and Los Angeles: University of California Press.

Cohen, Anthony P. 1985. *The Symbolic Construction of Community*. London: Tavistock.

Cohen, David W. 1980. "Reconstructing a Conflict in Bunafu: Seeking Evidence Outside the Narrative Tradition." In *The African Past Speaks*, ed. Joseph Miller, Hamden, Conn.: Archon.

————. 1986. "The Production of History," Position paper for the Fifth International Roundtable in Anthropology and History, Paris, 2–5 July 1986.

————. 1989. "The Undefining of Oral Tradition." *Ethnohistory* 36(1):9–18.

Colombia, República de. 1991. *Nueva constitución política de Colombia*. Pasto: Minilibrería Jurídica Moral.

————. Ministerio de Gobierno. 1983. *Fuero indígena: disposiciones legales del orden nacional, departamental y comisarial-jurisprudencia y conceptos*. Bogotá: Editorial Presencia.

————. Plan Nacional de Rehabilitación. 1990. *Fuero indígena colombiano: normas nacionales, regionales e internacionales, jurisprudencia, conceptos administrativos y pensamiento jurídico indígena*. Bogotá: Presidencia de la República.

Comaroff, John, and Jean Comaroff. 1992. *Ethnography and the Historical Imagination*. Boulder, Colo.: Westview Press.

Connerton, Paul. 1989. *How Societies Remember*. Cambridge: Cambridge University Press.

Cornejo Menacho, D., ed. 1992. *Indios: una reflexión sobre el levantamiento indígena de 1990*. Quito: ILDIS/Abya-Yala.

Correa, François. 1989. "Estado, desarrollo y grupos étnicos: la ilusión del proyecto de homogenización nacional." In *Identidad*, ed. M. Jimeno, G. I. Ocampo, and M. Roldán Bogotá: ICFES.

Crain, Mary M. 1989. *Ritual, memoria popular, y proceso político en la sierra ecuatoriana*. Quito: Abya-Yala.

————. 1990. "The Social Construction of National Identity in Highland Ecuador." *Anthropological Quarterly* 63(1):43–59.

Cummins, Thomas B. F. 1988. "Abstraction to Narration: Kero Imagery of Peru and the Colonial Alteration of Native Identity." Ph.D. diss., University of California, Los Angeles.

De Certeau, Michel. 1984. *The Practice of Everyday Life.* Trans. Steven Rendall. Berkeley and Los Angeles: University of California Press.

———. 1986. *Heterologies: Discourse on the Other.* Trans. Brian Massumi. Minneapolis: University of Minnesota Press.

———. 1988. *The Writing of History.* Trans. Tom Conley. New York: Columbia University Press.

Degregori, Carlos Iván. 1989. *Qué difícil es ser Dios: ideología y violencia política en Sendero Luminoso.* Lima: Ediciones El Zorro de Abajo.

———. 1990. *Ayacucho 1969–1979: el surgimiento de Sendero Luminoso.* Lima: Instituto de Estudios Peruanos.

Dening, Greg. 1988. *History's Anthropology: The Death of William Gooch.* Lanham, Md.: University Press of America/Association for Social Anthropology in Oceania.

Digges, Diana, and Joanne Rappaport. 1993. "Literacy, Orality and Ritual Practice in Highland Colombia." In *The Ethnography of Reading,* ed. Jonathan Boyarin. Berkeley and Los Angeles: University of California Press.

Diskin, Martin. 1991. "Ethnic Discourse and the Challenge to Anthropology: The Nicaraguan Case." In *Nation-States and Indians in Latin America,* ed. G. Urban and J. Sherzer. Austin: University of Texas Press.

Dorris, Michael. 1987. "Indians on the Shelf." In *The American Indian and the Problem of History,* ed. Calvin Martin. Oxford: Oxford University Press.

Dover, Robert, Katharine Seibold, and John McDowell, eds. 1992. *Andean Cosmologies through Time: Persistence and Emergence.* Bloomington: Indiana University Press.

Earls, John, and Irene Silverblatt. 1978. "La realidad física y social en la cosmología andina," *Actes 42 Congrès International des Américanistes,* 4:299–326. Paris: Fondation Singer-Polignac.

Eisenstein, Elizabeth L. 1966. "Clio and Chronos: An Essay on the Making and Breaking of History-Book Time." *History and Theory* 5(6):36–64.

Fabian, Johannes. 1983. *Time and the Other: How Anthropology Makes its Object.* New York: Columbia University Press.

———. ed. 1990. *History from Below: The 'Vocabulary of Elisabethville' by André Yav.* Amsterdam and Philadelphia: John Benjamins.

Fajardo, Dario. 1981. "Las luchas indígenas por la tierra en el Tolima durante el siglo XX." In *Indigenismo y aniquilamiento de indígenas en Colombia,* ed. N. S. de Friedemann, J. Friede, and D. Fajardo. Bogotá: CIEC.

Farriss, Nancy. 1987. "Remembering the Future, Anticipating the Past: History, Time and Cosmology among the Maya of Yucatan." *Comparative Studies in Society and History* 29(3):556–93.

Feierman, Steven. 1990. *Peasant Intellectuals: Anthropology and History in Tanzania.* Madison: University of Wisconsin Press.

Field, Les. 1991. "Ecuador's Pan-Indian Uprising." *NACLA Report on the Americas* 25(3):39–44.

Findji, María Teresa. 1992 "From Resistance to Social Movement: The Indigenous Authorities Movement in Colombia," in *The Making of Social Movement in Latin America: Identity, Strategy, and Democracy*, ed. A. Escobar and S. E. Alvarez. Boulder, Colo.: Western.

Findji, María Teresa, and José María Rojas. 1985. *Territorio, economía y sociedad páez*. Cali: Editorial Universidad del Valle.

Finnegan, Ruth. 1988. *Literacy and Orality: Studies in the Technology of Communication*. Oxford: Basil Blackwell.

Flores Galindo, Alberto. 1988. *Buscando un Inca: identidad y utopía en los Andes*. Lima: Editorial Horizonte.

Fogelson, Raymond. 1989. "The Ethnohistory of Events and Nonevents." *Ethnohistory* 36(2):133–47.

Foucault, Michel. 1970. *The Order of Things: An Archaeology of the Human Sciences*. Trans. pub. New York: Vintage.

Francisco, Alice E. 1969. "An Archaeological Sequence from Carchi, Ecuador." Ph.D. diss., University of California, Berkeley.

Friede, Juan. 1972. *El indio en lucha por la tierra: historia de los resguardos del macizo central colombiano*. Bogotá: La Chispa.

Friedlander, Judith. 1975. *Being Indian in Hueyapan: A Study of Forced Identity in Contemporary Mexico*. New York: St. Martin's Press.

Fundación para las Comunidades Colombianas. 1987. *Grupos étnicos, derecho y cultura*. Bogotá: Cuadernos del Jaguar and Fundación para las Comunidades Colombianas.

Garcilaso de la Vega, El Inca. 1960–65 [1609]. *Comentarios reales de los Incas*. Madrid: Biblioteca de Autores Españoles.

Gómez del Corral, Luz Alba. 1985. "Relaciones de parentesco en las relaciones de producción en la comunidad indígena de San Diego de Muellamués." Tesis de grado, Department of Anthropology, Universidad Nacional de Colombia, Bogotá.

González, Margarita. 1979. *El resguardo en el Nuevo Reino de Granada*. Bogotá: La Carreta.

González Echevarría, Roberto. 1990. *Myth and Archive: A Theory of Latin American Narrative*. Cambridge: Cambridge University Press.

Goody, Jack. 1977. *The Domestication of the Savage Mind*. Cambridge: Cambridge University Press.

———. 1987. *The Interface between the Written and the Oral*. Cambridge: Cambridge University Press.

Gow, David D. 1980. "The Roles of Christ and Inkarrí in Andean Religion." *Journal of Latin American Lore* 6(2):279–98.

Gow, Peter. 1990. "Could Sangama Read? The Origin of Writing among the Piro of Eastern Peru." *History and Anthropology* 5:87–103.

Gros, Christian. 1991. *Colombia indígena: identidad cultural y cambio social*. Bogotá: CEREC.

Gruzinski, Serge. 1985. "La memoria mutilada: construcción del pasado y mecanismos de la memoria en un grupo otomí de la mitad del siglo XVII." In *La memoria y el olvido*, Segundo Simposio de Historia de las Mentalidades. Mexico: Instituto Nacional de Antropología e Historia.

———. 1988. *La colonisation de l'imaginaire: sociétés indigènes et occidentalisation dans le Mexique espagnol, XVIᵉ-XVIIIᵉ siécle*. Paris: Gallimard.

Guaman Poma de Ayala, Felipe. 1980 [1615]. *El primer nueva corónica y buen gobierno*. Ed. John Murra and Rolena Adorno. Mexico City: Siglo XXI.

Gudeman, Stephen, and Alberto Rivera. 1990. *Conversations in Colombia: The Domestic Economy in Life and Text*. Cambridge: Cambridge University Press.

Guerrero, Andrés. 1989. "Curagas y tenientes políticos: la ley de la costumbre y la ley del estado (Otavalo 1830–1875)." *Revista Andina* [Cuzco] 7(2):321–66.

———. 1991. *La semántica de la dominación: el concertaje de indios*. Quito: Ediciones Libri Mundi.

Guerrero, Gerardo León. n.d. *Aspectos socioeconómicos de la Nueva Granada y el Distrito de Pasto a finales del período colonial*. Pasto: Gerardo León Guerrero.

Gutiérrez, Rufino. 1897. "De Tumaco a Pasto III." *El Repertorio Colombiano* [Bogotá] 14(5) and 15(1 & 4):324–48.

Halbwachs, Maurice. 1980. *The Collective Memory*. Trans. Francis J. Ditter Jr. and Vida Yazdi Ditter. New York: Harper Colophon.

Halverson, John. 1992. "Goody and the Implosion of the Literacy Thesis." *Man* (n.s.) 27:301–17.

Handler, Richard. 1988. *Nationalism and the Politics of Culture in Quebec*. Madison: University of Wisconsin Press.

———, and William Saxton. 1988. "Dyssimulation: Reflexivity, Narrative, and the Quest for Authenticity in 'Living History.'" *Cultural Anthropology* 3(3):242–60.

Hanson, Allan. 1989. "The Making of the Maori: Culture Invention and Its Logic." *American Anthropologist* 91(4):890–902.

Harris, Olivia. 1987. "*Phaxsima y qullqi*: los poderes y significados del dinero en el Norte de Potosí." In *La participación indígena en los mercados surandinos: estrategias y reproducción social, siglos XVI a XX*, ed. Harris, Brooke Larson, and Enrique Tandeter. La Paz: Centro de Estudios de la Realidad Económica y Social.

Harrison, Regina. 1989. *Signs, Songs, and Memory in the Andes: Translating Quechua Language and Culture*. Austin: University of Texas Press.

Hartmann, Roswith, and Udo Oberem. 1981. "Quito: un centro de educación de indígenas en el siglo XVI." In *Contribuções à antropologia em homenagem ao Professor Egon Schaden*. Sao Paulo: Coleçao Museo Paulista, serie ensaios 4.

Henao, Jesús María, and Gerardo Arrubla. 1938 [1910]. *History of Colombia*. Trans. J. Fred Rippy. Port Washington, N.Y.: Kennikat Press.

Hobsbawm, Eric J. 1972. "The Social Function of the Past: Some Questions." *Past and Present* 55:3–17.

———, and Terence Ranger, eds. 1983. *The Invention of Tradition*. Cambridge: Cambridge University Press.

Howard-Malverde, Rosaleen. 1981. *Dioses y diablos: tradición oral de Cañar Ecuador*. (*Amerindia*, special issue 1.) Paris: Association d'Ethnolinguistique Amérindienne.

———. 1990. *The Speaking of History: "Willapaakushayki" or Quechua Ways of Telling the Past*. London: Institute of Latin American Studies, University of London, Research Papers 21.

Huxtable, Ada Louise. 1992. "Inventing American Reality." *The New York Review of Books* 39(20):24–29.

Izko, Xavier. 1992. *La doble frontera: ecología, política y ritual en el altiplano central.* La Paz: Hisbol.

Jackson, Jean. 1989. "Is There a Way to Talk about Making Culture without Making Enemies?" *Dialectical Anthropology* 14:127–43.

———. 1991. "Being and Becoming an Indian in the Vaupés." In *Nation-States and Indians in Latin America,* ed. G. Urban and J. Sherzer. Austin: University of Texas Press.

Jimeno, Myriam, and Adolfo Triana. 1985. *Estado y minorías étnicas en Colombia.* Bogotá: Cuadernos del Jaguar and Fundación para las Comunidades Colombianas.

Keesing, Roger M. 1982. "*Kastom* in Melanesia: An Overview." *Mankind* 13(4):297–301.

Lame, Manuel Quintín. 1971 [1939]. *En defensa de mi raza.* Ed. Gonzalo Castillo-Cárdenas. Bogotá: Comité de Defensa del Indio. [English translation in Castillo-Cárdenas 1987.]

Lan, David. 1985. *Guns and Rain: Guerrillas and Spirit Mediums in Zimbabwe.* Berkeley and Los Angeles: University of California Press.

Landázuri, Cristóbal. 1990. "Territorios y pueblos: la sociedad Pasto en los siglos XVI y XVII." *Memoria* [Quito] 1(1):57–108.

Landsman, Gail H. 1988. *Sovereignty and Symbol: Indian-White Conflict at Ganienkeh.* Albuquerque: University of New Mexico Press.

———, and Sara Ciborski. 1992. "Representation and Politics: Contesting Histories of the Iroquois." *Cultural Anthropology* 7(4):425–47.

Langebaek Rueda, Carl Henrik. 1992. *Noticias de caciques muy mayores: orígen y desarrollo de las sociedades complejas en el nororiente de Colombia y norte de Venezuela.* Bogotá: Ediciones Uniandes, and Medellín: Editorial Universidad de Antioquia.

Lapierre, Nicole. 1989. *Le silence de la mémoire: à la recherche des Juifs de Plock.* Paris: Plon.

Layne, Linda L. 1989. "The Dialogics of Tribal Self-Representation in Jordan." *American Ethnologist* 16(1):24–39.

LeGrand, Catherine. 1986. *Frontier Expansion and Peasant Protest in Colombia, 1850–1936.* Albuquerque: University of New Mexico Press.

Lively, Penelope. 1987. *Moon Tiger.* Harmondsworth: Penguin.

Lockhart, James. 1982. "Views of Corporate Self and History in Some Valley of Mexico Towns: Late Seventeenth and Eighteenth Centuries." In *The Inca and Aztec States, 1400–1800: Anthropology and History,* ed. G. A. Collier, R. I. Rosaldo, and J. D. Wirth. New York: Academic Press.

———. 1985. "Some Nahua Concepts in Postconquest Guise." *History of European Ideas* 6(4):465–82.

López-Baralt, Mercedes. 1988. *Icono y conquista: Guamán Poma de Ayala.* Madrid: Hiperion.

Lord, Albert B. 1964. *The Singer of Tales.* Cambridge: Harvard University Press.

Lowenthal, David. 1985. *The Past Is a Foreign Country.* Cambridge: Cambridge University Press.

MacCormack, Sabine. 1991. *Religion in the Andes: Vision and Imagination in Early Colonial Peru*. Princeton, N. J.: Princeton University Press.

Mamani Quispe, Alejandro. 1988. *Historia y cultura de Cohana*. La Paz: HISBOL/ Radio San Gabriel.

Mamián, Doumier. 1992. "El pensamiento andino 'por la senda de Juan Chiles.'" *Mopa Mopa, Revista del Instituto Andino de Artes Populares* [Pasto] 8:25–41.

Mannheim, Bruce. 1991. *The Language of the Inka since the European Invasion*. Austin: University of Texas Press.

Mayer, Enrique. 1991. "Peru in Deep Trouble: Mario Vargas Llosa's 'Inquest in the Andes' Reexamined." *Cultural Anthropology* 6(4):466–504.

McDowell, John H. 1989. *Sayings of the Ancestors: The Spiritual Life of the Sibundoy Indians*. Lexington: University Press of Kentucky.

Mejía Piñeros, María Consuelo, and Sergio Sarmiento Silva. 1987. *La lucha indígena: un reto a la ortodoxia*. Mexico: Siglo XXI.

Melo, Jorge Orlando. 1989. "Etnia, región y nación: el fluctuante discurso de la identidad (notas para un debate)." In *Identidad*, ed. M. Jimeno, G. I. Ocampo, and M. Roldán. Bogotá: ICFES.

Miller, Joseph, ed. 1980. *The African Past Speaks*. Hamden, Conn.: Archon.

Momaday, N. Scott. 1977. *The Names: A Memoir*. New York: Harper and Row.

Moody, Roger, ed. 1988. *The Indigenous Voice: Visions and Realities*. 2 vols. London: Zed/IWGIA.

Moore, Sally Falk. 1986. *Social Facts and Fabrications: "Customary" Law on Kilimanjaro, 1880–1980*. Cambridge: Cambridge University Press.

———. 1989. "History and the Redefinition of Custom on Kilimanjaro." In *History and Power in the Study of Law*, ed. J. Starr and J. F. Collins. Ithaca, N.Y.: Cornell University Press.

Morales, Trino. 1979. "El movimiento indígena en Colombia." In *Indianidad y descolonización en América Latina: documentos de la Segunda Reunión de Barbados*. Mexico: Nueva Imagen.

Moreno Proaño, A. 1979. "Cronología de la vida de Fray Jodoco Ricke, fundador del convento de San Francisco de Quito (1498–1578)." *Boletín de la Academia Nacional de Historia* [Quito] 131–32:173–90.

Moreno Ruíz, Encarnación. 1970. "Historia de la penetración española en el sur de Colombia: etnohistoria de pastos y quillacingas, siglo XVI." Doctoral thesis, Universidad Complutense de Madrid.

Murra, John V. 1975. *Formaciones económicas y políticas del mundo andino*. Lima: Instituto de Estudios Peruanos.

Nash, June. 1979. *We Eat the Mines and the Mines Eat Us: Dependency and Exploitation in Bolivian Tin Mines*. New York: Columbia University Press.

Nora, Pierre. 1984. "Entre mémoire et histoire: la problématique des lieux." In *Les lieux de mémoire*, ed. Nora, vol. 1. Paris: Gallimard.

Oates, Joyce Carol. 1990. "Excerpts from a Journal: July 1989." *The Georgia Review* 44(1/2):121–34.

Ong, Walter J. 1982. *Orality and Literacy: The Technologizing of the Word*. London: Methuen.

Orlove, Benjamin S. 1991a. "La violencia vista desde arriba y desde abajo: narrativas oficiales y campesinas de encuentros conflictivos en la sierra sur del Perú." In *Poder y violencia en los Andes,* ed. Henrique Urbano, Cusco: Centro de Estudios Regionales Andinos Bartolomé de Las Casas.

———. 1991b. "Mapping Reeds and Reading Maps: The Politics of Representation in Lake Titicaca." *American Ethnologist* 18(1):3–38.

Ortiz Rescaniere, Alejandro. 1973. *De Adaneva a Inkarrí (una visión indígena del Perú).* Lima: Retablo de Papel.

Pachacuti Yamqui Salcamaygua, Joan de Santacruz. 1968 [1613]. "Relación de antigüedades deste reyo del Pirú." In *Crónicas peruanas de interés indígena,* ed. Francisco Esteve Barba. Madrid: Biblioteca de Autores Españoles.

Passerini, Luisa. 1987. *Fascism in Popular Memory: The Cultural Experience of the Turin Working Class.* Cambridge: Cambridge University Press, and Paris: Editions de la Maison des Sciences de L'Homme.

———. 1988. *Autoritratto di gruppo.* Florence: Giunti.

Pécault, Daniel. 1987. *Orden y violencia: Colombia, 1930–1954.* Mexico: Siglo XXI.

Phelan, John L. 1967. *The Kingdom of Quito in the Seventeenth Century.* Madison: University of Wisconsin Press.

Poole, Deborah A. 1988. "Landscapes of Power in a Cattle-Rustling Culture of Southern Andean Peru." *Dialectical Anthropology* 12:367–98.

———. 1990. "Accommodation and Resistance in Andean Ritual Dance." *The Drama Review* 34(2):98–126.

———. 1992. "Figueroa Aznar and the Cusco *Indigenistas:* Photography and Modernism in Early Twentieth-Century Peru." *Representations* 38:39–75.

Portelli, Alessandro. 1991. *The Death of Luigi Trastulli and Other Stories.* Albany: State University of New York Press.

Price, Richard. 1983. *First-Time: The Historical Vision of an Afro-American People.* Baltimore: Johns Hopkins University Press.

———. 1990. *Alabi's World.* Baltimore: Johns Hopkins University Press.

Price, Sally. 1989. *Primitive Art in Civilized Places.* Chicago: University of Chicago Press.

Radcliffe, Sarah A. 1990. "Marking the Boundaries between the Community, the State and History in the Andes." *Journal of Latin American Studies* 22(3):575–94.

Rafael, Vicente L. 1988. *Contracting Colonialism: Translation and Christian Conversion in Tagalog Society under Early Spanish Rule.* Ithaca, N.Y.: Cornell University Press.

Ramón Valarezo, Galo. 1987. *La resistencia andina: Cayambe, 1.500–1.800.* Quito: Centro Andino de Acción Popular.

———. 1992. "Ese secreto poder de la escritura." In *Indios: una reflexión sobre el levantamiento indígena de 1990,* ed. D. Cornejo Menacho. Quito: ILDIS/Abya-Yala.

Ramos, Alcida. 1988. "Indian Voices: Contact Experienced and Expressed." In *Rethinking History and Myth: Indigenous South American Perspectives on the Past,* ed. J. Hill. Urbana: University of Illinois Press.

Rappaport, Joanne. 1980–81. "El mesianismo y las transformaciones de símbolos mesiánicos en Tierradentro." *Revista Colombiana de Antropología* [Bogotá] 23:365–413.

———. 1982. "Territory and Tradition: The Ethnohistory of the Páez of Tierra-dentro, Colombia." Ph.D. diss, University of Illinois at Urbana.

———. 1985. "History, Myth and the Dynamics of Territorial Maintenance in Tierradentro, Colombia." *American Ethnologist* 12(1):27–45.

———. 1987. "Mythic Images, Historical Thought, and Printed Texts: The Páez and the Written Word." *Journal of Anthropological Research* 43(1):43–61.

———. 1988. "La organización socioterritorial de los Pastos: una hipótesis de trabajo." *Revista de Antropología* [Bogotá]4(2):71–103.

———. 1990a. "History, Law and Ethnicity in Andean Colombia." *Latin American Anthropology Review* 2(1):13–19.

———. 1990b. *The Politics of Memory: Native Historical Interpretation in the Colombian Andes.* Cambridge: Cambridge University Press.

———. 1992. "Reinvented Traditions: The Heraldry of Ethnic Militancy in the Colombian Andes." In *Andean Cosmologies through Time: Persistence and Emergence,* ed. Robert Dover, Katharine Seibold, and John McDowell. Bloomington: Indiana University Press.

———. n.d. "Object and Alphabet: Andean Indians and Documents in the Colonial Period." In *Records without Words,* ed. Elizabeth Boone and Walter Mignolo. Durham, N.C.: Duke University Press (*in press*).

Rasnake, Roger. 1988. *Domination and Cultural Resistance: Authority and Power among an Andean People.* Durham, N.C.: Duke University Press.

Reichel-Dolmatoff, Gerardo. 1972. *San Agustín: A Culture of Colombia.* New York: Praeger.

Rivera Cusicanqui, Silvia. 1986a. *"Oprimidos pero no vencidos": luchas del campesinado aymara y qhechwa, 1900–1980.* La Paz: HISBOL.

———. 1986b. "Taller de Historia Oral Andina: proyecto de investigación sobre el espacio ideológico de las rebeliones andinas a través de la historia oral (1900–1950)." In *Estados y naciones en los Andes,* ed. J. P. Deler and U. Saint-Geours. Lima: Instituto de Estudios Peruanos.

Rosero, Fernando. 1990. *Levantamiento Indígena: tierra y precios.* Quito: Centro de Estudios y Difusión Social.

Rostworowski de Diez Canseco, María. 1978. *Señoríos indígenas de Lima y Canta.* Lima: Instituto de Estudios Peruanos.

Rushdie, Salman. 1983. *Shame.* London: Picador.

Sallnow, Michael J. 1987. *Pilgrims of the Andes: Regional Cults in Cusco.* Washington, D.C.: Smithsonian Institution Press.

Salomon, Frank L. 1981. "Killing the Yumbo: A Ritual Drama of Northern Quito." In *Cultural Transformations and Ethnicity in Modern Ecuador,* ed. Norman Whitten, Jr. Urbana: University of Illinois Press.

———. 1982. "Chronicles of the Impossible: Notes on Three Peruvian Indigenous Historians." In *From Oral to Written Expression: Native Andean Chronicles of the Early Colonial Period,* ed. Rolena Adorno. Syracuse, N.Y.: Foreign and Comparative Studies, Latin American Series, no. 4.

———. 1986. *Native Lords of Quito in the Age of the Incas: The Political Economy of North Andean Chiefdoms.* Cambridge: Cambridge University Press.

———. n.d. "The Making and Reading of Native South American Historical Sources." In *Cambridge History of the Native Peoples of the Americas.* ed.

Stuart Schwartz and Frank L. Salomon. Cambridge: Cambridge University Press.

————, and George Urioste, eds. 1991. *The Huarochirí Manuscript: A Testament of Ancient and Colonial Andean Religion.* Austin: University of Texas Press.

Sánchez, Gonzalo. 1977. *Las Ligas Campesinas en Colombia.* Bogotá: Tiempo Presente.

Sanjinés, Jorge, and Grupo Ukamau. 1979. *Teoría y práctica de un cine junto al pueblo.* Mexico: Siglo XXI.

Sarmiento de Gamboa, Pedro. 1965 [1572]. *Historia indica.* Madrid: Biblioteca de Autores Españoles.

Schroder, Barbara. 1991. "Indians in the Halls of Academe: Rural Andean Peoples Confront Social Science." *Peasant Studies* 18(2):97–116.

Scott, James C. 1985. *Weapons of the Weak: Everyday Forms of Peasant Resistance.* New Haven, Conn.: Yale University Press.

Seligmann, Linda J. 1987. "Land, Labor and Power: Local Initiative and Land Reform in Huanoquite, Peru." Ph.D. diss., University of Illinois at Urbana.

————. 1989. "To Be In Between: The *Cholas* as Market Women." *Comparative Studies in Society and History* 31(4):694–721.

Sherbondy, Jeanette. 1979. "Les réseaux d'irrigation dans la géographie politique de Cuzco." *Journal de la Société des Américanistes* [Paris] 66:45–66.

Shopes, Linda. 1986. "Oral History and Community Involvement: The Baltimore Neighborhood Heritage Project." In *Presenting the Past: Essays on History and the Public,* ed. S. P. Benson, S. Brier, and R. Rosenzweig. Philadelphia: Temple University Press.

Silko, Leslie Marmon. 1981. *Storyteller.* New York: Arcade.

Skar, Sarah L. n.d. "On the Margin: Letter Exchange among Andean Non-Literates." In *The Multiplicity of Literacies,* ed. Eduardo Archetti. Oslo: Norwegian University Press (*in press*).

Smith, Gavin. 1989. *Livelihood and Resistance: Peasants and the Politics of Land in Peru.* Berkeley and Los Angeles: University of California Press.

Sontag, Susan. 1977. *On Photography.* New York: Delta.

Stern, Steve. 1982. *Peru's Indian Peoples and the Challenge of Spanish Conquest.* Madison: University of Wisconsin Press.

————. ed. 1987. *Resistance, Rebellion, and Consciousness in the Andean Peasant World, 18th to 20th Centuries.* Madison: University of Wisconsin Press.

Stock, Brian. 1990. *Listening for the Text: On the Uses of the Past.* Baltimore: Johns Hopkins University Press.

Street, Brian. 1984. *Literacy in Theory and Practice.* Cambridge: Cambridge University Press.

Sullivan, Paul. 1989. *Unfinished Conversations: Mayas and Foreigners between Two Wars.* New York: Alfred A. Knopf.

Taussig, Michael. 1987. *Shamanism, Colonialism, and the Wild Man: A Study in Terror and Healing.* Chicago: University of Chicago Press.

Tedlock, Dennis. 1983. *The Spoken Word and the Work of Interpretation.* Philadelphia: University of Pennsylvania Press.

Thomas, Nicholas. 1992. "The Inversion of Tradition." *American Ethnologist* 19(2):213–32.

Triana, Adolfo. 1980. *Legislación indígena nacional: leyes, decretos, resoluciones, jurisprudencia y doctrina.* Bogotá: América Latina.

Tyler, Stephen A. 1986. "On Being Out of Words." *Cultural Anthropology* 1:131–38.

———. 1987. *The Unspeakable.* Madison: University of Wisconsin Press.

Urban, Greg, and Joel Sherzer, eds. 1991. *Nation-States and Indians in Latin America.* Austin: University of Texas Press.

Urbano, Henrique. 1978. "La symbolique de l'espace andin." *Actes 42 Congrès International des Amèricanistes,* 4:335–45. Paris: Fondation Singer-Polignac.

Uribe, María Victoria. 1977–78. "Asentamientos prehispánicos en el altiplano de Ipiales, Colombia." *Revista Colombiana de Antropología* [Bogotá] 21:57–195.

———. 1985–86. "Etnohistoria de las comunidades andinas prehispánicas del sur de Colombia." *Anuario Colombiano de Historia Social y de la Cultura* [Bogotá] 13–14:5–40.

———, and Fabricio Cabrera. 1988. "Estructuras de pensamiento en el altiplano nariñense: evidencias de la arqueología." *Revista de Antropología* [Bogotá] 4(2):43–69.

Uribe Uribe, Rafael. 1907. *Reducción de salvajes.* Bogotá: El Trabajo.

Urton, Gary. 1984. "Chuta: el espacio de la práctica social en Pacariqtambo." *Revista Andina* [Cuzco] 2(1):7–44.

———. 1988. "La arquitectura pública como texto social: la historia de un muro de adobe en Pacariqtambo, Perú (1915–1985)," *Revista Andina* [Cuzco] 6(1):225–63.

———. 1990. *The History of a Myth: Pacariqtambo and the Origin of the Inkas.* Austin: University of Texas Press.

Vansina, Jan. 1985. *Oral Tradition as History.* Madison: University of Wisconsin Press.

Vidal, Hernán. 1985. *Socio-historia de la literatura colonial hispanoamericana: tres lecturas orgánicas.* Minneapolis: Institute for the Study of Ideologies and Literatures.

Vincent, David. 1981. *Bread, Knowledge and Freedom: A Study of Nineteenth-Century Working Class Autobiography.* London: Methuen.

Vining, Joseph. 1991. "Generalization in Interpretive Theory." In *Law and the Order of Culture,* ed. R. Post. Berkeley and Los Angeles: University of California Press.

Vizenor, Gerald. 1984. *The People Named the Chippewa: Narrative Histories.* Minneapolis: University of Minnesota Press.

Wachtel, Nathan. 1971. *La vision des vaincus: les indiens du Pérou devant la conquête espagnole, 1530–1570.* Paris: Gallimard.

———. 1982. "The Mitimas of the Cochabamba Valley: The Colonization Policy of Huayna Capac." In *The Inca and Aztec States, 1400–1800: Anthropology and History,* ed. G. Collier, R. Rosaldo, and J. Wirth. New York: Academic Press.

Warren, Kay B. 1978. *The Symbolism of Subordination: Indian Identity in a Guatemalan Town.* Austin: University of Texas Press.

Weismantel, M. J. 1988. *Food, Gender, and Poverty in the Ecuadorian Andes.* Philadelphia: University of Pennsylvania Press.

Williams, Brett. 1988. *Upscaling Downtown: Stalled Gentrification in Washington, D.C.* Ithaca, N.Y.: Cornell University Press.

Yates, Frances. 1966. *The Art of Memory.* Chicago: University of Chicago Press.

Zamosc, Leon. 1986. *The Agrarian Question and the Peasant Movement in Colombia: Struggles of the National Peasant Association, 1967–1981.* Cambridge: Cambridge University Press, and Geneva: United Nations Research Institute for Social Development.

Zuidema, R. Tom. 1964. *The Ceque System of Cuzco.* Leiden: E. J. Brill.

————. 1982a. "Bureaucracy and Systematic Knowledge in Andean Civilization." In *The Inca and Aztec States, 1400–1800: Anthropology and History,* ed. G. A. Collier, R. I. Rosaldo, and J. D. Wirth. New York: Academic Press.

————. 1982b. "Myth and History in Ancient Peru." In *The Logic of Culture: Advances in Structural Theory and Methods,* ed. I. Rossi. New York: J. F. Bergin.

————. 1983. "The Lion in the City: Royal Symbols of Transition in Cuzco." *Journal of Latin American Lore* 9(1):39–100.

————. 1990. "Ceques and Chapas: An Andean Pattern of Land Partition in the Modern Valley of Cuzco." In *Circumpacifica: Festschrift für Thomas S. Barthel,* vol. 1, ed. Bruno Illius and Matthias Laubscher. Frankfurt am Main: Peter Lang.

Zúñiga Eraso, Eduardo. n.d. *Realidad y perspectivas de los indígenas del sur de Colombia.* Manuscript kept in the Centro de Estudios Regionales, Banco de la República, Pasto.

————. 1986. "Resguardos de la cuenca interandina." *Revista de Historia* [Pasto] 8(59–60):9–36.

Index

Agricultural experimentation. See *Recuperación*, and economic innovation
AICO (Autoridades Indígenas de Colombia), 17, 114
AISO (Autoridades Indígenas del Sur Occidente). *See* AICO
Alpala, Hilarión, 53, 62, 127–129, 168
Alpala, José Manuel, 126, 129
Alpala, Lastenia, 60, 168: biographical sketch, 60; on Cumbe's tomb, 63–64; on loss of El Zapatero, 127–128; on repossession of Llano de Piedras, 148; on search for titles, 61–62; on sighting the Pacific, 64–65; on Urbano López, 137–139
Alpala, Miguel Angel, 80, 163: biographical sketch, 161. *See also* Grupo Artístico "Los Cumbes"
Alpala, Nestor, 88
Alpala, don Pedro, 48, 108
Amparos, 108–109, 116, 130
Ancuya, 28–32
Anderson, Benedict, 165
Andes (culture area): and Cumbal, 7–8, 40–41; essentialization of, 179n.3, 198–199n.17; and literacy, 97–98; symbolic motifs, 124, 137, 139, 143
Andoke, 190n.9
ANUC (Asociación Nacional de Usuarios Campesinos), Indigenous Secretariat, 15–16, 181n.17

Archives (*cabildo*), 144, 168: access to, 62–63, 66, 69–70, 118–119, 215n.1; inventory of, 67–69; rotation of, 47, 69
Arellano, Laureano Alberto, 9–10
Authors, subaltern: biographical sketches, 115, 117, 161–162; historical narratives of, 114–121; journalism, 15, 114; writing strategies, 98, 215n.3. *See also* Canacuán; *Chasqui Cumbe*
Aymara, 187n.12, 190n.9
Aza, Rosa Elena, 128–129

Bakhtin, Mikhail, 98
Barbacoas. *See* Camino de Barbacoas
Benjamin, Walter, 194n.25
Blessings, of children, 36, 92–96
Bloch, Marc, 76
Bolívar, Simón, 9, 103, 110, 116, 175
Bonfíl Batalla, Guillermo, 32
Boundaries: of agricultural fields, 83–89, 197; of *haciendas*, 141–142; of *resguardo*, 11–13, 80, 108, 119–120, 123, 134, 180n.9; of *veredas*, 139
Boyera, La, 8–9, 25, 51, 53, 88, 167
Bulls, symbolism of, 137–139, 209n.30

Cabildo: complicity in privatizations, 33–34; elections, 42–43, 45, 48, 186n.7; factionalism in, 45, 167–168; as family, 79; jurisdiction of, 10–11, 88, 111; meetings, 38–39; official history of, 57–58,

Historiography: European frameworks, 152–154, 189n.4; and legal discourse, 101, 115–117, 125, 174; and personal reminiscence, 19, 37, 55–56, 58, 64–66, 101, 114, 116–117, 150, 166, 171, 174, 190n.4. *See also* Historical truth; History

History: and antihistory, 175–176; correction of, 10, 52–53, 74, 89, 152; as dialogue with the dead, 100; hierarchy of sources for, 69, 88, 211n.7, 216n.6; interethnic negotiation of, 123, 135, 141, 198n.13; and militancy, 19, 58, 63, 115, 127–128, 159, 172, 175; vs. memory, 154, 175

Hitching post, symbolism of, 140-142

Holy Week, 152–153, 159–160, 212n.13, 213n.20

Identity. *See* Ethnic identity

Imagined community, 165

Inca, 41, 139

INCORA (Instituto Colombiano de Reforma Agraria), 8–10, 16–17, 26, 188n.22

Indian: and geographic displacement, 151, 158; and handicrafts, 151; historical category, 34, 135, 151, 158; legal category, 27–33; stereotypes of, 76, 90, 159, 169, 172. *See also* Ethnic identity; Law 89 of 1890

Indian law. *See* Legislation

Indian movement: history of, 14–17; ideology of, 18, 156–157; and images of Indians, 151. *See also* AICO; ANUC; CRIC; Lame, Manuel Quintín; ONIC

Indigenous Affairs, Division of, 8, 16, 26, 88

Intertextuality, 88, 94–95, 100–101, 106, 111, 120-121, 124–125, 173, 175. *See also* Historical narrative; Historiography; Literacy

Invented traditions, 124–125, 140, 143, 169. *See also* Staffs of office

Ipiales, 41

Juaspuezán, Darío, 209n.29

Lame, Manuel Quintín, 14, 153, 158; *Los pensamientos . . .* , 162–164

Lan, David, 215–216n.5

Land claims. *See* Repossession

Landholdings: and Camino de Barbacoas, 28–31, 55–56; usurpation of, 34, 55, 106, 136. *See also* Land tenure; *Resguardo*

Land tenure, 4, 33, 51, 56, 141, 183n.14. See also *Resguardo*

Laurel, El, 8–10, 26, 51, 53, 115–116, 167

Law 89 of 1890: and ethnic identity, 27–32; and evolutionary philosophy, 27–28, 34; historical context of, 26–27; as historical evidence, 27, 65, 68; images of, 25, 80, 116, 149–150; *resguardos*, liquidation of, 32, 34. *See also* Legislation

Legal discourse, 98, 126, 171, 173

Legal writing, polyphony of, 98–100, 107, 124–125

Legislation: as dominant discourse, 104, 174; as historical evidence, 27, 112, 171; Indian law, 125, 141, 143, 169; influence on narrative, 7, 25–28, 101, 174–175, 205n.2; multilayered nature of, 197n.12; and natural resources, 102–103, 112; property law, 125, 136, 141. *See also* Ethnic identity; Law 89 of 1890

Liadero, El, 103, 112–114

Liberal Party, 9–10, 30, 45, 161, 167–168, 180n.6, 191n.14

Libros de devoción, 47

Literacy: colonial-era, 101, 106–107, 193n.25, 202n.11, 202n.13; control of, 104, 124; as conversation, 98–100; ethnography of, 172–174; fixity of, 134, 173–174; and gender, 124; genres of, 22, 66–67, 73, 91, 93, 114–121, 173, 193n.25, 212n.12; and historical evidence, 88, 132–135, 144; journalism, 16, 114, 165, 181n.16; and legal codes, 62–63, 65; legal documents, 6, 56, 61, 67–69, 74, 95, 97–98, 100, 105–112, 134; legal writing, 101–104, 112, 114–117; and nationalism, 165; personal libraries, 67, 193n.21; secondary literacy, 62; subaltern literacy, 172, 199n.1; vs. oral accounts, 123–126, 133–137, 172, 175. *See also* Authors, subaltern; Historical narrative; Historiography; Legal writing

Lively, Penelope, 205–206n.4

Llano de Piedras: narratives of struggle, 147–149, 155; repossession of, 26, 53,